Building Flash® Web Sites

FOR

DUMMIES®

Building Flash® Web Sites For Dummies®

Cheat Sheet

Ten Flash Tips to Avoid Headaches

When creating content for your Flash Web site:

1. Use symbols for each graphic object you create.
2. Test your handiwork early and often by using the Test Movie command.
3. Don't lump all of your content into one movie. Instead, break a large site into several small movies that load into an interface.
4. Don't use a different frame rate when loading external content into your Flash interface.
5. Use symbol instances when at all possible instead of creating new content.
6. Create a separate layer for any ActionScript that is added to keyframes in the timeline.
7. Label keyframes with meaningful names.
8. Use symbol linkage to reference Library items with ActionScript.
9. Use comments with complex lines of ActionScript.
10. Label layers.

Flash Tools

Each Flash tool has a shortcut, which I've conveniently included in parentheses next to each tool.

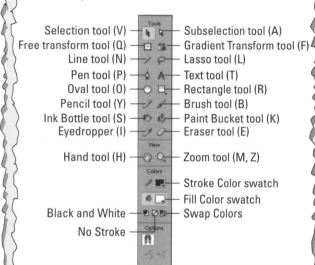

Selection tool (V) — Subselection tool (A)
Free transform tool (Q) — Gradient Transform tool (F)
Line tool (N) — Lasso tool (L)
Pen tool (P) — Text tool (T)
Oval tool (O) — Rectangle tool (R)
Pencil tool (Y) — Brush tool (B)
Ink Bottle tool (S) — Paint Bucket tool (K)
Eyedropper (I) — Eraser tool (E)

Hand tool (H) — Zoom tool (M, Z)

Stroke Color swatch
Fill Color swatch
Black and White — Swap Colors
No Stroke

Actions panel

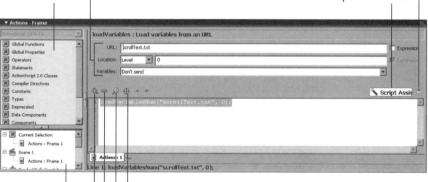

Parameters for the selected action

Actions books

ActionScript help

Script Assist button

List of ActionScript in movie

Insert a target path

Add a lin

Delete se

For Dummies: Bestselling Book Series for Beginners

Building Flash® Web Sites For Dummies®

Cheat Sheet

Tool Modifier Shortcuts

Tool	Modifier Action	Windows Shortcut	Mac Shortcut
Oval and Rectangle tools	Constrain shape to a circle or square	Shift-drag	Shift-drag
Oval and Rectangle tools	Draw from the center	Alt-drag	Option-drag
Oval and Rectangle tools	Constrain shape to a circle or square and draw from the center	Alt-Shift-drag	Option-Shift-drag
Line tool	Constrain lines to 45° increments	Shift-drag	Shift-drag
Line tool	Draw from the center	Alt-drag	Option-drag
Line tool	Constrain lines to 45° increments and draw from the center	Alt-Shift-drag	Option-Shift-drag
Brush and Pencil tools	Constrain strokes to vertical or horizontal	Shift-drag	Shift-drag
Pen tool	Add points	Click to add a straight point; click and drag to add a curve point	Click to add a straight point; click and drag to add a curve point
Selection tool	Use the Selection tool to move and rotate shapes while constraining direction	Shift-drag	Shift-drag
Selection tool	Move a selected element by one pixel	Select the object(s) and click an arrow key	Select the object(s) and click an arrow key
Selection tool	Move a selection by eight pixels	Select the object(s) and then press an arrow key while holding down the Shift key	Select the object(s) and then press an arrow key while holding down the Shift key
Selection tool	Use the Selection tool to create a copy of an object	Select the object and then Ctrl-drag	Select the object and then Option-drag
Subselection tool	Convert a corner point to a curve point	Alt-drag	Option-drag
Zoom tool	Switch between Zoom In and Zoom Out modes	Select the tool and then press Alt to zoom out; release the Alt key to change modes	Select the tool and then press Option to zoom out; release the Option key to change modes

Copyright © 2006 Wiley Publishing, Inc. All rights reserved.

Item 9220-9.

For more information about Wiley Publishing, call 1-800-762-2974.

For Dummies: Bestselling Book Series for Beginners

Building Flash® Web Sites

FOR DUMMIES®

by Doug Sahlin

Wiley Publishing, Inc.

Building Flash® Web Sites For Dummies®

Published by
Wiley Publishing, Inc.
111 River Street
Hoboken, NJ 07030-5774
www.wiley.com

Copyright © 2006 by Wiley Publishing, Inc., Indianapolis, Indiana

Published by Wiley Publishing, Inc., Indianapolis, Indiana

Published simultaneously in Canada

For general information on our other products and services, please contact our Customer Care Department within the U.S. at 800-762-2974, outside the U.S. at 317-572-3993, or fax 317-572-4002.

For technical support, please visit www.wiley.com/techsupport.

Wiley also publishes its books in a variety of electronic formats. Some content that appears in print may not be available in electronic books.

Library of Congress Control Number: 2006921152

ISBN-13: 978-0-471-79220-8

ISBN-10: 0-471-79220-9

Manufactured in the United States of America

10 9 8 7 6 5 4 3 2 1

1B/RX/QU/QW/IN

WILEY

About the Author

Doug Sahlin is a photographer, videographer, and Web designer living in Lakeland, Florida. He has written 16 books on computer graphics and office applications and co-authored 3 books on Photoshop and 1 book on digital video. Recent titles include *Digital Photography QuickSteps* and *How To Do Everything with Adobe Acrobat 7.0.* Many of his books have been bestsellers at Amazon.com. Doug's books have been translated into five languages. He uses Flash 8.0 Professional to create Web sites and multimedia presentations for his clients.

Dedication

Dedicated to the memory of my mother, Inez, my best friend and one of the kindest and wisest souls to walk the face of this earth.

Author's Acknowledgments

Thanks to Acquisitions Editor Steve Hayes for making this project possible. Special thanks to Project Editor Nicole Sholly and Copy Editor Andy Hollandbeck — an upstanding kind of guy and fellow Frank Zappa fan — for manicuring this work for public consumption. My sincere thanks to the Wiley editorial staff for their support and contribution to this work. Kudos to the lovely and talented Margot Maley Hutchison for being the best literary agent on the planet.

Thanks to fellow authors Ken Milburn and Joyce Evans for their continued support and friendship. Special thanks to my friend Bonnie Blake for creative inspiration. Thanks to my friends, mentors, and family — especially you, Karen and Ted. Special thanks to Niki the cat, the best companion an author could hope to have.

Publisher's Acknowledgments

We're proud of this book; please send us your comments through our online registration form located at www.dummies.com/register/.

Some of the people who helped bring this book to market include the following:

Acquisitions, Editorial, and Media Development

Project Editor: Nicole Sholly

Senior Acquisitions Editor: Steven Hayes

Copy Editor: Andy Hollandbeck

Technical Editor: Jim Kelly

Editorial Manager: Kevin Kirschner

Media Development Specialists: Angela Denny, Kate Jenkins, Steven Kudirka, Kit Malone, Travis Silvers

Media Development Coordinator: Laura Atkinson

Media Project Supervisor: Laura Moss

Media Development Manager: Laura VanWinkle

Editorial Assistant: Amanda Foxworth

Cartoons: Rich Tennant (www.the5thwave.com)

Composition Services

Project Coordinator: Erin Smith

Layout and Graphics: Carl Byers, Andrea Dahl, Joyce Haughey, Barbara Moore, Lynsey Osborn

Proofreaders: Leeann Harney, Jessica Kramer, Techbooks

Indexer: Techbooks

Publishing and Editorial for Technology Dummies

Richard Swadley, Vice President and Executive Group Publisher

Andy Cummings, Vice President and Publisher

Mary Bednarek, Executive Acquisitions Director

Mary C. Corder, Editorial Director

Publishing for Consumer Dummies

Diane Graves Steele, Vice President and Publisher

Joyce Pepple, Acquisitions Director

Composition Services

Gerry Fahey, Vice President of Production Services

Debbie Stailey, Director of Composition Services

Contents at a Glance

Table of Contents

Introduction

● ●

So you want to be a Flash Web designer, but you can't design Flash Web sites in a flash? It all takes time. And it also requires a modicum of knowledge, which is where this book comes in. If you've read other Flash how-to books, you know that they cover the sundry topics like how to create really cool animations with Flash. However, this book takes you to the next level and shows you how to create a Flash Web site from soup to nuts.

About This Book

Here are some of the things you can do with this book:

- ✔ Use it as a doorstop. (Kidding!)
- ✔ Plan a Flash Web site.
- ✔ Create a lean, fast-loading Flash interface.
- ✔ Create content for your Flash Web site.
- ✔ Create interactive Web sites with Flash.
- ✔ Optimize and publish your Flash Web site.
- ✔ Add eye candy to your Flash Web site.
- ✔ Create an e-commerce Flash Web site.
- ✔ Debug your ActionScript.
- ✔ Sharpen your ability to deal with clients.

Foolish Assumptions

In order to do most anything, you need some specific tools, just a bit of know-how, and perchance a bit of luck mingled with creativity. When you need to design a Flash Web site, you need the proper tools. For this book, that tool is Flash 8. And if you're going to do cool stuff, like encode your own video, you need Flash 8 Professional.

You should know your way around the Flash workspace. But don't worry; I do give you a brief refresher course on some of the basic Flash stuff, like creating animations, working with text, and so on. When you create animations, and for that matter format text, choose colors, and so on, you use the Properties Inspector to set the parameters for the object with which you are working. Therefore, you should have a working knowledge of the Properties Inspector. I also show you how to work with ActionScript. However, in order to follow along, you should have a basic knowledge of the Actions panel.

Another thing you should know is how to manipulate HTML documents. Although your main work in this book uses Flash, you still have to do some editing to the HTML document in which your Flash Web site is embedded. If you have working knowledge of an HTML editor, such as Dreamweaver, you're one step ahead of the game. Another benefit of Dreamweaver is the fact that you can use the software to upload files to the Web provider that hosts the Web site.

Conventions Used in This Book

I'm not a conventional kind of guy. But of course, without some kind of conventions, such as punctuation and grammar, people wouldn't be able to understand each other. This book is no different. Without conventions, you'd have no idea of what to do or when to do it. Therefore, we use the following conventions in this book. When you're asked to input information — you know, type something — the required input is **boldfaced.** When you see examples of ActionScript code, URLs, and e-mail addresses, these are in a monofont typeface, like so: `myEmail@myserver.com`. New terms are *italicized*.

What You Don't Have to Read

This is one of those nonlinear type of books, which means that you don't have to read it in order. Although the book can be read as a whole, feel free to jump to the section that contains the information you need. You'll get a good idea of what's in each section by reading the tips and notes. And of course, a picture is always worth a thousand words: You can look at the figures to get an idea of what's presented in each section; if the picture doesn't relate to the information you're looking for, feel free to skip that section. Also, you can feel free to skip any sections wearing a *Technical Stuff* icon.

How This Book Is Organized

Building Flash Web Sites For Dummies is split into five parts. You don't have to read the book sequentially, and you don't even have to read all the sections in any particular chapter. You can use the Table of Contents and the Index to find the information you need and quickly get your answer. In this section, I briefly describe what you'll find in each part.

Part 1: Building the Perfect Beast

In this part, I present information on how to plan your Flash Web site prior to building it. I show you several things you should consider prior to building the site, as well as techniques for working with clients. I show you how to create a mock-up for your client and how to begin gathering assets for your Web site before launching Flash.

Part 11: Fleshing Out Your Design

After you're done with the preliminaries, you can start creating some actual content, which is what this part is all about. First, I show you how to make an interface. I know what you're thinking: Why just an interface? Well, in order to have a lean and mean Web site, you create a fast-loading interface into which you load other content. In this part, I also show you how to create text for the Web site and how to create some spiffy navigation bars and buttons, as well as how to animate your site.

Part 111: Adding Bells and Whistles

So what's a Flash Web site without bells and whistles? *Boring!* In this part, I show you how to kick it up a notch. I introduce you to the wonders of ActionScript and what it can do for you, your site, or your client's site. I also show you how to create some spiffy things with ActionScript, like a clock that shows Web site visitors what time it is. Other interesting tidbits include how to create a Flash photo gallery, add video to your Web site, create an e-commerce site, and more.

Part IV: Sharing Your Site with the World

If you build it, they will come. But first you have to optimize the site for the viewing public and then publish it, the main topic of discussion in — you guessed it — this part of the book. First, I show you how to make your site lean and mean by getting rid of things that are not needed. I also give you other tips and techniques you can use to create a Skinny Minny Web site. Then I show you how to exterminate pesky little bugs in your ActionScript. And finally, I show you how to publish your site.

Part V: The Part of Tens

In the Part of Tens, you'll find three chapters. Each chapter contains ten tidbits — you know, useful nuggets of information — about creating Flash Web sites. I share with you some tips for creating trouble-free Flash Web sites, tips for dealing with clients, and tips for promoting your site. And I've done so much work on this introduction that I'm going to take this moment to take ten.

The appendix

Although Flash is super-popular, it's not the easiest application in the world to master. So I've added this handy appendix, which lists several Flash Internet resources. I waxed my board and actually surfed to each site to verify that it's still there as of this writing. But you know how the Net is . . . here today, gone tomorrow.

The color insert

Because this book is printed in black and white, I've included a color insert so that you can see at least some examples of what you can create with the techniques in the book in full, glorious color. In this section, you find screenshots of Flash Web sites under construction. You also find examples of images being optimized for use in Flash Web sites, as well as text being added to a Flash Web site. Because it's all in grand and glorious color, this section gives you, the reader, a visual feast and examples of what you can do when creating your own Flash Web site.

The companion Web site

I want to make Flash source files available to you, so this book has an accompanying Web site. The site is located at www.dummies.com/go/ flashwebsites. There, you can find folders for the chapters in this book. In each chapter's folder, you can find FLA files that give you an example of a project created using the topics covered in that particular chapter.

Icons Used in This Book

What's a *For Dummies* book without icons pointing you in the direction of really great information that's sure to help you along your way? In this section, I briefly describe each icon I use in this book.

The Tip icon points out helpful information that is likely to make your job easier.

This icon marks a generally interesting and useful fact — something that you might want to remember for later use.

The Warning icon highlights lurking danger. With this icon, I'm telling you to pay attention and proceed with caution.

When you see this icon, you know that there's techie stuff nearby. If you're not feeling very techie, you can skip this info.

I've placed several files on the Web for your use. This icon denotes an activity where you might want to first download the named file before continuing.

Where to Go from Here

Okay. So now that you've read this far, or maybe you started with this section of the intro, and you need someone to tell you where to go. Not a problem. If you want to plan your site and get everything ready to rock and roll before launching Flash, check out Part I. In Chapter 1, I give you the skinny on everything you need to do while designing a Flash Web site. In Chapter 2, I show you how to get all your ducks in a row by gathering all the information and assets you need to hit the ground running.

If you're a take-charge, grab-the-bull-by-the-horns, press-on-regardless kind of person, you'll find the information you need to start designing your site in Part II. In Chapter 3, I show how to create the site interface, whereas in Chapter 4, I show you everything you ever wanted to know — well almost — about Flash text but were afraid to ask. In Chapter 5, I show you how to add site navigation, and if you need motion in your Flash Web site, I show you how to get animated in Chapter 6.

If bells and whistles are your thing, or your client's thing, you can easily include them using Flash. If you want cool Flash stuff, mosey on over to Part III. Here I show you how to add cool things to your Web site with ActionScript and also show you how to add Flash eye candy to your site. If your site is going to be commercial, check out Chapter 10.

Part IV is all about finalizing your site and then publishing it. In Chapter 12, I show you how to optimize your site and get the bugs out of your Action-Script. In Chapter 13, I show you how to publish your site.

If you're in the mood for a hodge-podge of useful information about working with Flash, working with clients, and promoting your site, check out Part V, which is where you find the Part of Tens chapters. Each chapter contains ten — at least by my abacus — sections of useful information.

Part I
Building the Perfect Beast

In this part . . .

1 show you everything you need to know to hit the ground running. I show you all the steps involved in creating a Flash Web site and then show you how to begin laying out the Web site.

If you're working with clients, you'll find useful tidbits on how to deal with them and how to figure out exactly what they want. After you have that information in hand, you create a mockup for the client, a task I show you how to accomplish in this part.

Other topics of discussion include gathering materials for the Web site and optimizing images and video in other applications prior to working in Flash.

Chapter 1

Creating the Perfect Flash Site

*T*he first page of Chapter 1 is always an exciting place in any book. It's where you find out what's in store for you in the upcoming pages. Or hey, maybe you've already read three chapters and have just decided to restart at the beginning. (What a novel concept!) Well, you can get away with that when reading a book, but if you try to create an interface for your Flash site without first having done your homework, it's almost like trying to fly without knowing how to operate an airplane — but not nearly as hazardous to your health.

In this chapter, I show you the steps you go through to create a Flash site. And like anything else you build, there is a process. Whether you're creating a Flash site for your son's baseball team or for your boss — who plopped an unopened box on your desk that says "Flash Professional 8" and said, "Build me a Flash site" — if you don't approach the process logically, you're destined to have more than your share of headaches. Like the self-help gurus say, "Fail to plan, and you plan to fail."

Flash versus HTML . . . The Winner Is?

To Flash or not to Flash, that is the question. Whether 'tis nobler to create a ho-hum HTML Web site or to up the ante with a Flash design with more bells and whistles than . . . but I digress.

Flash has been around for a long time. In comparison, HTML is almost ancient. Flash has gone through a rapid growth and development spurt since Flash 4. HTML is now in version 4.0 and won't be developed anymore. In fact, HTML 4.0 has been around since 1998, which is practically the Jurassic age in regards to computers and Internet technology. Savvy designers have come up with all kinds of imaginative coding and workarounds to create some really cool Web sites with HTML. HTML designers use JavaScript to add interactivity to their designs. They write complex code to embed video and audio in their designs, and they use form elements to create interactive forms to gather information, to create virtual shopping carts, and so on. Or maybe they're lucky and have a good WYSIWYG (What You See Is What You Get) HTML application, like Dreamweaver, that takes care of a lot of the grunt work.

Either way, there's still a steep learning curve to create anything more complex than a hum-drum, text-only Web page sprinkled with the odd JPEG image or three. Simply put, modern-day Web designers need to know a lot. And they often have to resort to other colleagues in order to create the latest "all-singing, all-dancing" Web design that will blow the socks off their client's competitors.

However, when you want to have your cake and eat it too, nothing beats Flash. You have everything you need within the application to add all of the interactivity and WOW factor the law allows, and then some. Lots of people think of Flash as a really cool animation tool. But it's so much more than that. You can build high-powered, compelling Web sites with Flash. And the only time HTML comes into the picture is as the document within which you embed your Flash Web site. Figure 1-1 shows a cool Flash Web site.

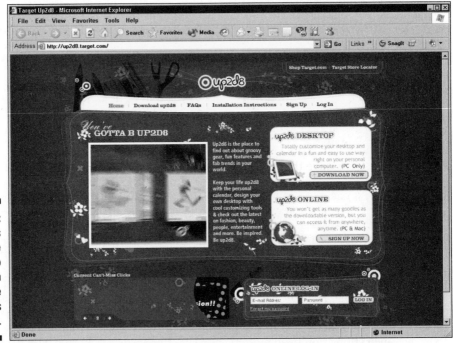

Figure 1-1:
Flash makes it possible for you to design interactive Web sites with pizzazz.

Within Flash is a powerful scripting language known as ActionScript, which bears a similarity to JavaScript. If the design you envision includes full-motion video, that's available from within Flash as well. In fact, Flash has its own video *codec* (an algorithm that compresses the movie when it is rendered, and decompresses the movie when it is viewed) called FLV (Flash Video). But that's only the tip of the iceberg. You say you want to gather information from customers at your Flash site? Piece of cake! You can design an artistic Flash form that makes its HTML brother look positively archaic. And you can do all of this within Flash. I show you how to incorporate these elements and more in your Flash Web design in the upcoming chapters.

Setting Goals for the Design

Before you can build the site, you need some kind of road map. Trying to create a Flash movie without a plan is like trying to drive from Florida to Alaska without a map or planned route. You may get there, but you'll end up taking a world of detours and wrong turns.

The easiest way to know where you're going with your Flash Web design is to interview the client. In fact, this step is an absolute necessity. After all, how can you create a proposal if you don't know what the client wants? If the Web site is for a friend or a family member, the interview process will probably be an ongoing give-and-take of ideas. After the goals for the design have been defined, put it in writing and get the client to sign off on it. Remember, no job is done until the paperwork is handled. And in the case of a Web design, no job should be started until the paperwork is handled. I discuss this issue in more depth in Chapter 2.

Planning Your Site

After you have the goals for your design on paper, it's time to put you design paper again. Yes, you read correctly. Only this time, you're not putting words on paper; you're sketching the design. The sketch doesn't have to be elaborate — just enough to give you a visual clue as to what the finished design will look like. You can create a series of sketches on a legal pad, an illustration application, or, if you're meeting with the client in a restaurant, a napkin works well as a makeshift sketchpad. If you prefer to be a little more elaborate, you can sketch your design and actually build different iterations of the design in Macromedia Fireworks (an application used to create graphics, edit images, and create HTML for Web sites). After the sketch is done, you'll know exactly what you need to build the site. The sketch also gives you an idea of what, if any, ActionScript you need to pull off the design. Don't worry, I show you everything you need to know about ActionScript for a Flash Web design in Chapter 7.

Gathering Assets for Your Site

After you create preliminary sketches for your site, it's time to get your ducks in a row, so to speak. In this phase of the project, you get or create everything that cannot be created in Flash and store it in a neat little folder. There's nothing worse than being two-thirds of the way into your project, with the creative juices flowing like a river in flood, only to discover that you don't have everything you need to complete the project.

The assets you gather will vary depending on what your design encompasses. If your site has a slide show, you'll gather the images, optimize them for Web site viewing, and size them to suit your design. Granted, you can do some of this work in Flash. However, a Web-friendly image editing application like Fireworks will give you more options. Other assets you may have to gather are sound clips and full-motion video. Animation? Forget it. You can do all that in Flash. Chapter 2 has more about gathering the necessary assets.

Building the Interface

Every good Web site needs an interface. In a nutshell, an *interface* is a graphic device that your viewers can use to navigate from one part of the site to another. The acronym for an interface is GUI — *graphical user interface.* The interface generally consists of a background, a banner, and navigation buttons. You can build most of the assets for your interface in Flash. However, some designers prefer to lay out the background for the interface in an application like Fireworks and then import the graphic into their Flash design.

You'll create many parts of the interface by using Flash drawing tools. When you create an object with Flash drawing tools, you create a vector object. *Vector objects* are graphic objects that can be scaled infinitely, that is, unless the object has a complex *gradient* (a fill that consists of two or more colors blended together in a linear or radial manner). Some Flash Web designers prefer to create their vector objects in a drawing application like Adobe Illustrator or CorelDraw.

Some Flash designers throw everything but the kitchen sink at their viewers. This is fine if you're creating a simple site with only a little navigation. However, when you add bells and whistles like video and full-color bitmaps, you run the risk of creating a Flash movie with a file size slightly smaller than the Trump Tower. When you create a site that big, trying to download it is like trying to drain an Olympic-size swimming pool with a garden hose; it takes a long time. I show you how to create a Web-friendly interface and then load content into the interface in order to manage a Flash Web site that has a humongous amount of content. Figure 1-2 shows a cool Flash interface, complete with a hideaway control panel that enables users to change interface colors and so on.

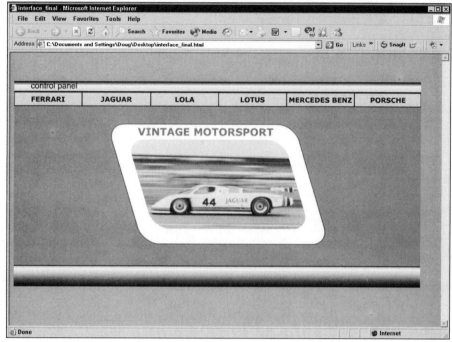

Figure 1-2:
You can create unique interfaces by using Flash.

Simplifying your workflow with symbols

So you have an idea for your Flash Web site, but you shudder at the thought of creating all the artwork. It's a good thing you decided to create a Flash Web site, because in Flash, anything you create can be converted into a symbol. Symbols come in three flavors: graphic, button, and movie clip. The beauty of symbols is that they're reusable. You can add a symbol wherever you need one without breaking the bandwidth bank. When you take a symbol from the Library and add it to the timeline, you create a symbol instance. When the instance is encountered, the Flash Player re-creates it from the information in the Library. Figure 1-3 shows a Library that lacks a live librarian but is chock-full of symbols.

And guess what? You can have a symbol within a symbol, which in Flash is known as *nesting*. This opens all manner of possibilities for the creative Flash Web designer. You can also house ActionScript in the Movie Clip symbol. This makes it possible for you to use the same ActionScript in other parts of your movie, or for that matter, in other movies. Now how cool is that? I give you a symbolic baptism by fire in Chapter 3.

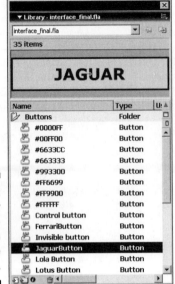

Figure 1-3:
You simplify
your work-
flow when
you use
symbols.

A tall tale of buttons and navigation menus

An important part of any interface is the navigation menu. The navigation menu consists of buttons. But you don't need to reinvent the wheel to create a navigation menu. Whenever you create a button, or for that matter any other symbol, it's stored in the Flash Library. Unlike your local library, you don't need a card to take something from the Library, you just do it. I show you how to create a navigation menu by creating one button, duplicating the button for the other links in your navigation menu, and then editing the duplicated buttons. It's really child's play after you get the hang of it.

If you have lots of content in your Web site, you might have to stuff the buttons into drop-down menus. Creating a drop-down menu might seem rather labor-intensive, especially if your site holds a whole lot of buttons that link to different content. Not to worry, in Chapter 5, I show you how to whip up a vertical or horizontal drop-down menu like the one in Figure 1-4 in no time. In this figure, the second row of buttons drops down when the Portfolio button is clicked.

Adding text and other delights

Sometimes you have to tell instead of show. When you're faced with this task, you need to create text. You may also need text for buttons. Creating text in Flash is almost as easy as working with your favorite word processor. The most basic form of Flash text is *static text*. When you create static text, it just sits there and gets the word out. You can make pretty static text by choosing a fancy font and rainbow colors, or you can create ho-hum text by using the basic Flash fonts dressed up in one of Halloween's favorite colors: jet black.

Flash offers two other forms of text: input and dynamic. *Input text* accepts information from your Flash site's visitors. This information can be stored in a variable. *Dynamic text* is just the opposite: It takes information from a variable and displays it within your Flash movie. You can use this dynamic duo to personalize a viewer's visit to your site. You can also use it to store a visitor's information when shopping in your Flash e-Store. I show you how to create fancy (and not-so-fancy) Flash text in Chapter 4.

Figure 1-4:
You can
stuff 50
pounds of
buttons into
a svelte
drop-down
menu.

Adding the WOW Factor

The indescribable WOW factor is something that can only be experienced with the senses. Sight and sound make a Flash site pop. And it's something that's hard to do with HTML, but relatively easy to do with Flash. You say you want to introduce your site with a bang? You can — literally. All the bells and whistles you need to create an award-winning Flash site that'll rock your visitors' worlds are included with Flash. All you have to do is harness the power. I show you how in Part III.

Making your site interactive with ActionScript

The thought of writing code strikes fear into the heart of any Web designer — with the exception of card-carrying geeks, also known as *Web developers.* Flash ActionScript, however, is a non-geek's answer to code. All you have to know is which action to use to pull off an effect. With Script Assist in Flash 8, you select the action and then fill in the parameters. You don't have to know how to enter code with Script Assist, which is a blessing after having to manually script everything in Flash MX 2004. You've probably seen plenty of Web sites with Flash intros. Virtually anyone with the slightest bit of Flashpertise can put together one of those. But what separates the men from the boys is the clever use of ActionScript.

The first place you'll use ActionScript is creating a preloader. A *preloader* is either a graphic, animation, or text that displays while enough content loads for the main Flash movie to play without interruption. Are preloaders necessary? Well, sometimes. If your audience accesses the Internet via a dialup connection, a preloader ensures that enough information loads to view your design without interruption. Some Flash designers go over the top with preloaders that contain so many bells and whistles that it loads slowly and needs a pre-preloader of its own. How's that for redundancy? In Chapter 8, I show you how to create a preloader, such as the one shown in Figure 1-5.

Figure 1-5:
You use
ActionScript
to create a
preloader.

If you want a unique menu, you can use ActionScript to create a drag-and-drop menu. Whether you create a cool drag-and-drop menu or a conventional navigation bar, when your visitors click a button, you can literally show them where to go. And when they get there, you can up the ante with ActionScript. You can use ActionScript for games, to create animated banners, to create moving menus, to add the time of day to your Web site, and much more. Figure 1-6 shows a Flash Web site with some ActionScript bells and whistles.

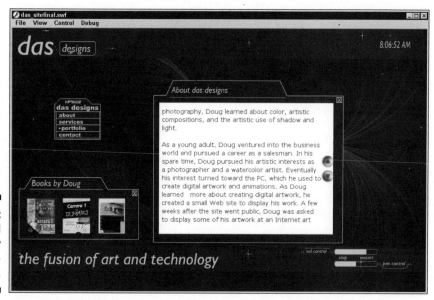

Get a move on with animation

The clever use of animation gets the attention of your visitors and has them returning on a regular basis. If you create a tricked-out navigation menu, you can use animation to instruct your visitors how to use it. And if you're really adventurous, you can use animation to create a text banner with text that dances or flies into position, such as the one shown in Figure 1-7.

Animation takes place on a timeline. The timeline is broken down into frames. The number of frames that occupy one second of the timeline is determined by the frame rate of the movie. The more frames you have, the smoother the motion. However, a higher frame rate increases the file size. You can find out all about frames and keyframes and blank keyframes, oh my, in Chapter 6.

If you've created animation in the past, you may have meticulously made changes on every frame to get it to work. However, with Flash, you can automate your animations. All you need to do is create a symbol, a few keyframes, and let *motion tweening* do the rest. Another cool way to attract attention is with an animated banner. I show you almost everything you wanted to know about animation but were afraid to ask in Chapter 6.

Figure 1-7:
You can
WOW your
audience
with dancing
text banners.

Flash has another form of automated animation known as *shape tweening.* Shape tweening can be used on editable shapes to change them into different shapes. Shape tweening isn't sophisticated enough to morph your ex-significant-other into a donkey, but it can create interesting animations.

Soundtracks and other operatic delights

Flash soundtracks can be a joyful noise or irritating enough to make your viewers hightail it without ever looking at your site. Everyone has different musical tastes; that's why there are so many music genres. Instead of subjecting your visitors to your personal taste in music, you can give them a choice. And to go with the choice, you can put the viewer in control of the experience with a sound controller. Now how cool is that? I show you how to add sound to your site in Chapter 8.

You can also add sound to buttons. If you're a photographer showing off your portfolio with a Flash Web site, what would be cooler than a shutter click when one of your visitors clicks a button? I show you how to make noisy buttons in Chapter 5.

Optimizing and Publishing Your Site

If you build it, they will come. But will they stay? The answer to that question is *no* if you create a Web site that takes a long time to load. The average Web surfer has the attention span of a sand flea, and that isn't very long. If you want your visitors to delve deeply into your site, you have to give them something to look at almost immediately. The secret to creating a quick-loading site is to carefully plan the site, create a skinny interface, and load content into the interface, which is what I show you how to do in this book. If you get to the eleventh hour and you have a 2MB site that takes eons to load, well, there's not much you can do except start all over again. But if you have a svelte siren of a Flash site, you can make the site load even faster by optimizing it. See Chapter 12 to find out how.

Testing your design

Test, test, and then test again. That should be the motto of every Flash designer. There's nothing more frustrating than being nearly finished, just to find a glaring error in your logic, or, for that matter, in the ActionScript, that prevents the site from doing all you wanted. It's in your best interest to test early and test often. You can do some testing in authoring mode, and do a full-fledged test in another window, as shown in Figure 1-8. I show you how to test your site in Chapter 13.

Figure 1-8:
You test
your site
prior to
publishing it.

Getting the bugs out

If your Web site contains ActionScript, variables, and dynamic text, you have a recipe for disaster if you don't know how to debug your site. Murphy's Law can and will raise its ugly head. But you can nip Murphy in the bud by using Flash's powerful debugger. You can track every variable in your Flash movie as well as in your ActionScript. However, even at the default frame rate, a snippet of ActionScript code executes in $\frac{1}{12}$ of a second. In other words, things happen so fast that you can't track them without a little help from a friend.

Those friends are known as *breakpoints* (not to be confused with the formerly popular *break dance*), which you place on complicated lines of ActionScript. A breakpoint stops ActionScript cold in its tracks when you debug your movie. After getting the skinny on what your code is doing, you resume the movie from within the Debugger (more on that in Chapter 12), shown in Figure 1-9.

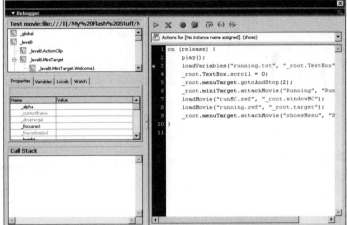

Figure 1-9:
You can nip
any glitches
in your
ActionScript
with the
Debugger.

Optimizing the beast

After you get the bugs out, you have some housecleaning to do. You need to optimize your Flash movie in order for it to load as quickly as possible. One of the first things you do is clean out the Library. Publishing a Flash movie with unused symbols in the Library is like preparing a car for the Indy 500 and leaving a whole bunch of extra parts in the engine compartment; the extra baggage makes the Web page load slower.

Other issues you'll deal with while optimizing the site are the quality of the images and the data rate of any sounds in your movie. Optimizing your Flash movie means it will load faster, which is a good thing for your site's viewers. I show you how to optimize your Flash Web site in Chapter 12.

Publishing and uploading your brainchild

After creating your Flash site, it's time to share it with the world, or at least with a few close friends. To convert your Flash document into a Flash movie, you publish it. When you publish the movie, you create an SWF file and an HTML file into which your movie is embedded. Or if you create a large Flash site, you publish several SWF files that load into your interface, which is yet another SWF file. The interface SWF file is embedded in an HTML document, which you also publish.

When you publish a Flash movie, you have several decisions to make that determine who can view your Flash movie. After you publish your Flash Web site, you upload it to your server. But not to worry, publishing and uploading a Flash movie isn't rocket science. I show you everything you need to know about publishing and uploading Flash movies, and maybe a little more, in Chapter 13.

Chapter 2

Before You Build Your Site

*I*t is always best to begin at the beginning. I know that sounds like useless advice, but many Web designers launch Flash as soon as they think they know where they're going. Then, lo and behold, they start assembling a Flash document for their Web site and find out that they don't have a clue. Planning and doing legwork before you actually start building the site takes time, but in the long run, it saves time. To quote George Harrison, "If you don't know where you're going, any road will get you there." In this chapter, I show you how to lay out a path that ensures success. You find out how to get your ducks in a row ahead of time by getting all the necessary information from your client and then gathering all of the assets you can't build in Flash.

Knowing Your Mission

The Empire State Building in New York City is a monument that has stood the test of time. The construction crew didn't just pull into town, set up some scaffolding, and start raising some steel. They had a well-thought-out plan of attack and a set of blueprints. Building a Flash Web site is not nearly as daunting as building a skyscraper, but it is a task best not left to chance. In the upcoming sections, I show you how to work with clients and get a grip on the audience that will be viewing your Flash Web site.

Working with clients

You probably know the old adage that the client is always right. But in reality, the client is always the client. When you work with a prospective client, your first task is to size him or her up. Does the client have a firm idea of the message he or she wants to get across with the site you'll be designing? If the client frequently changes his mind — you know, waffles — during your initial meeting, that's a red flag that he'll probably change his mind once or twice while you're creating the site. Be sure to factor this in when creating your proposal and, of course, when you're estimating the price you'll charge the client for your services.

Remember that the client is also sizing *you* up. When you're working with a client, you're in a sales situation: You're selling yourself and your services. Your initial session with the client will be give and take. The client will ask you a lot of questions, and you'll ask the client a lot of questions to get an idea of your client's needs. Sometimes it's appropriate to answer a question with a question. One very good question/answer is, "Why is that important to you?" The answer your client gives you is valuable information you can later use to overcome any objections.

Another thing you should do up front is establish your value. When you tell the client about your services, don't just blurt out facts. The client wants to listen to radio station WIIFM (What's In It For Me). So when you tell the client something — for example, that your Flash sites are fast-loading — you're telling the client a feature of your services. Back that up with why it's important for the customer. In this case, you tell the customer that your fast-loading site will prevent potential visitors from losing interest while waiting for content to load and surfing to another site.

Another good sales tool is a portfolio. You can use screen-capture hardware, such as SnagIt, to capture still images of your best Flash Web sites. You can then print these out on high-quality paper and put them in a professional-looking portfolio.

A picture is worth a thousand words. And if a picture is worth a thousand words, a moving picture must be worth a gazillion. In this regard, you can bring your laptop computer to the meeting with your client. Publish a few of your best Flash designs and store them on your laptop. Create desktop shortcuts to each Web site. Then, during the course of the client consultation, you can quickly show examples of your work by clicking the applicable shortcut.

Making it crystal clear with a client questionnaire

Whether you meet in person or do business over the Internet, you can get a solid grasp on your customer's expectations if you have the client fill out a questionnaire. Many Web designers have a questionnaire that potential clients can fill out and submit on their Web sites. The following is a list of useful questions you can ask your potential client to get a better idea of the type of Web site he or she desires:

- What type of business or organization are you trying to promote?
- Do you have a Web hosting service?
- Do you have a Web domain name reserved?
- Do you have a logo? If not, will you need me to design one?
- What is the purpose or goal of your Web site?
    - Promote products?
    - Sell products?
    - Create customer awareness?
    - Foster customer service?
    - Gather customer feedback?
    - Distribute company information via an internal Web site?
- How many sections will your Web site need?
- Will your customers be ordering products online?
- Will you provide the text for your Web site?
- Will you need full-motion video on your Web site?
- Do you want a soundtrack? If so, do you want me to provide a sound controller?

The answers to these questions will give you some of the information you need to prepare a quote.

Defining your target audience

After meeting with your client, you'll have a good idea of what your target audience is. This will determine a good deal of the content you'll add to your Flash Web site. The age and income level of your target audience determines the content for the site. For example, if you're creating a site for baby boomers, don't use a hip-hop soundtrack for background music. After you define your target audience, you'll know which part of the country or world they reside in. This will also give you an idea of what type of connection they use to surf the Internet, which will determine the bandwidth you can pump into your design.

What's the Bandwidth, Kenneth?

Another thing you'll identify when you define your target audience is the type of equipment they're likely to use to connect to the Internet. This factor determines the type of content you can put into your Flash Web site. If your target audience uses a DSL or cable modem, you have considerably more leeway than if your audience uses a dialup modem. The overall bandwidth pipeline is determined when your movie is finished. However, the techniques I show you to create Flash Web sites feature a reasonably svelte interface into which content is loaded.

However, the bandwidth issue is a factor with the individual content you load into the interface. For example, if your target audience accesses the Internet with a dialup modem, you'll have to apply more compression to the images and video that will be displayed. You will also have to use a lower frame rate to ensure that the content you load into the interface has a smaller file size and will load quickly. Importing Flash video is discussed in Chapter 9. I show you how to batch process video with the Flash 8 Video Encoder in an upcoming section in this chapter.

Soundtracks are another factor in bandwidth. For a dialup audience, you'll have to specify a lower bit rate so that the music streams into the viewer's Flash Player without any interruptions. I show you how to add background music to your site in Chapter 8.

A tale of two bandwidths

It's real simple when your entire target audience accesses the Internet in the same manner. But what happens when you have a mixed audience? Well, unfortunately, you end up creating two versions of your Web site: a skinny version for people who access the Internet with a dialup modem, and a more robust version with high-quality graphics, video, and sound. To head your viewers off at the pass, so to speak, you create an entry portal with links to the dialup and broadband versions, as shown in Figure 2-1.

Figure 2-1:
You create
an HTML
portal to
direct
viewers to
the version
of your site
that suits
their
connection
speed.

Do you need Freddy the Preloader?

Bandwidth is one issue, and the file size of each Flash movie that you load into the main interface is another. Even though you have a lean-and-mean interface, you can still run into a bandwidth issue with content you load into the interface. Flash movies are streaming content. The movie begins playing as soon as the Flash Player downloads enough information. However, you may have some frames with so much content that the Flash movie stops dead in its tracks. This is annoying enough. But the problem is exacerbated (love that word), when you've got an item such as a soundtrack that has already loaded and continues to play while the rest of the content pauses until enough information downloads for the movie to advance to the next frame. Talk about your bad lip-synch.

You'll be able to ferret out this information when your content is created. However, this doesn't help you at the beginning of the project, especially when you're creating a bid for the client. So do you have to waffle and tell the client that you *might* have to bill them additional for a preloader (which I discuss in Chapter 8)? No. You can safely assume that you should include a preloader in your bid if the following are to be included in the content:

✔ Streaming video

✔ Music soundtrack

✔ Extensive use of bitmap images, especially if they occur near the start of the movie

When you present a proposal to a client, leave a spot for the client to accept the proposal. Never begin work until the client returns the signed proposal.

Put Your Ideas Down on Paper

At this stage of the workflow, you have a pretty good idea of where you're headed. Your client has given you enough information to begin laying out the design. Now it's your turn to bring your client's vision to life. Before you launch Flash and start creating symbols and graphics with reckless abandon, take a deep breath and prepare to do some creative mind mapping in your favorite graphics application. After you have a rough handle on the design, you can start laying out different versions of the design for client approval.

Mind mapping your brainstorm

Most people think of *mind mapping* as visual graffiti filled with circles and words of wisdom. When you mind map to create a Flash Web design, you can jot the design down on paper. However, you'll have a lot more control if you use an illustration application or a good image editing/Web design application such as Fireworks. The following steps give you a starting point for your own creative mind mapping:

1. **Launch Fireworks.**

2. **Create a new document that's the same size as your Flash Web site.**

   The default size for a Flash document is 550 pixels by 400 pixels. Eventually, you're going to use a variation of your mind map to show your design ideas to your client. If you're going to provide the client with a printed image, specify an image resolution of 300 dpi. If you're going to e-mail images to your customer, specify an image resolution of 72 dpi.

3. **Use the drawing tools to map out the various sections of your Flash Web site.**

   Traditional design calls for a banner and a vertical or horizontal menu.

4. **When creating shapes, choose colors to suit your design.**

5. **Add images and text as placeholders for other content.**

   Figure 2-2 shows the results of a mind mapping session in Fireworks.

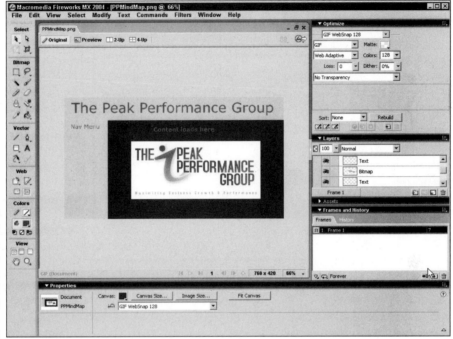

Figure 2-2:
You can use
an image
editing
application
to map out
your design.

You can create an effective color scheme by sampling colors from your favorite image.

Creating a storyboard

After you have a couple of ideas on how to assemble the site, your next job is to create a storyboard (or as some designers call them, *comps*) to present to the client. You can easily create multiple variations of an idea by using a Fireworks feature normally used for animation. To use Fireworks to create a storyboard of your Web design for client review, follow these steps:

1. **Launch Fireworks.**

2. **Open your mind-mapping session.**

3. **Refine the shapes and add text to the banner.**

4. **Flesh out the navigation menu section of the site by adding type to show each section of the site.**

5. **Add your client's logo and any images that will appear when the site opens.**

   Figure 2-3 shows one version of a Web site created in Fireworks.

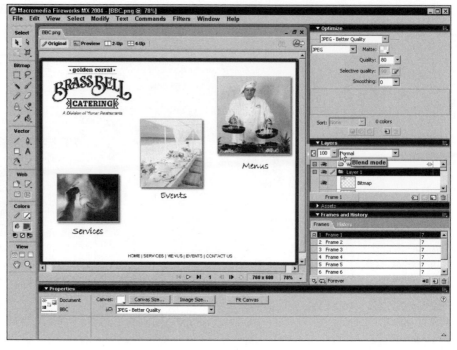

Figure 2-3:
You can
use an
application
like Fire-
works to
create a
mock-up of
your design.

6. **Open the Frames palette, select the first frame, and then click the New/Duplicate Frame icon.**

   Fireworks creates a carbon copy of the first frame.

7. **Create a variation of the first frame.**

   This will be the second design you present to the client. You can change the manner in which the menu is displayed, change the placement of objects, change colors, and so on. Figure 2-4 shows another variation of the design.

8. **Create additional frames to create different variations of the design.**

9. **After creating different variations of your design, choose File⇨Export to open the Export dialog box, shown in Figure 2-5.**

10. **Choose the desired file format in which to save the images and then, from the Save as Type drop-down menu, choose Frames to Files.**

11. **Name the document and then click Save.**

    After you export the frames, you'll have multiple files with the same base filename but appended with the number of the frame. You can now e-mail the individual versions to your client for consideration.

Figure 2-4:
Create a frame for each variation of your design.

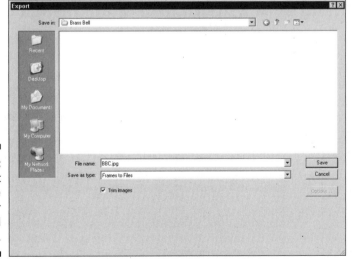

Figure 2-5:
You export each frame of your storyboard as a file.

You can achieve similar results in other image editing applications by duplicating the document and then making changes to the individual elements to create a variation of your original design. This process is easier if your image editing application features layers. If you own Photoshop CS or CS2, you can use the Layer Comps feature to manage alternate versions of the design.

When the client returns your e-mail with his or her choice, print a copy of the e-mail and save it in the client's file. If you really want to be efficient, have the client initial his or her choice and return it to you by mail.

Gathering Your Assets (Or, Wool Gathering)

Believe it or not, even though you have approval from the client to start with the design, you're still not ready to rock and roll in Flash. Flash does many things well and tries to do them all. However, there are still a few housekeeping details you need to tend to outside of Flash. In the upcoming sections, I show you how to deal with images, sounds, and video prior to beginning your design in Flash.

Creating and optimizing your images

If your Flash Web design calls for images, you should optimize your images in an image editing application prior to importing them into the Flash Library. Flash can apply wholesale compression to every image in your Flash documents; however, you always do best using a WYSIWYG (What You See Is What You Get) image optimization command in an application such as Photoshop or Fireworks. With these applications, you can also create montages and add text to create some really flashy images for your Flash document. The following steps illustrate how you can optimize an image for a Flash movie with Fireworks:

1. **Launch Fireworks and open the image you need to optimize.**

   The images you use in a Flash movie can come from a wide variety of sources: clip art, your client, your digital camera, a scanned image, and so on. The only real limit is your imagination. Figure 2-6 shows an image in Fireworks undergoing a complete makeover prior to entering the witness-protection program.

2. **Add sundry items in Fireworks, such as text, drop shadows, and other cool effects.**

Figure 2-6:
You optimize
images prior
to importing
them to
Flash.

3. **In the Optimize panel, shown in Figure 2-7, choose JPEG from the Export File Format drop-down menu.**

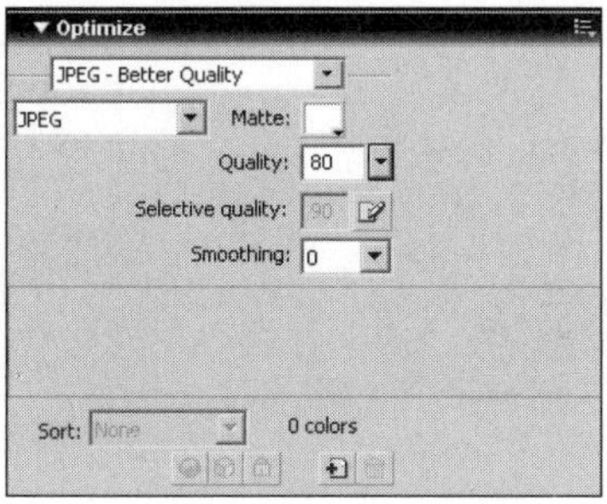

Figure 2-7:
You use the
Optimize
panel to fine
tune the
image for
use in Flash.

4. **In the Document window (refer to Figure 2-6), click the 2-Up button to display the original version of your image side by side with the image using the current optimization settings.**

5. **In the Optimize palette, click the Quality down arrow and then drag the Quality slider to determine image quality.**

Alternatively, you can enter a value between 0 (high compression, low image quality, small file size) and 100 (little or no compression, high image quality, large file size) in the Quality text field.

Use a value of 70 to 80 for any large images that will be prominent in your design. Of course, file size is a factor. You'll be able to see the file size with the current optimization settings by looking in the right pane of the Document window, as shown in Figure 2-8. You'll also be able to see the effects of your optimization on the quality of the image. If you begin to see individual pixels, you've gone way too far.

6. **Choose File⇨Export to open the Export dialog box.**

7. **From the Save as Type drop-down menu, choose Images Only.**

8. **Name the document and then click Save.**

If you're optimizing several images that will be shown in a Flash slide show, give the images the same name and append them with _01, _02, _03, and so on. When you import the images into Flash, Flash recognizes that you are importing images that appear to be part of an image sequence and gives you the option to import them to consecutive frames.

Figure 2-8:
Compare the optimized version with the original.

Rounding up sound bites for your site

Sound is a staple at many Flash Web sites. Flash Web designers use sound for buttons and add soundtracks to their Flash productions. Back in the Jurassic period of Flash development, Flash shipped with a library of button sounds. But, like the Jurassic period, button sounds have gone the way of the dodo. Therefore, you'll have to create your own or do some surfing on the Net to pick up some royalty-free sounds. You can also find royalty-free soundtracks at many of these sites. The easiest way to find sound for your Flash movies is to do a Google search. Listed here are a few sites where you can find royalty-free button sounds and soundtracks:

- ✔ **Flash Kit Sound Loops** (www.flashkit.com/loops): Here you can download a wide variety of free sound loops in various musical genres.

- ✔ **Flash Kit Sounds** (www.flashkit.com/soundfx): At this URL, you can download free sound effects that you can use for buttons and Flash games.

- ✔ **Shockwave.com** (www.shockwave-sound.com): This site features a wide array of reasonably priced sound loops that you can use in your Flash productions. You can preview sound loops prior to purchasing them.

- ✔ **Soundrangers.com** (www.soundrangers.com): Yet another site chock-full of a wide variety of reasonably priced, royalty-free sound loops. Loops can be previewed prior to purchase.

- ✔ **Loopsound.com** (www.loopsound.com): This site features a diverse collection of reasonably priced, royalty-free sound loops that can be previewed prior to purchase.

If you're the real creative type and you have a bit of musical background, you can create your own Flash soundtracks and button sounds by using applications like Sony Acid Music (Windows only) or Garage Band (Macintosh only). After you create a soundtrack for your production, save it as an MP3 file with a data rate of 128 Kbps. In Flash, you can optimize the soundtrack for the intended audience, a topic I discuss in Chapter 12. Figure 2-9 shows an Acid project under construction. With this application, you use royalty-free music samples to create your soundtrack. The software is quite sophisticated, enabling you to mix and match samples with different numbers of beats per measure. The software matches the beat of each sample to the project beat. The end result is a seamless sound loop that is perfect for a Flash soundtrack.

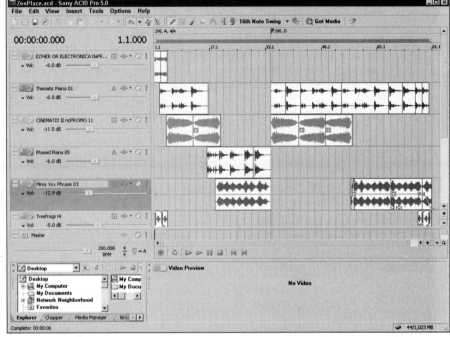

Figure 2-9:
You can
create your
own sound
loops by
using third-
party
software.

Adding vexing video

Video can be used to good effect at many Web sites. Fortunately for the Flash Web designer, video can be added fairly painlessly. And painless video is a good thing, especially if you're creating a Flash Web site for a dentist. But I digress. . . . Flash 8 Professional ships with a gem known as the Flash 8 Video Encoder, an application that enables you to encode supported video into the *FLV (Flash Video) format. From within the application, you can compress video to suit the connection speed of your intended audience. And with the Flash 8 Video Encoder, you can process multiple files while you're doing something more important, like catching up on your sleep or giving your cat a bath. To compress video using the Flash 8 Video Encoder:

1. **Launch the Flash 8 Video Encoder.**

   The Flash 8 Video Encoder application appears, as shown in Figure 2-10.

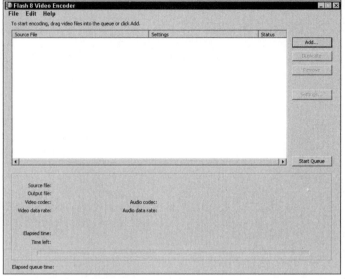

Figure 2-10:
You can
encode
multiple
video files
with the
Flash 8
Video
Encoder.

2. **Click the Add button.**

   The Open dialog box appears.

3. **Navigate to the video files you want to encode, select them, and then click Open.**

   The video files appear in the Flash 8 Video Encoder window, showing the default settings, as shown in Figure 2-11.

   At this stage in the encoding process, all files are selected, so you can apply the same settings to all files, or select an individual file and tailor the settings for that particular file. In most instances, you'll be applying the same settings to all files because they're all going in the same Web site.

   If you're creating alternate versions of the Web site for people who access the Internet with different equipment than your main target audience, click the Duplicate button to create a duplicate of each file to which you can apply settings that are appropriate for the type of equipment used by the target audience of your alternate Web site.

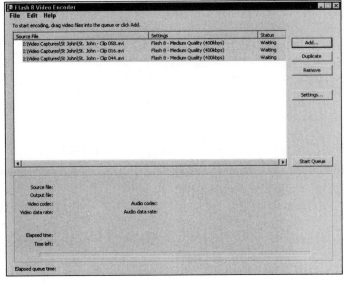

Figure 2-11:
How sweet
it is to be
encoded
by you.

4. Click the Settings button.

The Flash Video Encoding Settings dialog box, shown in Figure 2-12, appears.

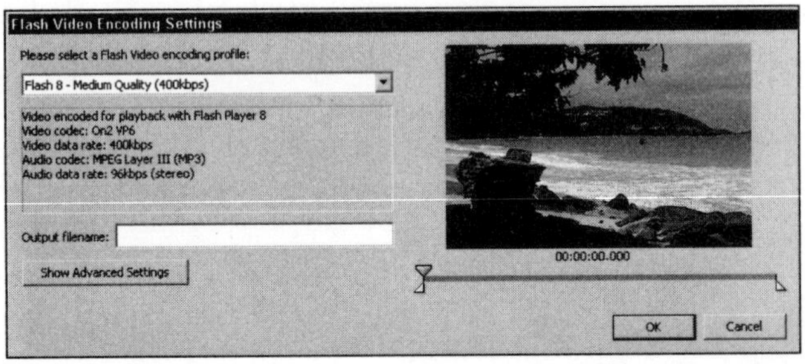

Figure 2-12:
Choosing
the
applicable
encoding
settings for
your target
audience.

5. Choose the desired setting from the Encoding Profile drop-down list.

You can choose from Flash 7 and Flash 8 Player presets. You can choose from settings applicable for modem users, or choose low-, medium-, or high-quality video. The default medium-quality setting is good for viewers who access the Internet with DSL modems. If your target audience accesses the Internet with high-speed cable modems, you can use the high-quality setting. Note that each setting has a different *data rate*, which is the amount of data transmitted to users' modems as measured in kilobytes per second. You can choose one of the defaults or modify a default by clicking the Show Advanced Settings button, as shown in the next step.

6. **Click the Show Advanced Settings button if you want to modify any default settings.**

   The Flash Video Encoding Settings dialog box reconfigures, as shown in Figure 2-13.

   The advanced settings enable you to encode both video and audio, which is the default, or you can encode either one or the other by deselecting the applicable check box.

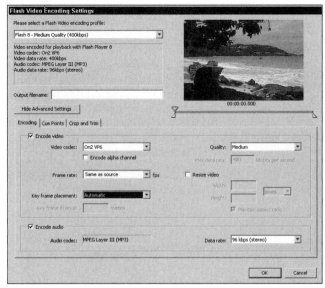

Figure 2-13: Specifying custom video settings.

7. **In the Encode Video section, set the following parameters:**

   - **Video Codec:** Click the down arrow and choose On2 VP6 (for the Flash 8 Player) or Sorenson Spark (for the Flash 7 Player).

   - **Quality:** Choose Low (150 kbps), Medium (400 kbps), High (700 kbps), or Custom. If you choose Custom, the Custom text field becomes available, which enables you to type the desired setting in kbps.

   - **Frame Rate:** Accept the default Same As Source option or choose the desired frame rate from the drop-down menu.

     The frame rate of the video must match the frame rate of the Flash movie in which the video plays.

   - **Resize Video:** Select this check box to reveal the Width and Height fields. Then type the desired values in either field if you have the Maintain Aspect Ratio check box enabled. If the video you are resizing was captured with an NTSC video camera, the aspect ratio of the original video is configured for a TV screen, and the pixels are rectangular. Because your video will be viewed on a computer monitor, you should deselect the Maintain Aspect Ratio check box and then enter the desired width and height. For a computer monitor, the aspect ratio is 3 to 2. An example of a video size for a computer monitor is 320 x 240 pixels.

- **Key Frame Placement:** Accept the default Automatic setting, and the Flash 8 Video determines how often *keyframes* are placed. A keyframe renders the entire frame, whereas the in-between frames render the portion of the video that has changed since the last keyframe. If you choose Custom from the Key Frame Placement drop-down menu, you can specify the interval between keyframes. A smaller interval between keyframes encodes a video with finer detail at the expense of a larger file size.

8. **In the Encode Audio section, specify the data rate for the audio from the Data Rate drop-down menu.**

   Choosing a high data rate ensures better-quality sound at the expense of a larger file size. You can render high-quality audio with a data rate of 80 kbps. If your video contains only the spoken word, you can get by with a data rate of 32 kbps and still have acceptable quality.

9. **Type a name in the Output Filename text field if your changes are for one video.**

   When you change settings for multiple videos, you cannot change the filename.

10. **Click OK to apply the custom settings.**

    The Flash Video Encoding Settings dialog box closes.

11. **Click Start Queue.**

    The Flash 8 Video Encoder processes your video files.

    The resulting file(s) will be in FLV (Flash Video) format, which you can then import into Flash, as outlined in Chapter 8.

If you want to encode your video later (I always encode my video while I sleep), choose File⇨Save Queue and then close the Flash 8 Video Encoder. When you next open the application, all of the files you saved are listed in the queue. Click the Start Queue button to process the files.

To store your processed files in a folder other than the folder from which the source files were opened, choose Edit⇨Preferences and then select the Place Output Files In check box. This enables the Browse button, which you use to specify the folder in which you want all processed files stored.

Part II
Fleshing Out Your Design

"Amy surfs the web a lot, so for protection we installed several filtering programs that allow only approved sites through. Which of those nine sites are you looking at now, Amy?"

In this part . . .

I show you how to use the information gathered from your client to begin laying out the site. First and foremost, I show you how to create a fast-loading interface into which your other content is loaded. Then I show you how to get the word out with text, a wordy topic that I whittle down into bite-sized chunks. And if plain old static text isn't enough to get the job done, I show you how to create input text boxes, so you can get information from Web site visitors, and dynamic text, which you use to impart to Web site visitors information that has previously been stored in a variable.

A Web site's not worth a flip without navigation, which is why I show you how to add navigation to your Web site in this part of the book. Another moving topic of discussion in this part of the book is animation. To motion tween or to shape tween, that is the question.

Chapter 3

Creating the Interface

· ·

· ·

*I*f you build it, they will come. Well, maybe not everyone will come, but you stand a better chance of having those who come stay if you create a user-friendly Flash Web site. Creating an attractive Flash design involves many factors. The biggest factor is creating a drop-dead gorgeous site that loads quickly. Web site visitors are a sophisticated bunch these days. When your site first appears, the design has to grab them by the throat and make them want to see more. On the other hand, the site has to load quickly. Otherwise, your potential visitor is gone in a New York minute. And that's pretty short. In this chapter, I show you the basics for creating a compelling interface.

Creating a Bandwidth-Friendly Flash Site

Many Flash Web sites throw everything at you, *including* the kitchen sink. Unfortunately, when you have a lot of material to show — say, for example, image and video galleries for a photographer and videographer's Web site — you end up with a site that loads sooooooooooo slowly that potential viewers take a quick exit, stage left. The only way to avoid this eventuality is to create a fast-loading interface into which the other content loads.

To begin designing your interface, you create a new document in Flash that is the size of the entire Web site. You then create all the bits that make up the interface, such as the navigation menu, the banner, and any images, such as your client's logo, that will appear in every section of the site. You then create a cavernous — or not-so-cavernous, depending on the amount of content in each section — space into which the other material loads. In Chapter 7, I show you how to load content into a target movie clip with ActionScript. This work is done in the Flash workspace, which is shown in all its glory in Figure 3-1.

Toolbar   Timeline

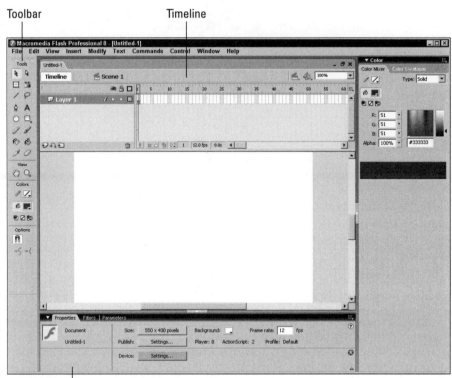

Figure 3-1:
It all begins
in the Flash
workspace.

Properties Inspector

Your graphical user interface (GUI) is created within a Flash document. You create the various bits by using the tools on the Flash toolbar. The fact that you're reading a book on Flash Web design leads your humble author to believe you already have a fundamental knowledge of Flash and the tools within. If you need a refresher course on the Flash toolbar, please refer to *Macromedia Flash 8 For Dummies,* by Ellen Finkelstein and Gurdy Leete (Wiley).

The size of your Flash movie depends on the desktop resolution used by your intended audience. The default size for a Flash movie is 550 x 400 pixels. However, you can safely assume that most Web surfers have a minimum desktop size of 800 x 600 pixels. When you factor in the size of a maximized Web browser and subtract the area needed for browser menu links, tools, and the status bar, this leaves you with an area of 760 x 420 pixels into which content can be loaded. Therefore, you're in good shape if you don't create a Flash interface larger than 760 x 420 pixels. Follow these steps to begin creating your Flash interface:

1. **Choose File⇨New to open the New Document dialog box, shown in Figure 3-2.**

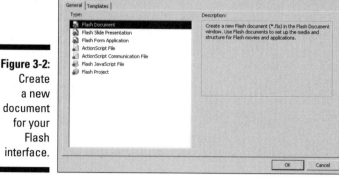

Figure 3-2:
Create
a new
document
for your
Flash
interface.

2. **Accept the default Flash Document option and click OK.**

   Flash creates a blank document with the default dimensions of 550 x 400 pixels, as shown in Figure 3-3.

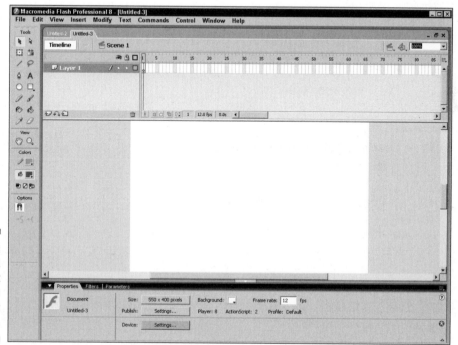

Figure 3-3:
A blank
document
needs to be
sized to suit
your design.

3. **Click the Size button in the Properties Inspector.**

   This opens the Document Properties dialog box, shown in Figure 3-4.

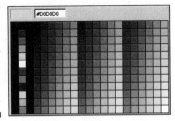

Figure 3-4:
To resize a
document,
you change
document
properties.

4. **Type the desired document dimensions in the width and height text boxes.**

   If you choose a dimension of 760 x 420 pixels and your viewers access your site with a desktop size of 800 pixels by 600 pixels, you'll have to modify the HTML document Top Margin to 0 pixels. Otherwise the default margin of 10 pixels causes a scroll bar to appear in the browser, and your viewers won't be able to see the whole movie.

5. **Click the background color swatch to reveal the Color Picker (see Figure 3-5) and then click the desired color swatch to set the background color.**

Figure 3-5:
Use the
Color Picker
to change
background
color.

Alternatively, if you know the hexadecimal code for the color, you can type it in the text box in the upper-left corner of the Color Picker. In fact, if your client specifies a color that is not in the Web 216 color palette, typing the number in the text box is the only way to ensure a match.

The background color you choose when setting up your Flash document determines the background color for the HTML document into which the Flash movie is embedded.

6. **Accept the default frame rate of 12 fps or type a different value in the Frame Rate text box.**

If your Flash movie includes video, you'll need to specify a higher frame rate. Even though at this stage of the workflow, you're building an interface into which your video will load, you must enter the video frame rate because the main movie determines the frame rate for all content.

Flash video should have a frame rate of 15 or 18 frames per second (fps).

7. **Click OK to apply the new document properties.**

Creating Symbols

To create a lean, mean Flash movie, you should always use symbols. When you create a symbol, it appears in the document Library, which means you can use the symbol in other places in your Flash movie without having to re-create it. Now how cool is that timesaver?

You can create symbols by using menu commands or by simply picking up your favorite drawing tool and going to work. After creating an object with a drawing tool, you can convert it into a symbol. You can also create a symbol by importing any file type supported by Flash and then converting that file into a symbol. In the upcoming sections, I give you a primer on Flash symbols and the creation thereof. Unfortunately, a full-blown dissertation on creating Flash symbols is beyond the scope of this book. After all, this is a book about Flash Web design. If you need a refresher course on creating Flash symbols, please refer to *Macromedia Flash 8 For Dummies* by Ellen Finkelstein and Gurdy Leete (Wiley).

Flash symbols 101

Flash symbols come in three flavors: button, graphic, and movie clip. Symbols are the lifeblood of a svelte Flash interface, and for that matter, any Flash movie. You can use a symbol repeatedly in a movie, and if you use a graphic symbol, you can change the symbol's characteristics by changing its properties. The following list gives a brief description of each symbol type and its uses:

✔ **Button:** A button symbol links to another part of your movie or to another Web page. You can create a simple one-state button or a complex multi-state button. You can also create invisible buttons as hot spots for areas of a Flash game or for a large portion of text that you want the viewer to read and then click to advance to another part in the movie.

> ✔ **Graphic:** A graphic symbol stores a graphic element that you create with the Flash drawing tools, or it houses a vector graphic you import. Graphic symbols can also be used to store bitmap objects.
>
> ✔ **Movie clip:** A movie clip symbol stores an animation. Movie clips can also be used to store bits of ActionScript.

Creating new symbols

You can create a new symbol from scratch. Doing so opens a new window in which you create the symbol. When you create a symbol, you can use multiple layers and multiple objects. Here's a quick cookbook recipe for a graphic symbol. I cover creating buttons in Chapter 5. Later in this chapter, in the "Creating a background symbol" section, I show you how to create a movie clip. Here's how you can create a graphic symbol:

1. **Choose Insert⇨Symbol to open the Create New Symbol dialog box, shown in Figure 3-6.**

Figure 3-6:
Create
symbols for
objects
you use
repeatedly.

2. **Type a name for the symbol, click the radio button to designate the type of symbol you want to create, and then click OK.**

   This opens a new window in which you create the symbol.

3. **Use the drawing tools to create a symbol.**

   Alternatively, you can import an object to the Stage and it will appear as part of the symbol.

4. **Add layers or objects to create the symbol you envision.**

   Figure 3-7 shows a symbol being created.

   If you already have a symbol in the Library that's similar to the object you need to create, drag it from the Library into the editing window. You can then use the Free Transform tool to size and position the symbol as needed. Putting a symbol within a symbol is known as *nesting* and is an effective way to decrease the file size of your published movie.

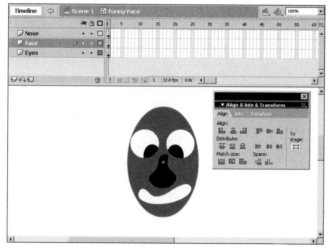

Figure 3-7:
You create symbols in a new window.

5. **Click the Scene button or the Back button to exit symbol-editing mode.**

   Your new symbol is added to the Library.

Converting objects to symbols

You can convert any object on Stage into a symbol. For that matter, you can select multiple objects and multiple frames and convert them into a symbol. This technique comes in handy when you create objects on Stage and decide you're going to use them in other parts of the movie. Follow these steps to convert objects into symbols:

1. **Select the objects you want to convert into a symbol. If necessary, select additional frames and keyframes.**

2. **Choose Modify➪Convert to Symbol to open the Create New Symbol dialog box (refer to Figure 3-6).**

3. **Click the applicable radio button to designate the type of symbol to which the objects will be converted.**

4. **Name the symbol and click OK.**

   The selected objects and frames are converted into a symbol and added to the document Library.

Creating instances of symbols

You can use a symbol as many times as needed to populate your Flash movie. This is known as creating an *instance* of a symbol. When you create an instance of a symbol, you add no overhead to the Flash movie because the Flash Player gets all the information needed to create a symbol instance from the symbol's definition in the document Library. Here's how to create an instance of a symbol:

1. **Navigate to the keyframe in which you want the symbol instance to appear.**

   Alternatively, navigate to a regular frame and then press F7 to create a blank keyframe.

2. **Choose Window⇨Library to open the document Library.**

   A small document Library is shown in Figure 3-8.

Figure 3-8:
The document Library stores all your symbols.

3. **Select the object you want to create an instance of and drag it on Stage.**

4. **Use the Free Transform tool to resize the instance as needed.**

   Resizing a symbol instance does not affect the original symbol.

To align a symbol instance to the Stage or to another selected object, choose
Window➪Align.

Editing symbols

Sometimes everything works according to Hoyle, and your Flash Web site
progresses perfectly. Other times, Murphy, the guy who wrote those infamous laws, rears his ugly head and turns your best efforts into a mockery.
Not to worry. Nothing regarding a symbol is cast in stone. You can edit a
symbol at any time. While editing a symbol, you can change the size of any
object in the symbol, change an object's color, introduce new objects to the
symbol, add more layers, and so on. When you edit a symbol, all instances of
the symbol are affected as well. After you edit a symbol, Murphy wipes the
smirk off his face. To edit a symbol, do one of the following:

- Double-click a symbol instance on the timeline to edit the symbol in
  another window.
- Double-click the symbol in the document Library to edit the symbol in
  another window.
- Choose Edit➪Edit In Place to edit the symbol on Stage. This command is
  especially useful if you're editing a symbol that needs to be edited relative to other objects on the timeline. For example, if you're editing a
  drop-down menu, the individual buttons will need to be edited regarding
  the drop-down menu system and other objects on Stage.

Working with Color

"Kodachrome, they give us those nice bright colors . . ." Just like in the Paul
Simon song, Flash has an object to give you nice bright colors. In fact, it's got
a couple of them. You can use color in many places in Flash. You use color for
text and objects you create. You can also mix up colors to change the color of
an object and to tint a symbol.

Mixing solid colors

You can mix solid colors for an object by clicking either the fill or stroke icon
prior to creating the object. You can also mix up a color and then apply it by
using the Paint Bucket tool to mix a solid color:

1. **Click the Fill or Stroke color swatch in the toolbar to open the Color
   Picker, shown in Figure 3-9.**

The fill determines the color characteristics of the object itself, while the stroke determines the color of the border around the object.

No Color icon

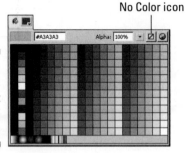

Figure 3-9:
You can fill
an object
with solid
colors.

2. **Click the desired swatch.**

   The preset swatches, unless you change them, are colors from the Web 216 color palette. These colors are Web safe and look the same on both Windows and Macintosh machines. If you want an object with no stroke or no fill, click the No Color icon.

3. **Accept the default Alpha value of 100 percent or enter a different value.**

   If you choose a value less than 100, objects from the underlying layers will be partially visible where the underlying object intersects the object you are creating.

4. **Select the drawing tool for the object you want to create and then create the object.**

   The object has the fill and stroke colors you specified.

Using the Ink Bottle and Paint Bucket tools

You can change the color of a stroke by using the Ink Bottle tool, or change the color of a fill by using the Paint Bucket tool. The Paint Bucket tool uses the color you mix in the Fill color swatch, and the Ink Bottle tool uses the color you mix in the Stroke color swatch.

Here's how you change the fill color of an object:

1. **Mix the desired color in the Fill color swatch.**

2. **Select the Paint Bucket tool.**

3. **Click inside the object to change its fill.**

And here's how you change the stroke color of an object:

1. **Mix the desired color in the Stroke color swatch.**
2. **Select the Ink Bottle tool.**
3. **Click inside the object to change its stroke.**

Creating colorful gradients

You can also fill an object with a colorful gradient. A *gradient* comprises multiple colors that are blended together. You can also edit a preset gradient and save it for future use. To fill an object with a color gradient, just click the Fill color swatch to open the Color Picker (see Figure 3-10) and then click the desired gradient preset.

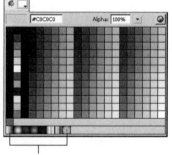

Figure 3-10:
You can use gradients to fill objects.

Gradient presets

You can also select a color by using the Swatches panel (Window⇨Swatches).

Using the Color Mixer

The Color Mixer makes it possible for you to mix up a custom color or gradient not found in the Swatches palette. The Color Mixer enables you to mix colors using the RGB (red, green, blue) or HSB (hue, saturation, and brightness) color model. You can also enter the hexadecimal equivalent for a color.

Follow these steps to mix a color by using the Color Mixer:

1. **Choose Window⇨Color Mixer to open the Color Mixer panel, shown in Figure 3-11.**

   The Color panel shows the current fill and stroke colors.

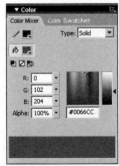

Figure 3-11:
You can use
the Color
Mixer to
specify
stroke and
fill colors.

2. **Click the stroke or fill color swatch to open the Color Mixer.**

3. **Choose a stroke or fill color that is close to the color you want to mix.**

4. **Type the R, G, and B values of the color, if known, in the R, G, and B text boxes.**

   Alternatively, you can drag inside the Color Well to choose a color and then drag the slider to the right to determine the hue of the color. As you drag the sliders, the values update in real time.

   You can also mix a color by typing the hexadecimal value of the color in the Hexadecimal text box.

5. **Accept the default Alpha value of 100% or type a different value in the Alpha text box.**

   If you specify a value below 100, the colors of the underlying objects show through where they overlap the object for which you're mixing the color.

You can also mix a gradient by using the Color Mixer:

1. **Choose Window⇨Color Mixer to open the Color Mixer.**

2. **Click the Fill color swatch and choose a preset gradient.**

   The Color Mixer reconfigures to show a Gradient Bar and a swatch that displays the gradient blend, as shown in Figure 3-12.

Figure 3-12:
You can mix
colorful
gradients
with the
Color Mixer.

3. To change a color in the gradient, click the desired color stop in the Gradient Bar and then specify the color by typing the R, G, and B values in the R, G, and B text fields, or by clicking inside the Color Well to specify the base color and then dragging the Hue slider to determine the color hue.

4. If desired, type an Alpha value less than 100 in the Alpha text field.

   This lets the colors of underlying objects show through where they intersect the object for which you are mixing the gradient.

5. To add another color to the gradient, click the Gradient Bar where you want the new color to appear and then mix the new color.

6. To remove a color from a gradient, click the applicable stop and drag it beyond the boundary of the Gradient Bar.

7. To change the position where a color appears in the gradient, click the applicable color stop and drag it to a new position.

8. To save a modified gradient, click the Option icon in the upper-right corner of the Color panel to open the Color Mixer options menu and choose Add Swatch.

   The new gradient appears in the Swatches panel for future use and also appears in the Color Picker when you click the Fill or Stroke color swatch.

You can convert a radial gradient to a linear gradient, or vice versa, by choosing the applicable option from the Type drop-down menu.

You can also use a bitmap as a fill. This option is handy when you want to fill an object with tiles of an image — for example, a client's logo. To fill an object with a bitmap, choose Bitmap from the Type drop-down menu and then navigate to the bitmap you want to use as a fill.

Using the Gradient Transform tool

When you fill an object with a gradient, it is scaled to fit the object. You can, however, change the way in which a gradient is displayed in an object by using the Gradient Transform tool:

1. Select the object.

2. Select the Gradient Transform tool.

   Handles appear around the object, as shown in Figure 3-13.

Width handle

Focal Point handle   Scale handle

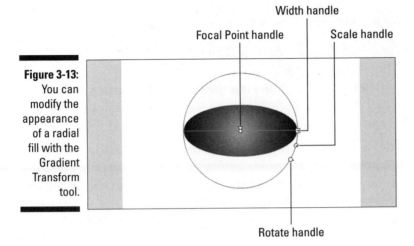

Figure 3-13:
You can
modify the
appearance
of a radial
fill with the
Gradient
Transform
tool.

Rotate handle

3. **Drag the Width handle to change the width of the gradient relative to the object.**

4. **Drag the Focal Point handle to determine where the center of the gradient appears in the object.**

5. **Drag the Scale handle to increase or decrease the size of the gradient relative to the object it is filling.**

6. **Drag the Rotate slider to rotate the fill.**

Fleshing Out the Interface

Now that you know all about how to create symbols and modify their colors, it's time to flesh out your interface. The final interface will have a banner, a navigation menu, and a place for content. Depending on your grand vision, or your client's grand vision, the contents may or may not have animation and may or may not have bitmap images. In the following sections, I show you how to flesh out the Flash document that will become the interface for your Flash Web site.

Creating Symbols for Content

At this stage of the project, I generally prefer to put placeholders for the content that match the ideas I came up with when mind mapping the Web site (see Chapter 2). I then add the needed elements, such as text, buttons, and other graphic symbols, that match my original vision. I use shapes that are the appropriate color and then convert them into symbols. The symbols function as more than placeholders; they contain a layer upon which other objects are placed.

Creating a banner symbol

The banner for a Flash Web site tells viewers what the site is all about. Even though the HTML document in which your Flash interface is embedded has a title, it's barely visible. To let the world know you've got a killer Flash Web site to show them, you create a banner that contains text and perhaps bitmap images. Begin by creating a shape that will be the basis for your banner:

1. **Select the Rectangle tool.**

2. **Click the Fill color swatch and choose the desired fill color.**

   The Background color you specify when creating the document is the color for the background of the HTML document in which the Flash interface movie is embedded. Choose a different color for the interface objects.

3. **If desired, click the Stroke color swatch and specify a color for the stroke.**

   I generally prefer to use no stroke around the banner.

4. **Create the shape that will be the basis for the banner.**

5. **Select the shape and, in the Properties Inspector, type the width and height for the banner in the W and H text boxes.**

6. **Press F8 to convert the shape into a symbol.**

   The Create New Symbol dialog box opens.

7. **Name the symbol** Banner.

8. **Select the Graphic radio button and then click OK to complete the conversion.**

   Figure 3-14 shows a placeholder for a banner.

If you're going to animate the banner, convert the shape to a movie clip symbol.

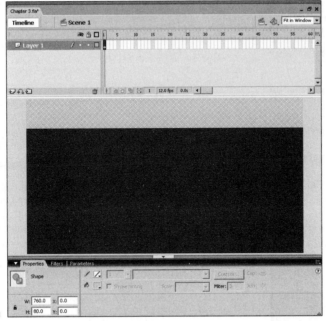

Figure 3-14:
You flesh out your design by creating shapes as place-holders for each element.

Creating a menu symbol

Your consultation with your client, combined with your mind-mapping and storyboard sessions, will determine the shape and placement of your menu. If you have more sections to display than you have space to display them, you need to create drop-down menus. This can easily be done after you've defined a shape for the menu content. If your menu is appearing beneath the banner, the shape should be high enough to overlap the text that will be used for the button shapes. I find that a horizontal menu between 25 and 30 pixels high is sufficient. If you're creating a vertical menu on the left side of the interface, the menu should be wide enough to display the longest menu selection with about 10 pixels to spare. Follow these steps to create a menu placeholder:

1. **Select the Rectangle tool.**

2. **Click the Fill color swatch and choose the desired fill color.**

3. **Create the shape that will be the placeholder for your navigation menu.**

4. **Select the shape and, in the Properties Inspector, type the width and height for your menu in the W and H text fields.**

5. **Align the placeholder to the left side of the interface.**

6. **Press F8 to convert the shape into a symbol.**

   The Convert to Symbol dialog box appears.

7. **Name the symbol** Menu **and then select the Graphic radio button.**

8. **Click OK to exit the Convert to Symbol dialog box.**

   Figure 3-15 shows the design with a menu symbol.

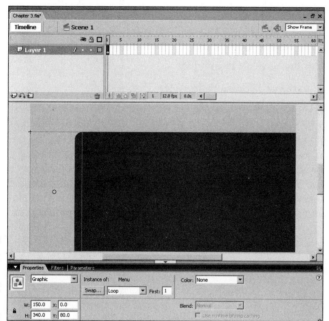

Figure 3-15:
Creating a
symbol for
the menu.

Creating a background symbol

Some Flash designers like to pop content other than a banner and navigation menu into their designs. However, this adds to the overhead of the site, which means it takes longer to load. If the client wants to include graphic content as the site opens, you can load it into the background symbol, which is actually a target for the content that will be loaded into the interface. You also use this symbol as a target for other content that loads into the interface. Here's how to create a background symbol:

1. **Choose Insert⇨New Symbol.**

   The Create New Symbol dialog box opens (refer to Figure 3-6).

2. **Click the Movie Clip radio button and name the movie clip** TargetMC.

3. **Click OK to enter symbol-editing mode.**

4. **Click the Back button to exit symbol-editing mode.**

   That's right. There's no graphic content for the background symbol. It functions solely as a target into which you load other content with ActionScript.

5. Drag the TargetMC symbol from the document Library and align it to the intersection of the menu and banner symbols.

In the design I've created, the menu has a curve, therefore I align it to the end of the curve where it intersects with the banner.

You can use the Properties Inspector to precisely align the TargetMC symbol. Type the horizontal position of the Menu symbol in the X text field and then type the vertical position of the Banner symbol in the Y text field.

6. Open the Properties Inspector.

7. In the <Instance Name> field, type TargetMC.

A symbol instance needs a unique name when you're referring to it with ActionScript. This is not the same as the name you gave the symbol. ActionScript does not recognize the name you gave the symbol, but it does recognize the instance name you assign in the Properties Inspector. ActionScript will be used on each button to tell the Flash Player which Flash movie to load into the named instance of the TargetMC symbol when the button is clicked. The interface with the background symbol is shown in Figure 3-16.

Figure 3-16:
Background symbols are place-holders for other content.

Creating a template for content

After you create the placeholder symbols for your interface, the next step is to create a document that will serve as a template for the content you load into the interface. The content all loads into the same area; therefore, you can create a single template and use this as the basis for all content you load into the interface. Here's how you can create a content template:

1. **Subtract the height of the banner from the height of the interface.**

   This dimension will be the height of your content template.

2. **If you have a vertical menu, subtract the width of the navigation menu from the width of the document.**

   If you have a horizontal menu, subtract the height of the menu from the result of Step 1.

3. **Create a new document.**

4. **Click the Size button.**

5. **Open the Properties Inspector and type the width and height of your template in the Width and Height text fields.**

6. **Click the Background color swatch and choose the same background color as specified in your Interface document.**

7. **Choose File⇨Save As to open the Save As dialog box.**

8. **Name the document** Template **and then click OK.**

Working with layers

If you've followed along with this chapter from paragraph one, all of your symbols are stacked on a single layer. When you have only three symbols, this doesn't present a problem. However, as you add to your project, a single layer just won't cut the mustard. Besides, some types of animation are not possible when you have more than one object on a layer.

Layers are like sheets of acetate placed on top of the objects on the underlying layer. You can see all of the objects until you add an object to the new layer, in which case, the objects on underlying layers directly underneath the topmost object will be eclipsed. Now that you have an idea of what function layers serve, it's time to serve some up.

Creating layers

The only way to efficiently organize content in any Flash document is with layers. Layers can be labeled to reflect their purpose. Animations should always be on separate layers. ActionScript should be on separate layers as well. To demonstrate how layers are created, follow these steps to create a layer on which your ActionScript for the Web site will reside:

1. **Right-click (Windows) or Control-click (Macintosh) the layer over which you want to create a new layer.**

2. **Choose Insert Layer from the Context menu.**

   Flash creates a new layer.

3. **Double-click the layer you just created.**

   This highlights the text, indicating you can type a new name for the layer, as shown in Figure 3-17.

Figure 3-17:
Rename
layers
for easy
identifica-
tion.

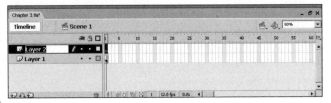

4. **Type a new name for the layer.**

   The name should reflect the layer's purpose, which in this case is storing ActionScript, hence the name in Figure 3-18.

Figure 3-18:
Rename a
layer to
reflect its
purpose.

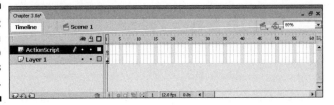

Distributing objects to layers

If you've been reading this chapter from the start, you know that I've created three symbols for the interface residing on one layer and a layer for ActionScript. If you haven't been reading this chapter from the start, you've missed some intriguing words of wisdom and the offhand joke or four. But you do know that one layer contains three symbols, and another layer is for ActionScript because I told you so in the first sentence of this section. Now, to get organized and distribute all the objects to their own layers, follow these steps:

1. **Select the objects you want to distribute to layers.**

2. **Right-click (Windows) or Control-click (Macintosh) the selection and choose Distribute to Layers from the context menu.**

   Flash distributes the selected items to layers and names them according to the name you gave the symbol, as shown in Figure 3-19. You did name each symbol, didn't you?

Figure 3-19:
Distribute
objects to
layers to
manage
complex
projects.

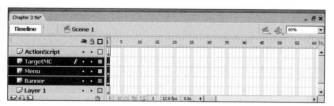

3. **Select the layer upon which the objects originally resided and press Delete to discard the layer because it is now empty.**

   Alternatively, you can select the layer and then click the icon that looks like a trashcan at the bottom of the Timeline window.

Managing layers

If you create a really complex document that has a lot of really neat content, which you proficiently stack on layers, you probably have a Flash document that really has a lot of layers. And that's difficult to manage with all the other stuff going on in the Flash workspace. In the upcoming sections, I show you how to rearrange the stacking order of layers and streamline the timeline by segregating layers that have similar functions in a layer folder.

Arranging the stacking order of layers

Objects on the uppermost layer eclipse items on the layer immediately underneath, and objects on that second layer eclipse items on the next lower layer, and so on. As you're working on your Flash project, you may decide that you need to rearrange the order in which the layers are stacked. To rearrange the layer order, in the left timeline window, simply select the layer you want to move and drag it up or down; continue in this manner until the layers are arranged as desired.

Here's a quick-and-dirty list of layer know-how you'll probably remember from Flash 101:

  ✔ **Hide a layer** by clicking the eye icon to the left of the layer's name.

  ✔ **Lock a layer** by clicking the lock icon to the left of its name.

✔ **Hide all layers** by clicking the eye icon above the uppermost layer. Click the eye icon again to reveal hidden layers.

✔ **Lock all layers** by clicking the lock icon above the uppermost layer. Click the lock icon again to unlock locked layers.

Creating a layer folder

Naming and rearranging layers are two ways you manage layers. The third is known as a *layer folder*. Layer folders are very handy when you create complex animations that span multiple layers. When you create a layer folder, you can collapse several layers to a single icon in the timeline window. When you need to access the layers within the folder, you expand the layer. Here's how you create a layer folder:

1. **Select the uppermost layer that you want to store in a layer folder.**

2. **Click the Layer Folder icon near the lower-left corner of the timeline window.**

   Flash creates an empty layer folder, as shown in Figure 3-20.

Figure 3-20:
Store
multiple
layers in a
layer folder.

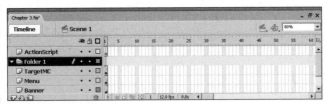

3. **Double-click the folder.**

   The text is highlighted, indicating that you can rename the folder.

4. **Type a new name for the folder.**

   Choose a name that reflects the folder's purpose in your project.

5. **Drag each layer you want to store in the folder to the folder name.**

   When you release the mouse button, the layer is indented, indicating that the layer has been successfully added to the folder.

6. **Add the other layers you want to store in the folder and, if necessary, rearrange the stacking order of layers in the folder.**

   Figure 3-21 shows a folder with three layers in it.

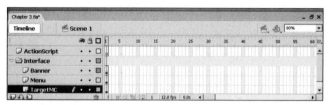

7. **Click the downward-pointing arrow to the left of a layer name to collapse it to a single icon in the timeline window, as shown in Figure 3-22.**

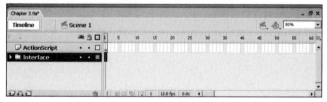

8. **Click the right-pointing arrow to the left of a layer name to expand the layer.**

Chapter 4

Getting the Word Out

*F*lash is all about motion and animation, but sometimes you've got to get the word out with text. A picture is worth a thousand words, which means you need at least a thousand words to describe a picture. And if you have to describe 10 or 15 pictures . . . yikes, that's a whole lotta text! In this chapter, I show you how to use the Text tool to add text to your Flash Web designs. I also show you how to format text so you've got, you know, Flashy text. And those clever Flash designers have also given you a way to receive and dispense information. These devices are known as *input text* and *dynamic text*. And if you have more text than you can fit in your Flash Web site, I show you how to deal with that, too. And you make them all with the handy-dandy Text tool, otherwise know as *Text-O-Matic*.

Using the Text Tool

Flash designers tried to cleverly disguise the Text tool, making it look like a child's building block with a capital A inside it. But I bet that didn't fool you one bit. Even though the Text tool may look simple, it is capable of doing many things. With it, you can create text that can be viewed on any machine, create a text box to fill an area, create text boxes to receive and display information, and so on.

Creating static text

In order to add text to your Flash Web site, you gotta use the Text tool. It's a law. The Text tool resides on the Flash toolbar. In this section, I show you how to create static text. Static text is your ho-hum get-the-job-done text when you need to add words of wisdom — or for that matter any words — to your Flash Web site. To create static text, follow these steps:

1. **Select the Text tool.**

2. **Choose Window⇨Properties to open the Properties Inspector, shown in Figure 4-1, and then choose Static Text from the Text Type drop-down menu.**

   I know there's a lot of stuff in the Properties Inspector. Not to worry, I show you how to format your text in the next section.

Figure 4-1:
You format text in the Properties Inspector.

3. **Click the spot on Stage where you want the text to appear.**

   A text box appears on Stage, as shown in Figure 4-2. At this point, you can begin typing and resize the text box when you're done. However, it's a good idea to size the text box ahead of time, as shown in the next step.

Figure 4-2:
You determine the area where text will appear and how large an area it appears in.

4. **Drag the square handle in the upper-right corner to resize the text box to the desired width.**

   If you double-click the square handle, it becomes a round handle, which means you can type 'til the cows come home and the text won't wrap to the next line. If you choose this option, press Enter or Return to start a new line of text.

5. **Type the desired text.**

   As you type, the text automatically wraps to the next line (unless you double-clicked the square handle). Figure 4-3 shows the results of using the Text tool.

"The quick brown fox jumps over the lazy dog."

Figure 4-3:
Static text can tell a tale to your Web site visitors.

Making text pretty

When you create text with the Text tool, the font parameters last used are applied to the text. This is all well and good when you're creating a bunch of text that is all the same. However, when you create the first block of text in a document, you need to tell Flash what you want the text to look like. You take care of these details in the Properties Inspector. From within the Properties Inspector, you can choose the text font, size, color, and a whole lot of other things. Follow these steps to format text:

1. **Select the Text tool.**

2. **Choose Window⇨Properties to open the Properties Inspector (shown in Figure 4-4), which you'll find directly below the Stage.**

3. **Choose Static Text from the Text Type drop-down menu.**

4. **Choose the desired font type from the Font drop-down menu.**

5. **Drag the Font Size slider to set the text size.**

   Alternatively, you can enter a value in the Font Size text field.

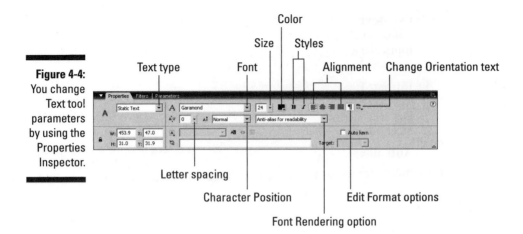

Figure 4-4:
You change
Text tool
parameters
by using the
Properties
Inspector.

Text type — Font — Color — Size — Styles — Alignment — Change Orientation text

Letter spacing — Character Position — Font Rendering option — Edit Format options

TIP

6. **Click the Text Fill color swatch to open the Color Picker and select the desired color from the preset swatches.**

   After clicking the Text Fill color swatch, you can click any item on Stage, or for that matter, anything in the Flash workspace, to sample the color directly beneath your pointer.

7. **Click the applicable style icon to boldface or italicize the text.**

8. **Click the applicable alignment icon to determine how the text will be aligned.**

   Your choices are left aligned, centered, right aligned, and justified.

9. **Click the Text Orientation icon and choose an option from the drop-down list.**

   Your choices are Horizontal; Vertical, Left to Right; and Vertical, Right to Left.

10. **Drag the Letter Spacing slider to determine the distance between each letter.**

    The default value of 0 uses the font's kerning information to determine spacing. You can increase or decrease the spacing between letters.

11. **Choose an option from the Character Position drop-down menu.**

    Your choices are Normal, Superscript, and Subscript.

12. **Choose an option from the Font Rendering drop-down list.**

    Your choices are as follows:

- **Use Device Fonts:** This option uses fonts installed on the viewer's machine. While this option offers the smallest file size because fonts are not embedded with the published file, the font you specify must be present on the user's machine.

- **Bitmap Text (No Anti-alias):** This option provides no anti-aliasing. Text is rendered with a sharp edge. This option increases the file size of the published SWF file. The text looks crisp at the published size, but scales poorly.

- **Anti-alias for Animation:** This option renders text for a smoother animation. This option creates a larger file because fonts are embedded with the published movie. If you specify a font size of 10 or smaller, the text will be hard to read.

- **Anti-alias for Readability:** This option is just what the doctor ordered if you're displaying copious amounts of text that you want the viewer to read. This option improves readability of small font sizes.

- **Custom Anti-alias:** This Flash Professional–only option opens a dialog box that enables you to specify the Sharpness and Thickness of the transition between text and the surrounding pixels. This option creates a larger file.

13. **Click the Selectable icon if you want to give your viewing audience the ability to select the text.**

14. **Type your text.**

15. **Click anywhere outside of the text box when you've finished typing your text.**

To edit text you've already created, select the Text tool and then click inside the text box. Use the Text tool to select all of the text, a single word, or a single letter. You can then change the parameters of the selected text by using the Properties Inspector.

After creating a block of text, click the Filters tab in the Properties Inspector. From within this tab, you can add a drop shadow, bevel text, make glowing text, and so on.

Formatting paragraph text

If your Flash Web design calls for paragraphs of text, you must format the text to determine whether the first line of text is indented, the distance between each line, and whether the text will have left or right margins. You set these parameters from within — you guessed it — the Properties Inspector:

1. **Choose Window⇨Properties to open the Properties Inspector and format the text as outlined in the previous section.**

2. **Click the Format Options icon to open the Format Options dialog box, shown in Figure 4-5.**

   In this dialog box, you set options for paragraph text.

Figure 4-5:
You set options for paragraph text by using the Format Options dialog box.

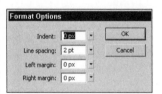

3. **Drag the Indent slider to specify the value in pixels by which the first line of text in each paragraph is indented.**

   Alternatively, you can enter a value in the Indent text field.

4. **Drag the Line Spacing slider to establish, in pixels, the space between each line.**

   Alternatively, you can enter the desired value in the Line Spacing text field.

5. **Drag the Left Margin slider to dictate the distance in pixels by which the text is offset from the left side of the text bounding box.**

   Alternatively, you can enter a value in the Left Margin field.

6. **Drag the Right Margin slider to set the distance in pixels by which the text is offset from the right margin.**

   Alternatively, you can enter a value in the Right Margin field.

7. **Click OK to close the Format Options dialog box.**

Checking your spelling, Aaron

Text is absolutely no good as a form of communication if it's not spelled correctly. Your client may supply you with text for the Web site, but that doesn't mean he or she bothered to spell check the documents before giving them to you. And no Flash Web designer in his right — or left — mind would publish a Web site with obvious typos. In order to ensure that your viewing audience sees text that is correctly spelled, you need to use Flash's spell check option. Before you can spell check text, you have to set up the Spell Checker.

Setting up the Spell Checker

When you set up the Spell Checker, you determine how Flash goes about checking the spelling. You can specify whether Flash checks the spelling in comments and labels or just in the text boxes you've created. To set up the Spell Checker, follow these steps:

1. **Choose Text⇨Spelling Setup to open the Spelling Setup dialog box, shown in Figure 4-6.**

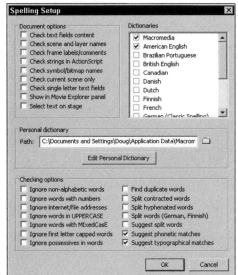

Figure 4-6:
Setting up
the Spell
Checker.

2. **Choose the desired options.**

   The options are self-explanatory, but you do have to choose some; otherwise, the Spell Checker won't work. I recommend that you include the following options when you set up the Spell Checker:

   • **Suggest Phonetic Matches:** This option gives you a list of suggestions that sound like the misspelled word.

- **Suggest Typographical Matches:** This option gives you a list of suggestions that contain letters in the misspelled word that are similar to words in the Spell Checker dictionary. For example, if you spell check *tex,* one of the suggestions is *text.*

3. **Click OK to exit the Spelling Setup dialog box.**

Using the Spell Checker

Your wonderful client sent you a document that contains all the text they want displayed on their Web site. And you, being the judicious, streamlined, workflow-oriented Flash Web designer, resort to the old cut-and-paste to populate your design with their text. But what happens if your client is a lousy speller or is mildly dyslexic? Yikes! A potential disaster is at hand, which is why the designers of Flash included a Spell Checker with the application, so you can guard against any misspelled words in your Flash design:

1. **Set up the Spell Checker as outlined in the preceding section.**

   You did read the last section, didn't you?

2. **Choose Text⇨Spell Checker.**

   The Check Spelling dialog box appears and finds the first misspelled word, as shown in Figure 4-7.

Figure 4-7:
Checking for misspelled words with the Spell Checker.

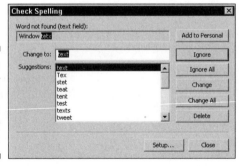

3. **Select one of the following options:**

   - **Add to Personal:** Adds the word to your personal dictionary and selects the next suspect word in the document.

   - **Ignore:** Ignores this instance of the suspect word and selects the next suspect word in the document.

- **Ignore All:** Ignores all instances of the suspect word and selects the next suspect word in the document.

- **Change:** Changes this instance of the suspect word to the word you choose from the list of suggestions or type into the Change To box.

- **Change All:** Changes all instances of the suspect word to the word you choose from the list of suggestions or type into the Change To box.

- **Delete:** Deletes the suspect word from the document.

4. **After Flash spell checks the document, a dialog box to that effect appears.**

    Now you can get back to the serious work of adding more cool stuff to your Flash Web site.

Adding text hyperlinks

Even though you'll be creating a full-fledged menu for your Flash Web site, you can also create hyperlinks from text. Many commercial Web sites like to have redundant links in their Web pages so that visitors can access pages from multiple places within the Web site. You can do the same with your Flash Web site.

Think of text hyperlinks as cross-references. You can also use text hyperlinks to connect to other Web pages, that is, on the ever-present but very important Links page. When you add text hyperlinks, you can specify where the linked URL opens.

To add a text hyperlink to your Flash Web design, follow these steps:

1. **Create a block of static text.**

    If you need a little help with this step, see the earlier section, "Creating static text."

2. **With the Text tool, select the portion of the text that will become the hyperlink.**

3. **Choose Window⊏⊐Properties to open the Properties Inspector.**

4. **Enter the URL for the hyperlink in the URL Link text box, shown in Figure 4-8.**

Figure 4-8:
You can
add text
hyperlinks
to any text
you select
with the
Text tool.

5. **Select the desired target for the hyperlink from the Target drop-down menu.**

Your choices are as follows:

- **_blank:** Opens the URL in a new Web browser window.

- **_self:** Opens the URL in the current Web browser window, which means your Flash Web site is no longer visible. This is generally not a good thing.

- **_parent:** Opens the URL in the parent of the current frame.

- **_top:** Opens the URL in the top frame in the current window.

When viewers hold their cursors over the hyperlink text, the pointing-finger cursor appears, which always seems to excite Web site visitors, as if they've discovered a deep dark secret instead of your carefully planted hyperlink. When the hyperlink is clicked, the viewer is magically transported to the URL you entered in Step 4. The URL opens in the window you selected in Step 5.

Creating an e-mail link

If you're creating a Web site for clients who want visitors to contact them, you need to add a Contact Us link somewhere in the design. Typically, Web designers add a Contact Us section to their designs, and you can do the same with Flash. However, it pays to be redundant. After all, some people may not even open the Contact Us section. To safeguard against people who don't visit the Contact Us section, add Contact Us links that open a blank e-mail document with the viewer's default e-mail application as follows:

1. **Create the desired text.**

   `Contact Us` or `Click Here For Additional Info` generally work well.

2. **Select the text with the Text tool.**

3. **Choose Window⇨Properties to open the Properties Inspector.**

4. **In the URL Link text box, enter** mailto: **followed by the e-mail address of the desired recipient, as shown in Figure 4-9.**

Figure 4-9:
Creating an
e-mail link
is almost
child's play.

5. **Select _blank from the Target drop-down list.**

That's all there is to it. When the document is published and viewers move their cursors over the hyperlink, the ubiquitous hand with the pointing finger appears, indicating a live hyperlink. When the hyperlink is clicked, the viewer's default e-mail application opens with the e-mail address you entered in Step 4.

Active Text for Fun and Profit

Static text gets the job done, giving information to your Web site visitors. But Flash can do so much more with text. Sometimes you don't want your text to be text at all, but rather prefer a bunch of individual letter shapes that you can bend, twist, move, and otherwise discombobulate. Flash's Break Apart command lets you do this.

If your design calls for getting information from your Web site visitors, you can do so by using a text input box, which is a field into which site visitors can input text. (Hmmm . . . inputting text into a text input box . . . truth in advertising . . . something that performs up to its name. How unique.)

And then there's dynamic text. The content of a dynamic text box is determined by a variable whose content can change at different points in your Flash movie. Dynamic text is a wonderful way to personalize information you present to visitors to your Flash Web site.

Breaking text apart

What was once united now is not. At least that's the case when you break apart text. When you break apart a block of text, you can select each letter of text, a useful task if you want to animate the letters. (Can you say *dancing text?*) If you apply the Break Apart command twice, you convert each letter into a vector object, which is a good thing if you want to create stylized letters. You can also apply a shape *tween* to a letter that has been converted into a vector object, which enables you to morph a letter into something else.

Here's how you break apart text into individual letters:

1. **Use the Select tool to select the block of text.**

2. **Right-click (Windows) or Control-click (Macintosh) the selected text block and choose Break Apart from the context menu.**

   Alternatively, you can press Ctrl+B (Windows) or ⌘+B (Macintosh) or choose Modify➪Break Apart to achieve the same result. Figure 4-10 shows text that has been broken apart into individual letters.

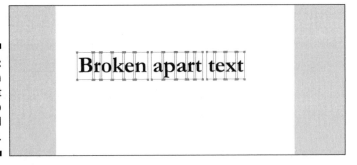

Figure 4-10:
You can break text apart into individual letters.

And here's how you break apart text into vector objects:

1. **Use the Select tool to select the block of text.**

2. **Right-click (Windows) or Control-click (Macintosh) the selected text block and choose Break Apart from the context menu.**

   Alternatively, you can press Ctrl+B (Windows) or ⌘+B (Macintosh) to achieve the same result.

3. **Repeat Step 2.**

   Figure 4-11 shows a block of text that has been broken apart into vector objects. Notice the difference between the objects in this figure and the text objects in Figure 4-10.

When you break apart text into vector objects, they can no longer be edited as text. You can, however, edit the individual objects with the Select tool, which is used to edit the path of the shape, or Subselection tool, which is used to edit the individual points that make up the shape.

Figure 4-11:
When you
break apart
text into
vector
objects,
they can no
longer be
edited as
text.

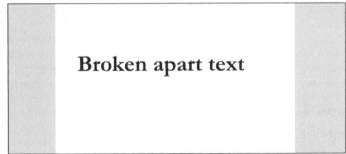

Broken apart text

Creating input text boxes

An input text box enables your Flash Web site visitors to input information, which is then stored in a variable. The contents of the variable can be used in other parts of your Flash movie; for example, you can display the contents of the variable in a dynamic text box. Here's how you create an input text box:

1. **Select the Text tool.**

2. **Choose Window⇨Properties to open the Properties Inspector.**

3. **Select the Input Text option from the Text Type drop-down menu.**

   The Properties Inspector is reconfigured to accept the parameters for input text.

4. **Specify the font attributes.**

   For a refresher course on formatting text, see the "Making text pretty" section, earlier in this chapter.

5. **Enter a name in the Var field, as shown in Figure 4-12.**

   This is the name for the variable that will store the information entered by the user.

Figure 4-12:
You create
input text
boxes to
accept
user-
provided
information.

6. **Drag the Text tool on Stage to define the area that will be occupied by the input text box.**

After entering a name in the Var field, you've provided Flash with everything it needs to know in order to store the information entered by visitors to your Flash Web site. To demonstrate the one-two punch of input text and dynamic text, I suggest you create a new document, follow the preceding steps, and then follow the steps in the next section to create a dynamic text box using the same Var name you used with the input text box. When the movie is published or tested (Ctrl+Enter [Windows] or ⌘+Return [Macintosh]), the text entered in the input text box is mirrored in the dynamic text box.

Creating dynamic text

A dynamic text box enables you to display information that is stored in a variable. Dynamic text boxes are wonderful ways to display information previously input by a user or information you've assigned to a variable. For example, you can use a dynamic text box to display information entered by a Web site visitor — shipping information, for example. Follow these steps to create a dynamic text box:

1. **Select the Text tool.**

2. **Choose Window➪Properties to open the Properties Inspector.**

3. **Select the Dynamic Text option from the Text Type drop-down menu.**

   The Properties Inspector is reconfigured to accept the parameters for dynamic text.

4. **Specify the font attributes.**

5. **Enter a variable name in the Var field.**

   This is the name of the variable that contains the information you want to display in the dynamic text box, as shown in Figure 4-13.

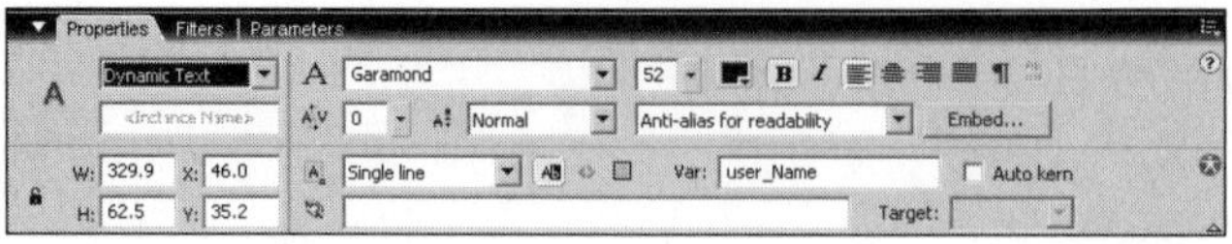

Figure 4-13:
To display data in a dynamic text box, you enter the applicable variable name.

Make sure you type the variable name correctly. Misspelled or mis-capitalized variable names translate into buggy Flash movies.

6. **Drag the Text tool on Stage to define the area occupied by the dynamic text box.**

When the movie is published, the dynamic text box displays the information stored in the variable that contains the same name you entered in the Var field in Step 5.

Stuffing 50 Pounds of Text in a 30-Pound Bag

Sometimes you have more text than room. That's like TMS syndrome — Too Much Stuff and not enough room to store it. But unlike TMS syndrome, there is an answer when you have more text than space to put it in; the answer is the TextArea component. To use the TextArea component in a Flash movie, follow these steps:

1. **Choose Window⇨Components.**

2. **Click the plus sign (+) to the left of the User Interface category to display the choices shown in Figure 4-14.**

3. **Drag the TextArea component on Stage.**

4. **Select the Free Transform tool.**

5. **Click the TextArea component and use the handles to resize the box to the desired area, as shown in Figure 4-15.**

6. **Choose Window⇨Properties to open the Properties Inspector and click the Parameters tab to reveal the parameters shown in Figure 4-16.**

7. **Enter the text for the TextArea component in the Text field.**

Create the text for the TextArea component in your favorite word processing application. Select the text and press Ctrl+C (Windows) or ⌘+C (Mac) to copy the text to the clipboard. Then place your cursor inside the TextArea component Text field and press Ctrl+V (Windows) or ⌘+V (Mac) to paste the text into the field.

Figure 4-14:
User Interface components augment your Flash design.

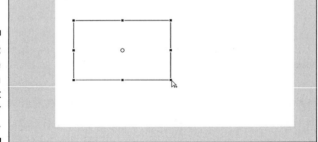

Figure 4-15:
Resize the Text Area component to suit your production.

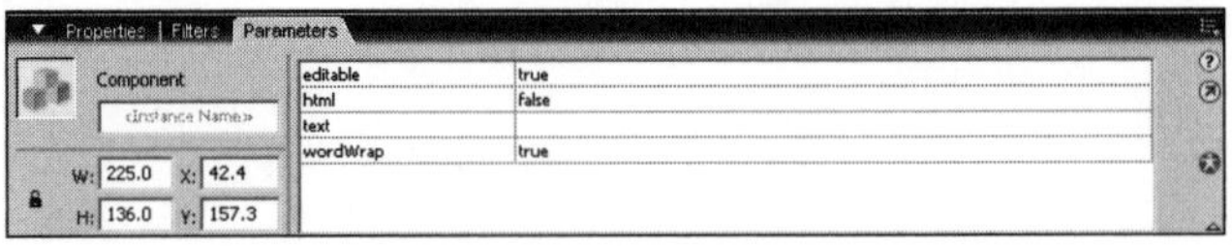

Figure 4-16:
Every component has parameters. It's a Flash law.

8. **After entering text in the Text parameter field, a vertical scroll bar appears inside the component, as shown in Figure 4-17.**

Figure 4-17:
A vertical scroll bar is added after you enter text into the component.

9. **Press Ctrl+Enter (Windows) or ⌘+Return (Macintosh) to test the movie.**

The movie opens in another window, and you can test the scroll bar, as seen in Figure 4-18.

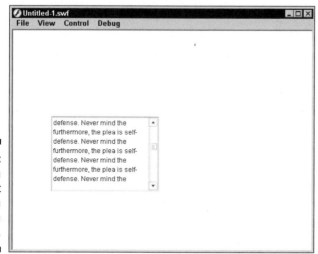

Figure 4-18:
A TextArea component can hold a whole lotta text.

Chapter 5

Adding Site Navigation

*N*o doubt you've seen your share of buttons while surfing the Net. And if you've designed HTML Web pages, you've created buttons. HTML buttons can be moderately cool, but when it comes to compelling buttons, the King of Cool is Flash. With Flash, you can create simple buttons, multi-state buttons, buttons that dance, buttons that sing, and buttons that sing and dance. Most Flash site navigation needs are handled with a navigation bar of neatly arranged buttons. But if you or your client wants to stuff a whole lotta content into the Flash Web site, you're going to need some drop-down menus. Okay, if you're ready to navigate, hang on; point your compass to True North and venture into the wonderful world of Flash navigation.

Button, Button, Build Me a Button

When you build a button, you create a symbol. You can create carbon copies of symbols wherever you need them, and this applies to buttons as well. However, when you create navigation for a site, you generally have different labels on each button. Buttons can be duplicated in the document Library and then edited to change label text.

Building a basic button

A basic button gets the job done. When you click it, something happens. The button has no frills, no bells, and no whistles. It clicks; therefore, it is — a button, that is. Basic buttons are the trick when you need to give your viewers a device to take care of some mundane task such as submitting a form. Here's how to create a basic button:

1. **Choose Insert⇨New Symbol.**

   The New Symbol dialog box opens.

2. **Enter a name for your new symbol, select the Button behavior type, and then click OK.**

   Flash enters symbol-editing mode. The button timeline is shown in Figure 5-1.

Figure 5-1:
An empty button timeline is a terrible thing to waste.

3. **Click the Up frame and use any of the drawing tools to create an object.**

   As soon as you create the shape, a dot fills the frame, signifying it is a keyframe.

   You can also use a Library symbol as the basis for your button shape.

4. **Align the object to the center of the Stage, as shown in Figure 5-2.**

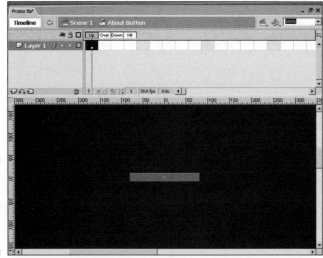

Figure 5-2:
A basic button only uses one frame.

5. **Click the Back button or current scene button to exit symbol-editing mode.**

The button is added to the Library. To create an instance of the button, drag it from the Library to the Stage.

A button with many states

A multi-state button changes when the viewer holds his or her cursor over the button. When the button is clicked, it changes yet again. This wizardry is achieved by using the other frames in the button symbol timeline. When you create a multi-state button, you can use as many layers as needed to get the job done. A multi-state button has four states:

✔ **Up:** The graphic you add to this frame is displayed when the button is first seen.

✔ **Over:** The graphic you add to this frame is displayed when a user holds his or her cursor over the button.

✔ **Down:** The graphic you add to this frame is displayed when the button is clicked and held down.

✔ **Hit:** The graphic you add to this frame is not seen or heard; it merely defines the *target area* for the button, that is, the area that defines where the pointing-hand cursor appears — you know, the clickable area. You can use this state to define the target area for a miniscule — read *tiny* — button graphic or for a graphic that has an irregular shape, such as a star.

To create a multi-state button, follow these steps:

1. **Choose Insert⇨New Symbol.**

The New Symbol dialog box opens.

2. **Enter a name for your new symbol, select the Button behavior type, and then click OK.**

Flash enters symbol-editing mode.

3. **Click the Up frame and use any of the drawing tools to create a graphic.**

Alternatively, you can use a graphic symbol from the Library.

To create the ever-present pill shape for a button, use the Rectangle tool with the Set Corner Radius modifier enabled. Enter a value of about 50 points for the Corner Radius and drag the tool on Stage to create the button shape.

4. **Create additional layers as needed.**

As a rule, you'll need an extra layer for text.

5. **Click the Over frame and choose Insert⇨Blank Keyframe.**

   Alternatively, right-click (Windows) or Control-click (Macintosh) and select Insert Blank Keyframe from the context menu.

   Press F6 to create a new keyframe, which in essence copies the graphic from the previous frame. Change the graphic color so viewers see something different when hovering their cursors over the button.

6. **Use any of the drawing tools to create an object for the Over frame or select a symbol from the document Library. Make any additions or changes to the other layers in your button.**

   For this example button, I used the same graphic from the Up frame, but I changed the color of the text. After you create the graphic for the Over frame, you've occupied two states of the button timeline, as shown in Figure 5-3.

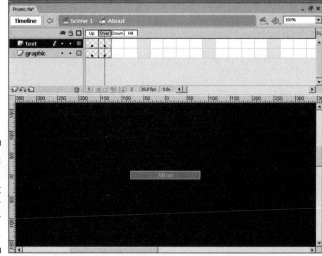

Figure 5-3:
You create a different graphic for the Over frame.

7. **Click the Down frame and either choose Insert⇨Blank Keyframe or press F7.**

   Alternatively, you can press F6, which copies the contents of the previous keyframe, and then use the Transform tool to change the graphic or to change the color of the graphic or button text.

8. **Use any of the drawing tools or use a Library symbol to create the Down frame graphic.**

9. **Choose Window⇨Align and then use the Align panel to align the graphic to the center of the Stage, as shown in Figure 5-4.**

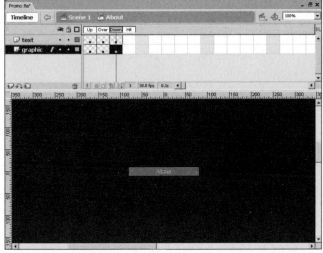

Figure 5-4: A graphic in the Down frame can still have an upbeat attitude.

10. **Click the Hit frame and insert a blank keyframe by pressing F7.**

Alternatively, you can press F6, which copies the contents of the previous keyframe, and then use the Transform tool to change the graphic or to change the color of the graphic or button text.

11. **Create a graphic for the Hit frame.**

The shape you use for the Hit frame is not seen in the published movie. The graphic you create for the hit frame should be slightly larger than the biggest shape in the button's preceding frames, but not so large that it will interfere with the target areas of other buttons that will be in close proximity in the published movie. This step is not needed if the graphics in the preceding frames are the same size.

12. **Click the Onion Skin icon to see how the shapes relate to each other, as shown in Figure 5-5.**

13. **Click the Back button or current scene button to exit symbol-editing mode.**

The button is added to the Library. To create an instance of the button, drag it from the Library to the Stage.

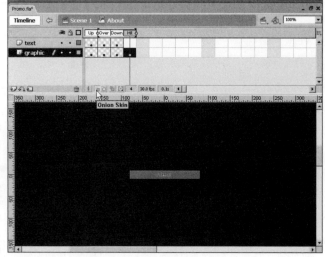

Figure 5-5:
Enable
onion skins
to see how
the frames
relate to
each other.

Saying Goodbye to Boring Buttons

If you've been reading straight through this chapter, you have seen the basic button and the multi-state button; now say hello to the WOW buttons. Well, *WOW* may be too strong a word, but the buttons you're about to find out how to create are definitely more exciting and are guaranteed to get your viewer's attention . . . with the possible exception of the invisible button, which just hides out and waits to be clicked.

Creating animated buttons

Multi-state buttons are cool, but you can up the ante by using animated buttons on your Flash Web site. When you create an animated button, you add an animation in the form of a movie clip to one button state. The logical state would be the Over state. The animation you add can be as long as you want because it plays only when the user's cursor is over the button. Here's how to create an animated button:

1. **Choose Insert⇔New Symbol.**

   The New Symbol dialog box opens.

2. **Enter a name for your new symbol, select the Button behavior type, and then click OK.**

   Flash enters symbol-editing mode.

3. **Click the Up frame and use any of the drawing tools to create a graphic.**

   Alternatively, you can use a graphic symbol from the Library.

4. **Click the Over frame and choose Insert⇨Blank Keyframe.**

   Alternatively, right-click (Windows) or Control-click (Macintosh) and select Insert Blank Keyframe from the context menu.

5. **Select the Movie Clip symbol that contains the animation for the Over state from the document Library.**

   For information on creating animations, see Chapter 6.

6. **Click the Down frame and choose Insert⇨Blank Keyframe.**

   Alternatively, right-click (Windows) or Control-click (Macintosh) and select Insert Blank Keyframe from the context menu.

   To have the same graphic in the Up and Down frame, select the Down frame and then press F6. This copies the contents from the Up frame into the Down frame.

7. **Click the Hit frame and then create a graphic slightly bigger than the largest graphic in the previous frames.**

8. **Click the Back button or current scene button to exit symbol-editing mode.**

   When viewers position their cursors over the button, the animation plays.

Building a noisy button

Another way-cool button is a noisy button. When you create a noisy button, you can have a different sound for each state, with the exception of the Up state. If you added a sound to the Up state, it would play all the time — not a good thing. Therefore, the logical state for button sounds would be Over or Down, but not both. If you added a sound to both states, one sound might still be playing when the viewer clicks the button and the other sound starts playing. Talk about your sensory overload. Creating a noisy button is pretty easy:

1. **Choose File⇨Import⇨Import to Library to open the Import to Library dialog box, shown in Figure 5-6.**

   When using a sound for a button state, choose a short one because the sound plays in its entirety when the user accesses the button state.

2. **Select the sound for your button and then click Open.**

3. **Create a multi-state button by following the directions in previous sections of this chapter.**

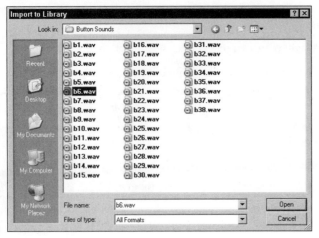

Figure 5-6:
You can
import a file
directly
to the
document
Library.

4. **Create a new layer.**

5. **Name the layer** Sound.

6. **Select the desired keyframe (Over or Down) and then choose Insert⇨Blank Keyframe.**

7. **Choose Window⇨Library to open the document Library.**

   Alternatively, press F11.

8. **Drag the sound file from the Library to Stage.**

   The selected keyframe shows a waveform icon, as shown in Figure 5-7.

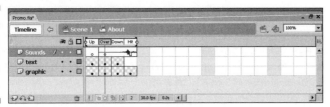

Figure 5-7:
Adding
sound to a
button
frame.

9. **Click the Back button or current scene button to exit symbol-editing mode.**

Creating an invisible button

You can use an invisible button to designate a hot spot in your published Flash Web site. Invisible buttons can be used in Flash games or when you have a lot of text you want visitors to read before going to the next part of your Flash Web site. Here's how to create an invisible button:

1. **Choose Insert⇨Symbol.**

   The Create New Symbol dialog box appears.

2. **Enter a name for the symbol and select the Button behavior type.**

3. **Select the Hit frame and choose Insert⇨Blank Keyframe.**

4. **Select one of the drawing tools.**

5. **Use the selected tool to create the desired graphic for the Hit frame.**

   If you're creating an irregularly shaped hot spot, use the Pen tool for point-to-point control over the final shape of the invisible button.

6. **Click the Back button or current scene button to exit symbol-editing mode.**

   The invisible button is safely tucked away in the document Library until you drag it on Stage.

Figure 5-8 shows an invisible button behind a block of text. When you see an invisible button in authoring mode, it's anything but invisible. In fact, it's light blue, but it's invisible when the document is published.

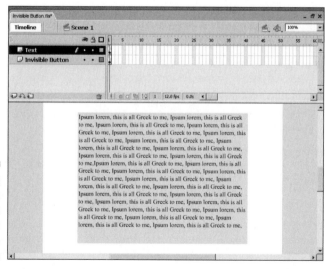

Figure 5-8:
An invisible button is neither seen nor heard.

Hanging Out at the Navigation Bar

A navigation bar is a neat way to arrange the buttons that your viewers will use to navigate through your Flash Web site. When you create a navigation bar, it can be vertical or horizontal. Aesthetics, client preference, and your artistic vision will dictate your choice. When you create a navigation bar, you could jam 50 buttons into a small space, but the text would be almost impossible to read and the buttons almost impossible to select. If you need to stuff copious buttons into a menu, you have to resort to one or more drop-down menus. It's the aesthetics thing, you know. The following sections show you how to create a navigation bar and a drop-down menu.

Bellying up to the nav bar

When you create a navigation bar, you decide whether to use all or part of the available vertical or horizontal area available to you. Unless your Web site has only a few sections, you'll probably use up all of the available area. After you determine how much room you'll need for your navigation bar, you populate it with buttons. The beauty of working with symbols in Flash is that you don't have to create each and every button from scratch. The following steps show you how to determine the size of the base button for your navigation bar:

1. **Determine the amount of vertical or horizontal space you have available for a navigation bar.**

   If you're creating a vertical navigation bar, deduct the height of the site banner, if one is part of your design, from the height of the document.

2. **Divide the available width (if creating a horizontal navigation bar) or height (if creating a vertical navigation bar) by the number of sections in your site.**

   This tells you the maximum width the button can be for a horizontal navigation bar or the maximum height the button can be for a vertical navigation bar.

3. **Determine how wide or tall the button will actually be.**

   Chances are that if you're creating a horizontal navigation bar, you'll use all of the available space. If you're creating a vertical navigation bar, you won't be using the available space unless you have a lot of menu items. In this case, decide how high the button will be based on the button text and aesthetics. I generally don't exceed a height of 25 pixels for a button. This allows plenty of room for text, and then some.

4. **Create a multi-state button using a separate layer for button text, as shown in Figure 5-9.**

   This button will serve as the basis for the other buttons in your navigation bar.

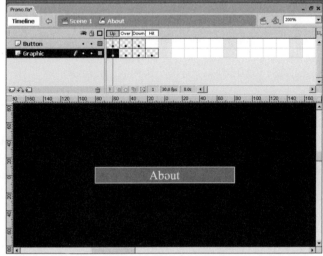

Figure 5-9:
Create the
first button
for your
navigation
bar.

For a refresher course on creating buttons, refer to the "A button with many states" section, earlier in this chapter.

Duplicating buttons

After you create the first button for your navigation bar, you can flesh out the rest of the navigation bar from within the document Library. This involves a bit of high jinks in the form of duplicating and then editing buttons:

1. **Choose Window⇨Library to open the document Library.**

2. **Right-click (Windows) or Control-click (Macintosh) the first button you created for your navigation bar and then choose Duplicate from the context menu.**

   This opens the Duplicate Symbol dialog box, shown in Figure 5-10.

3. **Name the duplicated symbol.**

   Give the symbol a meaningful name, such as the section of the Web site to which the button will be linked.

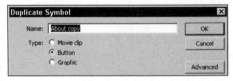

4. **Click OK to create a duplicate symbol and close the Duplicate Symbol dialog box.**

5. **Repeat Steps 2 through 4 to create the remaining buttons for your navigation bar.**

6. **Edit each button in turn and change the button text to reflect the section of the Web site to which it will link.**

Building a navigation bar

After you create the buttons for your navigation bar, putting the beast together is child's play. Thanks to a little Flash magic known as *swapping symbols* (a practice that is approved in all 50 states and most surrounding countries), you can quickly create a navigation bar, as follows:

1. **Choose Window⇨Library to open the document Library.**

2. **Drag one of the buttons for your navigation bar on Stage and align it as previously determined when you mind mapped your site.**

   You did mind map your site, didn't you? (I tell you how in Chapter 2.)

3. **Select the button and then hold Shift+Alt (Windows) or Shift+Option (Macintosh) while you drag the button.**

   This creates a duplicate of the button and constrains the motion to the axis in which you are dragging.

4. **Release the mouse button when the duplicated button is aligned to the edge of the button from which it was created.**

5. **Repeat Steps 3 and 4 until you've fleshed out your navigation bar, as shown in Figure 5-11.**

   Now you have enough buttons, but they all say the same thing.

Figure 5-11:
Create
multiple
instances of
a button to
flesh out
your
navigation
bar.

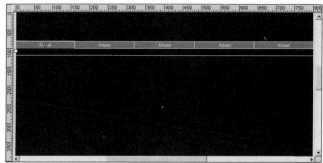

6. **Select the second button on your navigation bar.**

7. **Right-click (Windows) or Control-click (Macintosh) the button and choose Swap Symbol from the context menu.**

   This opens the Swap Symbol dialog box, shown in Figure 5-12.

Figure 5-12:
Swap
symbols to
complete
the
navigation
bar.

8. **Choose the desired symbol and click OK.**

9. **Select the next button and repeat Steps 7 and 8.**

10. **Repeat Step 9 until you've swapped each symbol and completed your navigation bar, as shown in Figure 5-13.**

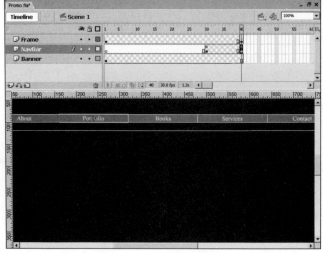

Figure 5-13:
Swap symbols to complete your navigation bar.

Assigning actions to buttons

After you create buttons, you have to assign actions to them. Otherwise, they're just pretty Flash symbols that just remain stationary and do nothing. The upcoming sections get you up to speed on how to add actions to buttons.

ActionScript is covered in greater detail in Chapter 8.

Actions applied to buttons occur when the user's mouse interacts with the button's target (Hit frame) area. Actions commonly used with buttons transport the user to another part of the movie or to another Web site or load additional content into the interface.

Actions are applied to a button's *instance,* which means you can have multiple instances of buttons with different actions applied to each. Even though buttons have four frames, you cannot apply actions to them as you can with keyframes on the timeline.

The following steps show you how to assign an action to a button:

1. **Select the button on Stage and choose Window⇨Actions.**

   The Actions panel appears, as shown in Figure 5-14. Notice that the panel says "Actions – Button," indicating that any script you create will be applied to a button. If the dialog box does not say this, you have not properly selected the button.

Action books

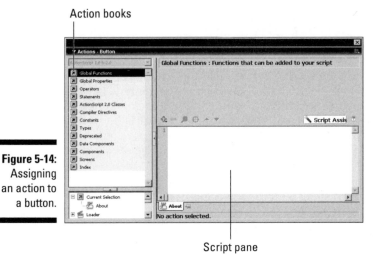

Figure 5-14:
Assigning
an action to
a button.

Script pane

2. **Select the desired action from an action book and drag it into the
   script pane.**

   In Figure 5-15, the goto action has been added to the script. This action
   resides in the Timeline Control action book. Notice that the preceding line
   of script reads on (release) {, which means this will occur when the
   button is released. This is known as an *event.* The default on (release)
   event is added automatically when you add actions to a button while
   working in Script Assist mode.

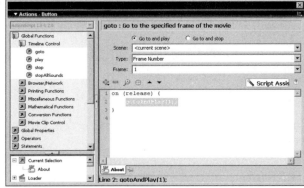

Figure 5-15:
The event
determines
when a
button
action
executes.

Assigning the proper event to a button action

You can assign multiple actions to buttons, and you can have different actions occur depending on which event occurs when a user interacts with a button. For example, when a user passes his or her mouse over a button, you can have a movie clip play and then stop when the user's mouse is beyond the hit area of the button. By default, Flash adds the `on (release)` event whenever you add an action to a button. You can assign a different event to trigger an action by following these steps:

1. **Select the line of script that contains the code** `on (release) {`.

   The Actions dialog box reconfigures to show the events that can trigger an action, as shown in Figure 5-16.

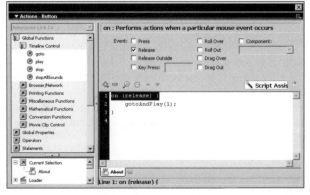

Figure 5-16: Choose the desired event that will trigger a button action.

2. **Choose the desired action by selecting the applicable check box. Choose from the following events:**

   - **Press:** This event triggers an action on the down stroke of a user's mouse click.

   - **Release:** The default event applies an action on the upstroke of a user's mouse click.

   - **Release outside:** Choose this event to have an action occur when the user releases the mouse outside of the button's target area.

   - **Key Press:** Select this event to have an action occur when the user makes a keyboard entry. If you select the Key Press event, a text field appears, as shown in Figure 5-17. Type the keyboard value in the text box. Note that you can also press Enter, Return, or Backspace if you want the user to press the same to trigger the ActionScript code associated with the button.

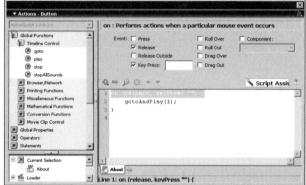

Figure 5-17:
Enter the desired keyboard entry in the text box.

- **Roll Over:** Select this event to trigger an action when the user's mouse is over the button.

- **Roll Out:** Select this event to have an action occur when the user's cursor rolls outside the button's target area.

- **Drag Over:** This event triggers an action when the user's mouse is clicked while over a button, rolls outside of the button, and then rolls back over the button with the mouse button still held down.

- **Drag Out:** This event triggers an action when the user's mouse is clicked while over the button and then rolls outside of the button's target area.

It is possible to apply multiple events to a single On Mouse Event action. Be sure to delete unwanted events to prevent scripting errors.

Creating a drop-down menu

If you have more menu selections than you have room, your only solution is to create a drop-down menu. When you create a drop-down menu, you create enough buttons to flesh out the drop-down menu and then create a movie clip that contains all of the buttons in your drop-down menu. The movie clip is actually an animation. I know; I haven't covered animation yet. Consider this your baptism by fire. To create a drop-down menu, follow these steps:

1. **Create enough buttons to flesh out the drop-down menu.**

   You can do this in the document Library by duplicating and editing buttons as outlined in the "Duplicating buttons" section, earlier in this chapter.

2. **Select the button on your navigation bar that will open the drop-down menu.**

3. **Press F8 to convert the selected button into a symbol.**

   This opens the Convert to Symbol dialog box, shown in Figure 5-18.

Figure 5-18:
Creating the movie clip that will be the drop-down menu.

4. **Name the symbol** Drop Down, **choose the Movie Clip behavior type, and then click OK to convert the button into a movie clip symbol.**

   If you have more than one drop-down menu, add further identification to the name you assign — for example: **Portfolio Drop Down**.

5. **On Stage, right-click (Windows) or Control-click (Macintosh) the movie clip symbol you just created and then choose Edit In Place from the context menu.**

6. **Select the first button; then hold down Shift+Alt (Windows) or Shift+Option (Macintosh) and drag down to create a duplicate of the button. Release the mouse button when the top of the duplicated button is aligned to the bottom of the button from which it was created.**

7. **Repeat Step 6 on the second button to create another duplicate.**

8. **Create enough additional duplicates for all of the choices on your drop-down menu.**

9. **Right-click (Windows) or Control-click (Macintosh) the second button and choose Swap Symbol from the context menu.**

10. **Choose the desired button symbol from the Swap Symbol dialog box.**

11. **Repeat Steps 9 and 10 for the remaining buttons on your drop-down menu.**

12. **Select the buttons, right-click (Window) or Control-click (Macintosh), and then choose Distribute to Layers from the drop-down menu.**

Flash distributes the buttons to layers, as shown in Figure 5-19.

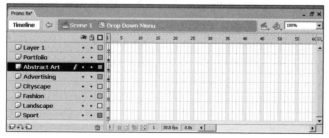

Figure 5-19: Distributing the drop-down menu buttons to layers.

13. **Select Layer 1 (which is now empty) and delete it.**

Animating the menu

Now that you have all the buttons for your drop-down menu, it's time to animate the menu. To animate the menu, you use the Motion Tween method of animation. Consider this your introduction to Flash animation, a topic that I cover in detail in Chapter 6:

1. **Select the tenth frame on the first layer and then Shift-click the tenth frame on the last layer.**

2. **Press F6.**

Flash creates keyframes on the tenth frame of each layer.

3. **Select the fifth frame on the first layer and then Shift-click the fifth frame on the last layer.**

4. **Right-click (Windows) or Control-click (Macintosh) and choose Create Motion Tween from the drop-down menu.**

A right-pointing arrow appears between the first and last keyframes of each layer, and the background is a light blue, as shown in Figure 5-20.

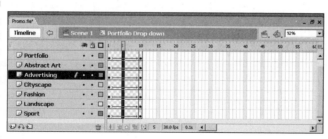

Figure 5-20: Your first step in animating the menu is creating a Motion Tween.

5. Select the fifth frame on the first layer and then Shift-click the fifth frame on the last layer.

6. Press F6 to convert the frames to keyframes.

7. If necessary, rearrange the order of the layers so that the topmost layer contains the first button in the drop-down menu.

8. Select the first keyframe, which automatically selects the first button.

9. Shift-click the remaining buttons in your drop-down menu.

10. Choose Window⇨Align to open the Align panel, shown in Figure 5-21.

Figure 5-21:
Align the
buttons for
when the
menu is
collapsed.

11. Deselect the To Stage option and then click the Align to Top icon.

12. Repeat Steps 8 through 11 for the buttons on the tenth keyframe.

Coding the menu

After animating the menu, you apply ActionScript code to the timeline and buttons to make the menu expand when the first button is clicked and collapse when a choice is made from the drop-down menu. Don't worry; it isn't complicated ActionScript:

1. Right-click (Windows) or Control-click (Macintosh) the uppermost layer and choose Insert New Layer from the context menu.

2. Rename the layer Actions.

3. Select the fifth frame and then press F6 to convert it to a keyframe.

4. Select the tenth frame and then press F6 to convert it to a keyframe.

5. Select the first keyframe.

6. Choose Window⇨Actions to open the Actions panel.

7. Choose Global Functions⇨Timeline Control and then drag the Stop action into the Script pane, as shown in Figure 5-22.

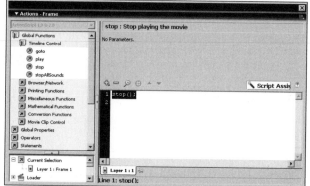

Figure 5-22:
Adding the
stop action
to a
keyframe.

8. **Repeat Step 7 on the fifth keyframe.**

9. **Select the tenth keyframe.**

10. **Choose Global Functions⇨Timeline Control and then drag the** `gotoAndPlay` **action into the Script pane.**

11. **Click the Go To and Stop radio button and accept the default parameter to go to the first frame, as shown in Figure 5-23.**

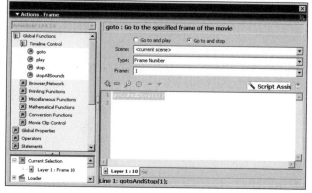

Figure 5-23:
Adding the
code for the
last
keyframe in
the drop-
down menu.

12. **Select the button that will open the drop-down menu in the first keyframe.**

13. **Choose Window⇨Actions to open the Actions panel.**

14. **Choose Global Functions⇨Timeline Control and then drag the** `play` **action into the Script pane, as shown in Figure 5-24.**

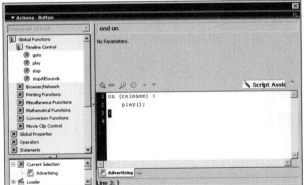

Figure 5-24:
Adding the
play action
to a button.

15. Select the second button on the fifth keyframe.

16. Choose Global Functions⇨Timeline Control and then drag the play
action into the Script pane.

On a typical drop-down list, you would precede the play action with the
action you wanted performed before the drop-down menu closes. Figure
5-25 shows an action that will load additional content into the interface.
Don't worry, I show you how to do this in Chapter 7.

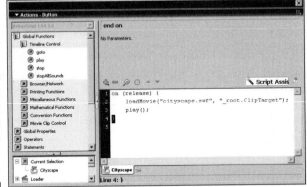

Figure 5-25:
Typical
ActionScript
for a button
in a drop-
down menu.

17. Repeat Step 16 on the remaining buttons in your drop-down menu.

Chapter 6

Get a Move On and Animate the Site

Animation is a staple of many Flash movies. However, some Flash design-ers take animation way over the top. When everything is moving, a viewer has no idea what the designer wants him or her to watch. There are lots of places you can use animation. You can use animation to amuse your viewers, to create a unique banner, or to create an introduction to your Flash Web site. Flash has many types of animations: frame-by-frame, motion tween, shape tween, and, for you control freaks, animating along a motion path. Animation in Flash can be daunting. In this chapter, I show you how to work with frames and keyframes, plus how to use this knowledge to create anima-tions. And if you'd like, you can be animated while reading this chapter. Your pets will be endlessly amused.

Animation 101: A Tale of Frames and Keyframes and Blank Keyframes

Before you can create any animation in Flash, you need to know how to work with frames and keyframes. If you've already mastered this task, feel free to skip the upcoming sections. However, if you're a neophyte, or if you're a bit rusty on your animation techniques, read on.

Working with frames

When you create a new document in Flash, you have a single empty keyframe with which to work. If you go through life creating one-keyframe Flash Web sites, you won't attract many visitors, or for that matter, clients. To create an animation, you need to add frames and keyframes and then manipulate their positions on the timeline. A *keyframe* is a place in your animation where you introduce a major change, whereas *frames* duplicate the information from the previous keyframe. For example, if you create a Flash slide show, you add a keyframe to display a new image. The number of frames after the keyframe determines how long the image is displayed. Then you add another keyframe to display the next image, and so on. Sometimes you need just a few keyframes, sometimes a whole lot; it depends on the complexity of your animation. If you are working with multiple layers, you need to coordinate the position of the frames on each layer, synchronizing the climax of one object's motion with the beginning of another's.

Creating frames

Frames are placeholders along the timeline. When you add a frame to a layer's timeline, you create a copy of the graphic elements of the previous keyframe along with it. You also use frames to fine tune an animation's timing, as you find out in the upcoming sections. Adding a single frame to the timeline is easy:

1. **Click the spot on the timeline where you want to add the frame.**

2. **Choose Insert⇨Timeline⇨Frame.**

   Flash adds a frame to the Timeline.

If one frame is good, two must be better, right? Well, only if you need to extend the duration between keyframes. But sometimes you need to add 5, 10, or 20 keyframes to the timeline. Here's how you create multiple frames:

1. **Click the spot on the timeline where you need to add frames.**

2. **Drag to the left or right to increase the size of the selection.**

   As you drag, you select more frames.

3. **Choose Insert⇨Timeline⇨Frame to add the exact number of frames that you selected to the Timeline.**

   Alternatively, press F5. Flash adds the same number of frames you selected in Step 2 to the right of the selected frames.

Deleting frames

Sometimes you need to delete frames. For example, if the sequence of events between keyframes is just too slow, deleting frames speeds things up. To delete a selected frame or a selected range of frames, do one of the following:

- ✔ Choose Insert⇨Timeline⇨Remove Frames.
- ✔ Press Shift+F5.

Working with keyframes

Keyframes make animations happen. An animation without keyframes is, well, static; nothing moves. You create keyframes at the point in the timeline where you want major changes or events to occur in your animation. You can use keyframes to change an object's position on Stage, to introduce another object into the movie, to add a sound event to the movie, or to add an action to a movie. Keyframes are also needed when you create motion tween and shape tween animations. These keyframes are versatile characters.

Creating keyframes

When you add a keyframe to the Timeline, it is blank unless you have an object in the preceding keyframe. You can create either a keyframe, which duplicates the content of the previous keyframe, or a blank keyframe, which is a place-holder for an object you've yet to create, or in the case of ActionScript, a script you've yet to write. When you create a blank keyframe, an unfilled dot appears within the frame's border. If regular frames precede the blank keyframe, an unfilled rectangle appears in the previous frame to indicate the end of the previous frame range. A *frame range* consists of a keyframe and subsequent frames that copy the keyframe's content along the timeline. A filled keyframe is signified by a filled dot within the frame's boundaries, as shown in Figure 6-1. To create a keyframe, follow these steps:

1. **Click the spot on the timeline where you want to add a keyframe.**

2. **Choose Insert⇨Timeline⇨Keyframe.**

   Alternatively, you can press F6. Flash adds a keyframe to the timeline.

Frame range

Blank keyframe

Figure 6-1:
You create
a keyframe
at the spot
in your
animation
where you
want a
change to
occur.

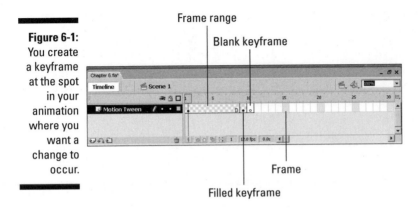

Frame

Filled keyframe

Creating blank keyframes

You create a blank keyframe where you need a placeholder for a future event change. Creating a blank keyframe is also a convenient way to end the previous frame range prior to introducing a new symbol, sound, or action. Inserting a blank keyframe in a sequence of frames clears all objects on a layer's frames from that point forward or until you create a new keyframe farther down the timeline. The following steps show how to create a blank keyframe:

1. **Click the spot on the timeline where you want to add a blank keyframe.**

2. **Choose Insert⇨Timeline⇨Blank Keyframe.**

   A blank keyframe appears on the timeline. A rectangular icon appears in the previous frame's border, signifying the end of the previous frame range. Alternatively, you can press F7.

Animating Symbols with Motion Tweening

The lowest common denominator in Flash animation is the ever-present and omnipotent keyframe. The most difficult form of Flash animation is known as frame-by-frame animation, which uses a whole lot of keyframes. When you play back a frame-by-frame animation, objects don't move when there is a gap between keyframes. Frame-by-frame animations (which I describe briefly in the "Creating frame-by-frame animations" sidebar) are tedious work. Fortunately, Flash has an easier way to create animations: *tweening*. When you use tweening to animate an object, Flash interpolates the difference between keyframes and redraws the object on frames between keyframes to fill in the blanks, so to speak. When you play back the animation, there are no gaps, and smooth animation occurs.

There are two types of tweening animation: *motion tweening*, which interpolates changes in an object's position between keyframes (and which is the subject of this section); and *shape tweening*, which transforms an object's shape from one keyframe to the next (the subject of a later section, "Animating Objects with Shape Tweening"). I show you how to create sophisticated animations using both forms of tweening.

Cartoonists are masochists. To create a few seconds of animation, they draw dozens of pictures — one for each frame — a technique similar to creating a frame-by-frame animation. If you've ever created a stick figure animation that goes through a range of motion on each page of a pad of paper, you know what it's all about. To create a cool animation in Flash, you need to create some keyframes, change the object in each keyframe, and then apply motion tweening. When you add motion tweening, Flash takes care of the magic, moving and redrawing the object on each in-between frame. You can create a motion tween animation using editable objects or symbols. However, only symbols can be used if you're going to animate along a motion path. Therefore, it's best to get in the habit of using only symbols when creating motion tween animations. To create a motion tween animation, follow these steps:

1. **Create a shape in the first keyframe and then convert it into a symbol by pressing F8.**

   Alternatively, select a symbol you've already created from the Library and drag it on Stage.

2. **Determine how long the animation will be, advance to the final frame, and then insert a keyframe by pressing F6.**

   The number of frames you'll need per second of animation is determined by the frame rate of your movie. If the frame rate is 12 fps, 36 frames equal 3 seconds of animation.

3. **Change the object's position in the final keyframe.**

   You use the Move tool to move the object to a different position. You can also change the position, size, and orientation of the object with the Free Transform tool.

4. **Right-click (Windows) or Control-click (Macintosh) a frame between the keyframes that you just created, or right-click (Windows) or Control-click (Macintosh) the first keyframe in the animation, and then choose Create Motion Tween from the context menu.**

   The background of the in-between frames is tinted a light blue with an arrow connecting the beginning and ending keyframes, indicating that you've successfully created a motion tween animation.

5. **To preview the animation, click the Controller's Play button.**

   Alternatively, press Enter or Return. Figure 6-2 shows a motion tween animation.

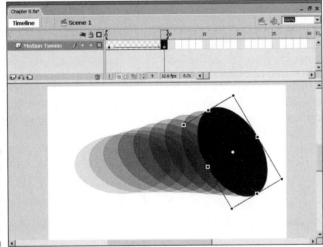

Figure 6-2:
Creating a motion tween animation.

You can also use your good friend the Properties Inspector to create a motion tween animation. Click any frame between keyframes, open the Properties Inspector, and choose Motion from the Tween menu (see Figure 6-3).

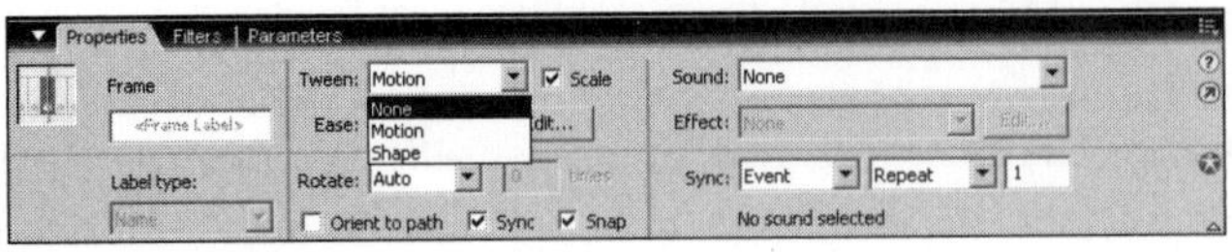

Figure 6-3:
Creating a tween animation by using the Properties Inspector.

Removing a motion tween

Sometimes you just plain goof and add a motion tween where you shouldn't have. If, after previewing your movie, you decide the animation was done in haste, or is not in good taste, not to worry. You can easily remove a motion tween as follows:

1. **Select the first frame in the motion tween sequence or any of the in-between frames.**

2. **Open the Properties Inspector (by choosing Window⇨Properties).**

3. **Click the triangle to the right of the Tween field and choose None from the drop-down menu.**

   Alternatively, choose Insert⇨Timeline⇨Remove Tween. The motion tween goes bye-bye.

In search of the perfect motion tween

After you preview your motion tween animation, you may think that's all there is. But wait, there's more. You can tweak the motion tween to suit your production. In real life, motion is not linear. Objects accelerate and decelerate. You can mimic these laws of motion by tweaking the motion tween as follows:

1. **Select any frame in your motion tween animation.**

2. **Choose Window⇨Properties to open the Properties Inspector.**

   The controls for a motion tween animation are shown in Figure 6-4. By default, the Scale check box is selected. If you've changed the size of the object between keyframes, this scales the object incrementally during the course of the animation.

Figure 6-4:
Tweaking a motion tween animation.

3. **Drag the Ease slider to determine how the motion begins and ends:**

   - **Drag the slider down or enter a value between 0 and –100 to have motion start slowly and end quickly.** This eases in the motion and would be the choice for a car accelerating from a stoplight.

   - **Drag the slider up or enter a value between 0 and 100 to have the animation start quickly and end slowly.** This eases out the animation and would be the choice for an object coming to a stop.

Creating custom easing

If you really want to take your viewers for a ride, you can use *custom easing* to control the manner in which an object moves from one keyframe to the next. For example, you can have the object accelerate rapidly at the start of the animation, slow down in the middle, and then speed up at the end of the animation. You make this magic happen by creating a custom curve, an option that is available only in Flash Professional. Here's how you create custom easing:

1. **Create a motion tween as outlined previously.**

2. **Choose Window⇨Properties to open the Properties Inspector.**

3. **Click the Edit button to the right of the Ease field.**

   This opens the Custom Ease In/Ease Out dialog box, shown in Figure 6-5. By default, the graph has a linear curve, which indicates that the motion between keyframes will occur in a linear fashion — in other words, the object moves from point A to point B at the same rate of speed.

   Before opening the Custom Ease In/Ease Out dialog box, use the Ease slider to change the manner in which the animation occurs. This changes the curve, which you can further modify by adding and moving points in the Custom Ease In/Ease Out dialog box.

4. **Click the curve to add a point.**

   When you add a point, two handles appear that enable you to change the curve between the current point, the preceding point, and the next point. These work similarly to the handles on a Bezier curve in an illustration application such as CorelDraw or Adobe Illustrator.

5. **Drag the handles to shape the curve.**

   You can also click and drag the point to another spot on the curve.

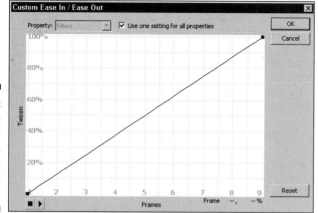

Figure 6-5:
For the
ultimate
control,
create a
custom
ease curve.

6. **Continue adding points to the curve and positioning the handles to precisely control the animation from keyframe to keyframe.**

   Figure 6-6 shows an ease in/out curve with a couple of points. In the case of this animation, the animation starts slowly between the first two points, and then accelerates rapidly as indicated by the sharp spike in the curve. After the third point, the animation slows markedly as indicated by the downhill curve. The animation ends rapidly as indicated by the sharp uphill curve between the forth and fifth points.

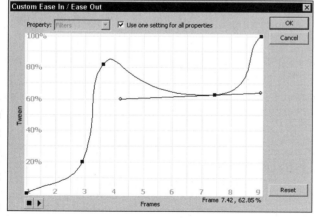

Figure 6-6:
Adding
points to the
ease in/out
curve.

Taking an object for a spin

When you create a motion tween animation, you can also spin an object. Granted, you can change an object's rotation with the Free Transform tool, but there's an easier way. Be careful not to preview an animation with a rotating object in front of your pet cat. They've been known to get dizzy and cough up hairballs while viewing frenetic animation.

Here's how you rotate an object:

1. **Set up a motion tween animation as outlined previously.**

   You did read the instructions on creating a motion tween animation, didn't you?

2. **Click the first keyframe or one of the in-between frames and then open the Properties Inspector (Window⇨Properties).**

3. **Choose one of the following options from the Rotation drop-down menu:**

   • **None:** Select this option, and the object does not rotate.

   • **Auto:** Select this option if you manually rotated the object in either the first or the last keyframe. When the animation is played, the object rotates in the direction requiring the least motion.

   • **CW:** Select this option to rotate the object clockwise between keyframes.

   • **CCW:** Select this option, and the object rotates counterclockwise between keyframes.

4. **If you select the CW or CCW option, the Times option becomes available. Enter the number of times that you want the object to rotate between keyframes.**

   You must enter a whole number in this field. That's right, you can't rotate an object 3.25 times; it's a Flash law.

Editing your animation

Animations are fun. And with the right client, they can be profitable. However, it's rare that you get an animation that's to your liking right out of the box. You may have to do some subtle tweaking to get the animation just the way you want it. To fine tune your animation, press Enter or Return to preview the animation in the authoring workspace and do one of the following:

✔ Delete one or more frames between the starting and ending keyframes to speed up a motion tween animation.

✔ Add one or more frames between the beginning and ending keyframes to slow down the sequence of events in a motion tween animation.

✔ Insert a keyframe in the middle of a motion tween. The new keyframe will have an instance of the symbol as it appears at that point in the animation. You can then change the position of the object or transform it.

Animating along a Motion Path

When you create a motion tween animation and add a motion path into the equation, the object stays stuck-like-glue to the motion path during the course of the animation. This is an easy way to create cool effects like a letter sliding along a curve. When you animate along a motion path, you can even have the shape orient to the path. Now how cool is that? But your first step in a motion path animation is creating the path that the object will follow.

Creating a guide layer

On a motion guide layer, you use drawing tools to create the motion path that you want a symbol to follow. When the movie is published, the motion guide layer and its path are not visible. To create a motion guide layer:

1. **Create a motion tween animation as outlined previously, but do not move the second instance of the symbol.**

2. **Right-click (Windows) or Control-click (Macintosh) the animation layer and then select Add Motion Guide from the context menu.**

   A new layer appears above the animation layer. The animation layer is now a guided layer. Animation layers linked to and guided by motion guide layers are indented, as shown in Figure 6-7.

Figure 6-7:
Guide layers
show
objects
where to go,
just like tour
guides
show
tourists
where to go.

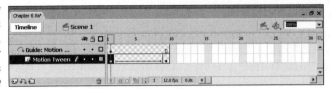

Creating a motion path

A motion path is to a symbol what railroad tracks are to a train; it guides the object along the path to which you want it to adhere. You can create a motion path with any of the drawing tools, although some Flash Web designers limit themselves to the Line tool or the Pencil tool. You can also create interesting motion paths with the Pen, Oval, and Rectangle tools. Using the Pen tool to draw a path gives you precise point-by-point control. If you use the Oval or Rectangle tool to create the path, create the path with no fill; all you need is the object's outline for the path. A path that you create with either the Oval or Rectangle tool will be closed, which is not a good thing because motion paths need to have a beginning and ending. However, you can easily open a path with the Eraser tool.

After creating the motion path, you should lock the motion guide layer to prevent accidentally altering the path. Just click the dot on the motion guide layer beneath the lock icon at the top of the timeline.

Getting objects to follow a motion path

Just because you create a motion path, don't expect the designated object to follow it. Oh no, you have to grab the object by the scruff of the neck and drag it to the motion path. (If it kicks and scratches, turn off your computer because it may have a virus.) Talk about leading your horse to water. But in this case, when you align an object to a motion path, it will follow. When you align the instance to the path, remember to drag it by its *registration point* (the dot with the cross-hair, which by default is in the center of the symbol, unless you specified otherwise when creating the symbol). As you drag the instance toward the motion path, the black circle becomes larger, signifying that you can align it precisely to the path, which you can do by following these steps:

1. **Select the animation layer and then select the first frame of the motion tween.**

2. **Select the Arrow tool and make sure the Snap To modifier (it looks like a magnet) is enabled.**

   With the Snap To modifier enabled, the registration point of the object you select with the tool develops a magnetic attraction to objects you drag it toward.

3. **Select the instance by its registration point and then align it to the start of the motion path.**

   In most cases, the registration point is the center of the item.

4. **Select the last frame of the motion tween.**

5. **Drag the instance until it aligns to the end of the motion path.**

   Figure 6-8 shows a symbol instance properly aligned to a motion path.

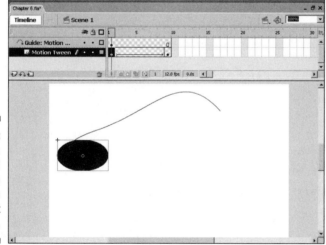

Figure 6-8:
Align a symbol instance to a motion path, and it will follow.

Orienting a symbol instance to its motion path

Sometimes you have to send symbols to symbol obedience school. Otherwise, they won't properly orient themselves with the path to which you've so meticulously attached them. When you orient a symbol to a motion path, the symbol changes orientation during the course of the animation. This isn't important for a circle, but if you have an oval or irregular shape, it is important. Picture a car going up an incline. It won't be parallel to the ground as it moves uphill; it will be parallel to the incline, which is what happens when you orient an object to a path. To orient a symbol instance to its path, follow these steps:

1. **Create a motion tween animation in which a symbol instance follows a motion path.**

2. **Align the symbol instance to the path in the first and last keyframes.**

3. **Select any frame in the animation.**

4. **Open the Properties Inspector (Window⇨Properties).**

   By now you should know that all of the cool stuff you can do to a motion tween animation happens in the Properties Inspector.

5. **Select the Orient to Path check box, as shown in Figure 6-9.**

   When the animation is played, the object will orient to the motion path as it moves.

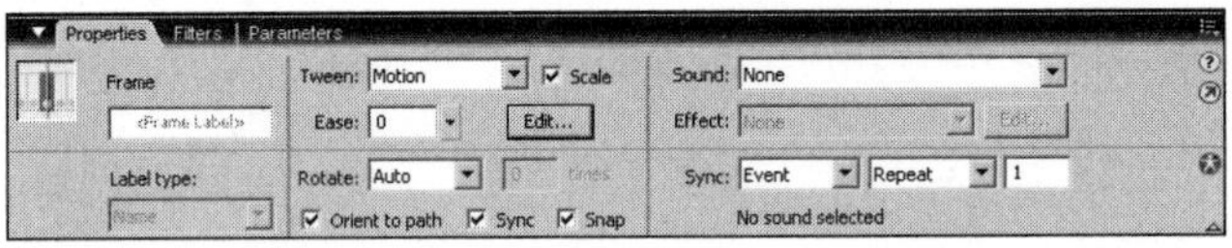

Figure 6-9:
Orient
yourself, my
little symbol
instance.

Linking additional motion tween animations to a layer guide

After you create a perfectly good motion path on a guide layer, you can use it for other motion tween animations you create. Suppose you want to have the letters of your client's business name cascade down a ski slope? You can easily do so by linking additional animations to a layer guide that hugs an image of a ski slope. Before you move the next letter down the slope, make sure you leave a couple of frames for the preceding letter to scoot down the slope; otherwise, the letters will travel in lock-step and it will look as though the word is traveling as a whole instead of a letter at a time. To link additional layers to a layer guide, do one of the following:

✔ **If the layer that you want to link to the motion guide layer is above it, select the layer and drag it directly beneath the motion guide layer.**
   When the selected layer can be linked to the guide layer, the guide layer icon becomes highlighted.

✔ **If the layer that you want to be guided by the motion guide layer is
below the motion guide layer, select the layer and drag it *directly*
below the motion guide layer.** If there are other layers linked to the
guide layer, you can drop the selected layer anywhere in the guide
layer's stack. When you have several guided layers, the rules of layer
hierarchy apply and objects on upper layers eclipse objects on lower
layers. When the layer can be successfully linked to the guide layer, the
guide layer icon becomes highlighted.

✔ **Right-click (Windows) or Control-click (Macintosh) a layer directly
beneath a guided layer, choose Properties from the context menu,
and then select Guided in the Layer Properties dialog box.**

Animating Objects with Shape Tweening

A shape tween animation morphs one shape into another. As in motion
tweening, you create the starting and ending shapes in keyframes, and Flash
fills in the blanks by redrawing the object on the in-between frames. With
shape tweening, you transform editable shapes instead of symbols because
the shape of a symbol instance cannot be edited and therefore will not work
in this type of animation.

With shape tweening, you're not restricted to transforming only an object's
shape. You can also change an object's color, size, and location.

Shape tweening has slightly different options than motion tweening. With
shape tweening, you cannot automatically rotate a shape or make it follow a
motion path. Another limitation is the inability to apply effects to editable
objects. Here's how you create a shape tween animation:

1. **Select the beginning frame for the animation and then use any of the
   drawing tools to create a shape.**

2. **Determine how long the animation will be, select the ending frame for
   the animation, and then insert a keyframe by pressing F6.**

   The shape from the first keyframe is copied into the new keyframe.

3. **Modify the size, shape, location, color, or any combination of these
   parameters to create the shape that you want the first shape to change
   into.**

   You can also delete the shape and create an entirely new shape.

4. **Open the Properties Inspector (Window➪Properties).**

5. **Click the triangle to the right of the Tween field and then select Shape from the menu.**

The shape tween frames are tinted green, and an arrow appears, connecting the starting and ending keyframes, as shown in Figure 6-10.

Figure 6-10:
Look ma, I
made a
shape
tween
animation.

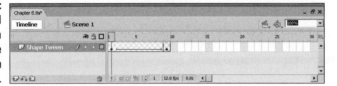

6. **Press Enter or Return to preview the animation.**

Figure 6-11 shows a shape tween animation in which a square is being morphed into an oval. To display the shapes on the in-between frames, onion skins have been enabled.

Figure 6-11:
Can I use
shape
tweening
to morph
Donald
Trump's
bank
account
into mine?

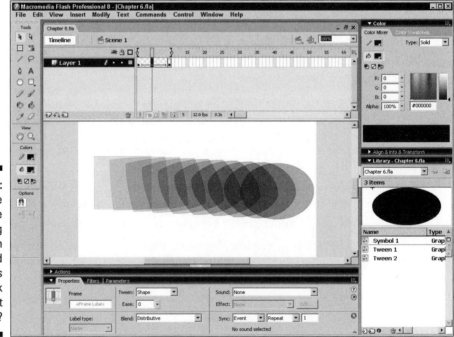

If you inadvertently try to apply shape tweening to a symbol, a triangular warning icon appears to the right of the Ease field. Click the icon and Flash displays a warning dialog box telling you that shape tweening cannot be applied to symbols or grouped objects.

Removing a shape tween

Did you ever have one of those days when you just couldn't make up your mind? To tween or not to tween . . . ? Well, if you decide to shape tween and then need to un–shape tween, do one of the following:

- Open the Properties Inspector (Window➪Properties), click the triangle to the right of the Tween field, and choose None.

- Right-click (Windows) or Control-click (Macintosh) either the first frame or one of the in-between frames and then choose Remove Tween from the context menu.

Modifying a shape tween animation

What can be created can be modified. If your shape tween animation isn't all you'd hoped it would be, you can easily modify it to morph as you envisioned:

1. **Select any frame in the animation.**

2. **Open the Properties Inspector.**

   Figure 6-12 shows how the Properties Inspector is configured for a shape tween animation. The Properties Inspector's chameleon-like persona enables it to change parameters whenever you choose a different item.

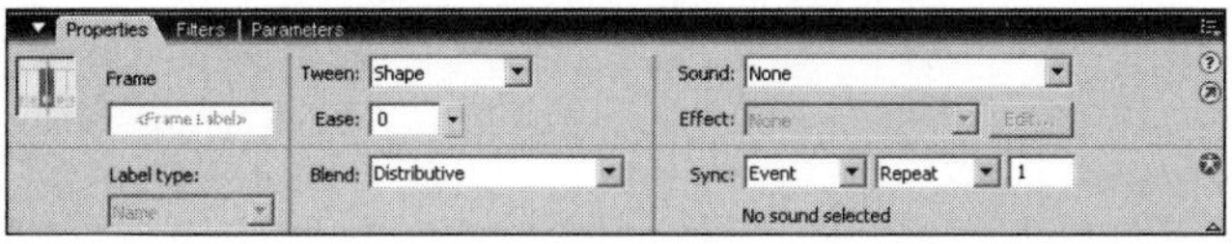

Figure 6-12:
Yes,
Virginia, you
can modify
a shape
tween
animation.

3. **In the Ease section, drag the slider to determine how the transition begins and ends.**

   You have the following options available:

   - To have the transition begin slowly and end quickly, drag the slider down or enter a value between 0 and –100.

   - To have the transition begin quickly and end slowly, drag the slider up or enter a value between 0 and 100.

4. **Choose one of the following options in the Blend section to determine how one shape blends into the next:**

   - Distributive blends one shape into another by using smooth, flowing curves.

   - Angular preserves pointy corners and straight lines when Flash draws the shapes on the in-between frames.

With shape tweening, it is possible to morph several shapes on a single layer. However, the results are unpredictable, especially when the shapes that you are tweening change positions. Flash doesn't read minds and therefore has no way of determining which shapes should cross paths instead of going in a straight line. When you apply shape tweening to multiple objects, it's always best to create each animation on its own layer.

Creating frame-by-frame animations

If you're a real masochist, a real glutton for punishment who likes to do more than your fair share of work, you can animate the old-fashioned way, *frame by frame*. If you've already mastered the art of creating shape tween animations, you know how to morph one object into another. If you've mastered the art of creating motion tween animations, you know that this is the obvious choice for creating an animation in which an object moves from one point to another. So when would you create a frame-by-frame animation? One of the only logical choices I can think of is when you want to create an animation in which letters appear as though they're being typed one at a time. To create an animation like this, you simply type the word and then create enough additional keyframes for each letter of the word. Then you select the next-to-last keyframe and remove one letter. Continue in this manner until you reach the first keyframe, which will have only one letter. To really simulate an old-fashioned typewriter, create an additional layer and add a typewriter sound to the first keyframe. Duplicate the keyframe so that the sound is heard when each letter appears.

Creating a shape tween animation for complex objects

Most of the time, Flash does a wonderful job of morphing one shape into another. However, when you have an object with obtuse, and maybe obscene, angles, Flash needs a helping hand. You supply the helping hand by adding Shape Hints. Shape Hints tell Flash which part of Object A should morph into which part of Object B. You get your first clue that a shape tween animation has gone bad when you preview it. Figure 6-13 shows a shape tween animation in need of a helping hand. Notice that onion skins have been enabled so the in-between shapes can be seen.

Adding shape hints

A shape hint is a dot with a letter in the center. You add a shape hint to a specific location on the object in the beginning keyframe and then move the shape hint to the desired location on the object in the last keyframe. This gives Flash a hint (clever use of wording, Flash designers!) as to which area on shape A should morph into which area on shape B. You can add up to 26 shape hints to a shape tween animation.

Figure 6-13: A shape tween in need of remedial help.

After you determine that shape hints are needed, your next step is to decide where to place the hints on each shape. You can drag the playhead from frame to frame and examine each in-between shape as Flash redraws it. Enable onion skins to view the in-between shapes of several frames at once. If you notice any jarring or unnatural transitions, you know exactly where to place each shape hint. When a shape tween animation plays, your viewer should have an inkling of what the new shape will look like as Flash redraws the shape on the in-between frames. To add shape hints:

1. **Create a shape tween animation in which a simple shape transforms into a complex one.**

2. **Preview the animation to determine the problem areas on each shape. Press Enter or Return to preview the animation in the authoring workspace.**

3. **Click the Onion Skin button to enable onion skins.**

Onion skins make it possible for you to view several frames at once. The objects on frames other than the one currently selected are of lower opacity.

4. **Click the first frame of the animation and choose Modify⇨Shape⇨Add Shape Hint.**

A shape hint appears in the middle of the shape. Shape hints are round circles surrounding a letter of the alphabet. A shape hint's letter is how you determine which shape hints on the first shape correspond to the shape hints on the last shape. For example, if you are morphing a circle into a star, you might place the first shape hint with the letter *a* on a point on the circle that you want to transform into one of the points of the star. When you position the shape hints on the star, you would place the shape hint with the letter *a* on the applicable star point. Shape hints on beginning shapes become yellow after they are positioned; they're green on ending shapes.

5. **Drag the shape hint to a trouble area on the first shape.**

6. **Repeat Steps 4 and 5 for each problematic area on the first shape.**

Apply shape hints counterclockwise in alphabetical order.

7. **Select the last keyframe in your animation.**

The shape hints that you applied in the first frame are stacked in a neat little pile.

8. **Click a shape hint to select it and then drag it to its corresponding position on the animation's ending shape.**

Remember to apply the shape hints in alphabetical order with counterclockwise rotation as you did on the first shape in the animation. Figure 6-14 shows the animation previously seen in Figure 6-13 with shape hints applied.

Figure 6-14:
Shape hints
can save
the day on
problematic
shape
tween
animations.

Editing shape hints

After you add a few or a bunch of shape hints to a shape tween animation, preview the animation by pressing Enter or Return. If the animation still isn't up to snuff, you may need to add another shape hint or three. Here are some additional modifications you may have to do with shape hints:

✔ To delete a shape hint, select it and drag it off Stage. The shape hint is removed from both shapes.

✔ To delete all shape hints, choose Modify➪Shape➪Remove All Hints.

Animating Image Sequences

In the Jurassic period of Flash, you'd use image sequences when you wanted to emulate full-motion video in a Flash movie. But with the advent of the Flash video encoder and the FLV codec, this is no longer needed. However, there is still a place for image sequences: a slide show. If you're creating a Flash Web site for a photographer, an image sequence is a wonderful way of displaying selected images as a slide show. With a bit of preliminary work, you can import the images into Flash in the order in which they will appear:

1. **Edit the images in your favorite image editing application, optimizing them for the Flash movie in which they will appear.**

2. **When you save each image, append the filenames with _01, _02, and so on.**

   The reason for the sequential numbering will soon be apparent.

3. **Launch Flash and create a new document.**

4. **Select the solitary keyframe in your new document.**

   Alternatively, you can create a new Movie Clip symbol, if there's going to be other content besides the slide show, and select the first keyframe in the movie clip.

5. **Choose File➪Import➪Import to Stage.**

   The Import dialog box shown in Figure 6-15 appears.

6. **Select the first image from your image sequence.**

   It's always best to begin at the beginning, right?

7. **Click Open.**

   Flash displays the warning shown in Figure 6-16.

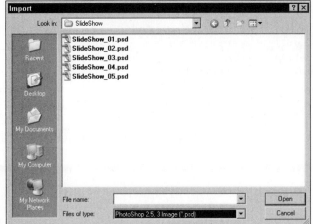

Figure 6-15:
In Flash, you
can import
without
having to
pay a tariff.

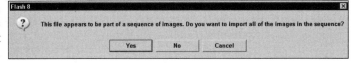

Figure 6-16:
Flash is
one smart
application.

8. **Click Yes.**

   Flash imports every image in the image sequence and places each image on its own keyframe.

9. **If needed, align the images to the center of the Stage.**

   After aligning the images to center Stage, you need to add additional frames; otherwise, the images will fly by so fast that your viewers will never get the chance to appreciate them.

   To align every image in the sequence, click the Edit Multiple Frames icon near the bottom of the Timeline window. Choose Edit⇨Select All and then use the Align panel to center all images to Stage center.

10. **Select the first keyframe and then press F5 to add additional frames.**

    If your movie frame rate is 12 fps, add 23 frames to display the image for 2 seconds, 35 frames to display the image for 3 seconds, and so on.

11. **Repeat Step 10 for the remaining keyframes in your slide show.**

    Your timeline should resemble Figure 6-17.

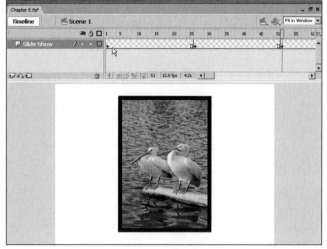

Figure 6-17:
You can
easily
convert a
sequence of
images into
a slide
show.

Part III
Adding Bells and Whistles

The 5th Wave   By Rich Tennant

"Maybe it would help our Web site if we showed our products in action."

In this part . . .

I show you how to add your bells, and I show you how to add your whistles to a Flash Web site, which, incidentally, is why I call this part "Adding Bells and Whistles." Talk about your truth in advertising. If it's ActionScript you need to know, it's ActionScript I show you how to use. ActionScript is so much more than code. I show you how to use ActionScript to add useful items like clocks and pre-loaders to your Web design.

But bells and whistles are more than ActionScript, as you'll see when I show you how to add cool things like Flash photo galleries and full-motion video to your Web designs. But wait, there's more. In this part, I also show you how to add Flash eye candy and how to create e-commerce Flash sites.

Chapter 7

Making Your Site Interactive

*W*hen you create your Flash Web site, you increase the horsepower when you add cool animations, but you turbocharge the site when you add ActionScript. With ActionScript, you can load additional content into your Flash interface and use variables to dispense and store information — the variables giveth, and they taketh away. ActionScript is similar to JavaScript, but with one important exception: You don't have to know code to create ActionScript. All you have to do is know how to use the Actions panel and master the actions you use frequently. In this chapter, I show you the stuff you need to know to make your site interactive.

Adding Sizzle to the Steak with ActionScript

When you need to do something that's illegal, immoral, or fattening, use ActionScript. Kidding! But seriously folks, ActionScript is what you need to take your site from "Oh look, Ethel, it's another Flash site" to something that will rock your viewer's world. ActionScript, like the proverbial well, is deep. But you don't have to dive to dizzying depths to add sizzle to your site. And you don't have to learn all 4,258 actions to add interactivity to your site. (Well, there aren't that many, but there are more actions than I'd care to learn in this lifetime.) Just internalize the ones you need to know and tackle the rest at your convenience.

Introducing ActionScript classes, objects, and methods

Objects, classes, methods, and properties — whew, that's a mouthful — are the building blocks of ActionScript programming. These terms are all related, and understanding how they interact is one of the keys to mastering ActionScript. ActionScript neophytes are often surprised to discover that they have been creating objects since they first began using Flash. In fact, everything you create in a Flash movie is an object. In a Flash movie, ovals, imported images, and blocks of text are all individual objects. You can also create your own objects by using ActionScript code. For example, you can create an instance of the Date object — a bachelor's favorite action — which retrieves the current date and time from the computer used to view your Flash Web site.

Objects are identified by unique names and are also referenced by their location on a particular level. An object exists within a hierarchy in a movie and is called on not only by its established unique name but also by its location within the hierarchy. Objects may remain static through one part of the movie but change later. The Movie Explorer provides a graphical representation of your movie and the objects within it. The Movie Explorer (open it by choosing Window⇨Explorer) represents the objects in your movie as a visual outline, as shown in Figure 7-1.

Objects have properties, and properties describe objects. An object's properties are what make it unique. For example, you set properties for text objects with the Properties Inspector. When creating a block of text, you choose the font type, font color, and font size, all of which are properties of the text object. All of these properties contribute to making a unique block of text.

You can change many object properties with ActionScript code. For example, you can position an object on stage by modifying its _x and _y properties or change the height of an object by modifying its _height property.

A *class* describes everything an ActionScript programmer needs to know about an object. It might help to think of a class as information that defines an object's properties, methods, and event handlers. Properties such as height, width, and position are often included in a class. The *methods* describe what you can do when using ActionScript with an object. For example, the getMinutes method of the Date object retrieves the current minute of the hour from the computer viewing your Flash Web site.

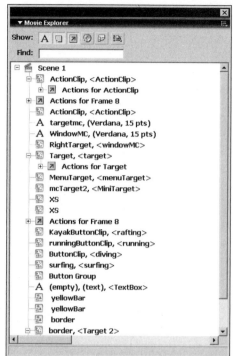

Figure 7-1:
Explore your
movie with
the Movie
Explorer.

A class can be thought of as an object that makes other objects. When you create an object from a class, it is known as an *instance* of the class. To understand this, look at the Date object. The Date object is an ActionScript object that contains methods that retrieve the current date and time from the host computer. Before you can use any of the Date object's methods, you must first create an instance of the Date object, like in the following code:

```
myDate=new Date();
curHour=myDate.getHours();
curMintues=myDate.getMinutes();
```

The first line of code creates an instance of the Date object, while the second and third lines of code use methods of the Date object (getHours and getMinutes) to retrieve the current hour and minute from the host computer. Don't worry, I show you how to keep time with the Date object in Chapter 8.

If you are an experienced ActionScript user, you will probably agree that creating ActionScript in Flash 8 is more powerful and intuitive than ever. The new Script Assist feature takes a lot of the drudgery out of hand-coding

ActionScript. This powerful new feature will benefit ActionScript veterans and beginners alike. In the upcoming sections, you see how to use ActionScript to add interactivity to your Flash productions.

Using the Actions panel

When you need to create ActionScript for a button, keyframe, or movie clip, you open the Actions panel. In the default workspace, the Actions panel is docked with the Properties Inspector, directly beneath the Stage. If you're doing a lot of scripting, you may find it convenient to float the panel in the workspace. If you float the Actions panel, it remains where you float it until you decide to move it, dock it, or revert to the default panel layout. The Actions panel can be accessed by using one of these methods:

- ✔ Choose Window➪Actions.

- ✔ Press F9.

- ✔ If the title bar is displayed in the workspace but the panel itself is closed, click the title Actions to open the panel. Click Actions again to close the panel.

Figure 7-2 shows the Actions panel displaying a simple script that loads a movie when a button is clicked. Notice that the title bar is labeled "Actions – Button," indicating that the script is written for a button symbol. Because you can also create ActionScript for keyframes and movie clips, the title bar changes to reflect the object for which you are creating a script. Before you begin writing a script, make sure the Actions title bar displays the proper object.

Figure 7-2:
Actions –
Button
means you
better be
creating
script for a
button.

If you're new to Flash, the first time you open the Actions panel, you may think you've opened Pandora's box. There's a whole lotta stuff in this panel, as you can see in Figure 7-2. Notice that the panel is divided into three parts. The split window on the left displays the Actions books (top) and shows every script you've created in the movie (below). The large window on the right side of the panel is the Script pane; it shows the script you are currently authoring. When you have a lot of scripts or need to sift through the Actions books, you use the up and down buttons or the scroll bar. You create ActionScript in this pane by doing one of the following:

- ✔ Manually type the code in the Script pane.
- ✔ Click the Add Action button, select an ActionScript group, and then select an action.
- ✔ Open one of the Actions books and drag an action into the Script pane.
- ✔ Open one of the Actions books and double-click an action.
- ✔ Open one of the Actions books, right-click (Windows) or Control-click (Macintosh) an action, and then choose Add to Script from the context menu.

Flash MX 2004 marked the introduction of ActionScript 2. Much to the chagrin of Web designers and non-geeks (read *non-developers*), the only way you could flesh out ActionScript was to manually enter the parameters for each action. (Talk about your exercises in frustration.) Fortunately for us mere mortals, the designers of Flash 8 included a Script Assist button in the Actions panel. When you click this baby, the Parameters pane we non-geeks grew to know and love in Flash 4 through Flash MX (may you rest in peace, except maybe on eBay) appears, as shown in Figure 7-3.

There are a ton of Actions books. And within Actions books, you'll find more Actions books. Throughout this chapter, instead of telling you to click this book, then click that book, and then double-click this action, I tell you something like the following: choose Global Functions⇨Timeline Control and then double-click the `stop` action. This simply means that you open the Global Functions book, then open the Timeline Control book, and then double-click the `stop` action to add it to your script.

Figure 7-3: Look Ethel, the parameters are back in town.

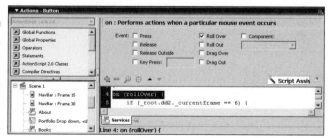

Assigning an action to a keyframe

You assign an action to a keyframe when you want something to happen at that particular point in your Flash movie. Actions you assign to a keyframe can be as simple as a stop action, which stops the movie dead in its tracks, awaiting further input from the viewer; or they can be complex, multiline codes that define variables and evaluate whether a certain set of conditions is true before transporting the viewer to another part of the movie or executing the next lines of code. Here's how you add an action to a keyframe:

1. **On the timeline, select the keyframe to which you want to assign the action(s).**

   On the timeline, keyframes are frames with black dots in them. If a keyframe doesn't appear where you want to add ActionScript, select the desired frame and press F6 to convert it to a keyframe.

2. **Choose Window⇨Actions to open the Actions panel, shown in Figure 7-4.**

   Notice that the panel is labeled Actions – Frame.

3. **Use your favorite method of applying actions to script the keyframe.**

   To reward anyone who is reading this chapter in its entirety, I don't list every possible way to apply an action to a frame. For those who haven't read the chapter in its entirety — we know who you are; Big Brother is watching — refer to the "Using the Actions panel" section of this chapter, which, for your convenience, immediately precedes this section.

4. **Click the Script Assist button.**

   Without the Script Assist button, you must manually enter the parameters for the selected action in the Script pane, which is difficult work if you're not an experienced ActionScript coder or a card-carrying geek.

5. **Add actions as needed to finish scripting the keyframe.**

   Figure 7-4 shows an ActionScript written for a keyframe. When you apply actions to a keyframe, you see a lowercase *a* in the keyframe's position on the timeline.

   In Figure 7-4, notice the panel with three text boxes above the first line of code in the Actions panel. You use these Parameters text boxes to modify available parameters for an action. I discuss the Parameters text boxes as needed throughout the course of the chapter.

   Notice the status line at the bottom of the Actions panel. This indicates the line of the script you are currently working on along with the code contained in that line.

Figure 7-4:
Frame —
Actions,
not pixels.

When you create ActionScript for keyframes, create a new layer and label it **Actions**. When you need to create ActionScript for a keyframe, select the Actions layer, create a keyframe at the desired spot, and then add your ActionScript. Doing so makes it easier to debug a Flash movie.

I cover assigning actions to buttons in Chapter 5.

Navigating with ActionScript

When you navigate with ActionScript, it becomes the steering rudder for your Flash Web site. The ActionScript code you create, when executed, takes your viewers to another part of the movie or to another Web page.

Putting a halt to your movie

Sometimes you need to stop a movie. You can add a `stop` action to the main timeline or to a movie clip's timeline. For example, you might stop the movie when you want viewers to read a large block of text. After they read your words of wisdom, they click a button to resume the movie. You can also add a `stop` action to a movie clip, as shown in Chapter 5 (where I show you how to create a drop-down menu). Here's how you stop a movie:

1. **Select the keyframe where you want the movie to stop.**

   If the frame you selected isn't a keyframe, convert it to one by pressing F6.

   It looks like you can apply an action to a frame; however, the action is assigned to the preceding keyframe on the timeline.

2. **Choose Window⇨Actions.**

   The Actions panel opens.

3. **Choose Global Functions⇨Timeline Control and then double-click the `stop` action.**

   Or if you prefer, click the plus (+) button in the upper left of the Script pane and choose Global Functions⇨Timeline Control⇨stop. The `stop` action is added to the selected keyframe. Figure 7-5 shows a stop action being added to a keyframe.

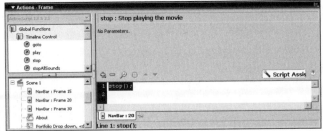

Figure 7-5:
Whoa there
movie! Now
stop!

After you stop a movie, you can play it again by adding the play action to a button.

Using the goto action to pass a frame and collect $200

You use the goto action to navigate to a specific frame in the movie. If you're into making scenes (and who isn't?), you can use the goto action to navigate to another scene in your movie. Navigating to a different scene comes in handy when you create a preloader or intro to your Flash movie. Here's how you add the goto action to a movie:

1. **Click the frame to which you want to apply the action.**

   If the frame isn't already a keyframe, press F6 to convert it to one.

2. **Choose Window⇨Actions.**

   The Actions panel opens for business.

3. **Click the Script Assist button.**

   The Script Assist button is your friend and enables you to choose parameters rather than manually entering them in the Script pane.

4. **Choose Global Functions⇨Timeline Control to open the group.**

   The Timeline Control group is assembled and ready for action.

5. **Double-click** goto.

   Flash adds the line of code gotoAndPlay(1); to your script, and the parameter text boxes, shown in Figure 7-4, make an appearance. The default parameters for the goto action tell the Flash Player to "go to and play frame 1 in the current scene." To have the Flash Player go to a specific frame and stop, select the Go To and Stop option, which you find directly above the Script pane. With this option selected, the Flash

Player goes to the specified frame and stops, awaiting further instructions before proceeding to another part of the movie. You specify whether to Go To and Play or Go To and Stop by clicking the proper radio button directly above the Script pane.

6. **Choose the desired parameters from the following drop-down lists:**

   • **Scene:** Accept the default <current scene> option or choose a different scene from the drop-down menu.

   • **Type:** Frame Number lets you manually enter the number of the frame in the Frame text box, and Frame Label lets you choose the name of a labeled frame from the Frame drop-down list. Your other choices are Expression, Next Frame, and Previous Frame.

   You can learn more about labeling frames and expressions by reading *Macromedia Flash 8 For Dummies* by Ellen Finkelstein and Gurdy Leete (Wiley).

   • **Frame:** Enables you to manually enter the desired frame number in the text field if you choose Frame Number as the Type, or enables you to choose a previously labeled frame from the drop-down list if you choose Frame Label as the Type.

Navigating to another Web page with the getURL action

You use the getURL action to direct your viewer to outside content you want them to see. I know what you're thinking: Why would I want my viewers to go elsewhere? Well, you may want to add a Links section to your site. But when you direct someone to another Web site, you can do so in a new window, which means your masterpiece is still available in its very own browser window. To add the getURL action to a script, follow these steps:

1. **Select the object or keyframe to which you want to apply the action.**

2. **Choose Window⇨Actions.**

   The Actions panel opens.

3. **Choose Global Functions⇨Browser/Network.**

   The Browser/Network group of actions invites you to peruse its *stuff* — a technical, non-geek term for "a lot of things."

4. **Click the Script Assist button.**

   Non-geeks need all the help we can get. The Script Assist button enables the parameter text boxes.

5. **Double-click the getURL action.**

   Flash adds the action to your script, and the parameter text boxes open.

6. In the URL field, type the address of the Web page you want to open, as shown in Figure 7-6.

Be sure to use the proper syntax — for example, `http://www.dasdesigns.net`.

By default, Flash opens the URL in the same window.

Figure 7-6:
Sending
your
viewers to
another
Web page
with the
getURL
action.

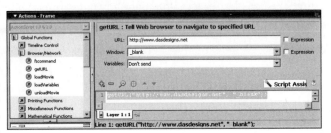

7. To open the URL in another window, click the triangle to the right of the Window field and choose one of the following:

- `_blank` opens the linked document in a brand-new, unnamed browser window.

- `_parent` loads the linked document in the window of the frame that contains the link. If the frame isn't nested, the linked document loads in the full browser window.

- `_self` loads the linked document in the same frame or window as the link.

- `_top` loads the document in the full browser window, removing all frames.

8. In the Variables field, accept the default option, Don't Send, or click the triangle to the right of the field and choose either Send Using Get or Send Using Post.

You can send variables to another Web page by using the Send Using Get option or forward the variables used in a form to an e-mail address by using the Send Using Post option in combination with a CGI script.

9. Close the Actions panel to apply the script.

When the movie is published and the action is executed, the movie loads to the desired URL.

Loading External Movies into Your Flash Site

You have a lot of information to stuff into your Flash site. If you read Chapter 3, you know I'm an advocate of breaking a lot of information down into byte-size pieces. If you didn't read this masterpiece of technical wizardry written in non-techno lingo, you might want to take a gander at that chapter and learn how to break your Flash Web site into an interface into which other content is loaded before delving any further. In the upcoming sections, I show you how to use ActionScript to load external content into your teeny-weenie interface.

Understanding levels

It may help you to think of the different levels of a Flash movie like you think of layers on the timeline. The bottom layer of the timeline is like the bottom level of the movie. Any objects in movies that you load into levels above the main movie eclipse objects directly beneath them on the main level.

The main movie's level is Level 0. You can have as many as 99 levels in a movie. Think of a skyscraper with Level 0 (the main movie) as the ground floor . . . with a glass ceiling. When nothing is happening on the ground floor, all you see is the movie's background color. When action occurs on the time-line, the background color is eclipsed by the action. When you load a movie into Level 1, it's similar to getting tenants on the second floor. When action occurs on Level 1 and one of the Level 1 objects moves over an object in Level 0, the object on the lower level is hidden. If, however, you load a movie into Level 0, it's a new group of tenants moving into the offices on the first floor; the new stuff replaces the old.

Loading movies into targets

You use the `loadMovie` action to load a published Flash movie. In most cases, you assign the `loadMovie` action to a keyframe or a button. The action has two parameters that you use to specify the destination for the movie you're loading and whether any variables will be sent from the loaded movie. Adding the `loadMovie` action to a script is fairly easy:

1. **Select the object or keyframe to which you want to assign the action.**

2. **Choose Window⇨Actions.**

   The Actions panel opens.

3. **Click the Script Assist button.**

4. **Choose Global Functions⇨Browser/Network.**

   The Browser/Network group gets ready to rumble.

5. **Double-click** `loadMovie`.

   Flash adds the action to the script, and the parameter text boxes appear above the Script pane.

6. **In the URL parameter text box, type the path and title of the movie you're loading. Enter the directory where the movie can be found, along with the movie's title (for example:** `myflashmovie.swf`**).**

7. **In the Location field, choose one of the following:**

   • **Level:** Choose the default setting when you're loading the movie into a level in the main movie.

   • **Target:** Choose this option when you're loading the movie into a target movie clip within the movie.

When you have a large amount of content, you always load into a target movie clip. For more information on creating and positioning a target movie clip, see Chapter 3.

8. **In the blank field to the right of the Location field, enter the number of the level or the path in which you're loading the movie.**

   Choose any level from 0 to 99, but remember that if you load the movie into Level 0, you erase the base movie. Figure 7-7 shows the ActionScript for loading a movie into a target movie clip called `targetMC` when a button is released.

Figure 7-7:
Lock and load external content into a target movie clip.

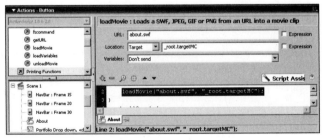

9. **Click the triangle to the right of the Variables field and choose one of the following:**

   • **Don't Send:** Choose this setting (the default) if no variables are associated with the movie you're loading.

   • **Send Using GET:** Choose this option when you have a small number of variables to work with. The option appends the variables to the end of the URL.

   • **Send Using POST:** Choose this option if you have more than a handful of variables.

Unloading movies

When you load a new movie into the same level where one is playing, the new movie replaces the old movie. When movies are playing on multiple levels and you're loading new content, you need to use the unloadMovie action to clear the deck. Here's how to assign the unloadMovie action to a keyframe or object:

1. **Select the object or keyframe to which you want to apply the action.**

2. **Choose Window⇨Actions.**

   The Actions panel opens.

3. **Click the Script Assist button.**

4. **Choose Global Functions⇨Browser/Network.**

   The Browser/Network actions group assembles, waiting for you to make a choice.

5. **Double-click** unloadMovie.

   The unloadMovie action is added to your script, and the parameter text boxes appear.

6. **Click the triangle to the right of the Location parameter text box and choose one of the following:**

   • **Level:** Choose the default option if the movie you want to unload is loaded into a level.

   • **Target:** Choose this option if the movie you've unloaded is loaded in a target.

7. **In the field to the right of the Location field, depending on the option you chose in Step 5, enter either the number of the level from which the movie is to be unloaded or the target path to the movie that you want to unload.**

Giving Flash a Brain (Variables 101)

You add a variable to a movie whenever you need to capture some data entered by someone viewing your movie or to store data that you want displayed on demand or used in conjunction with other elements of your movie. For example, if you create a quiz game, you create one string variable for a correct answer and one for an incorrect answer. The variable that is displayed depends on the answer entered by the movie's viewer.

Similar to everything else in life, variables have a certain set of guidelines that must be adhered to in order for ActionScript to perform as originally planned. If you didn't plan, consider this your virtual verbal punishment. Lack of planning is the main reason that ActionScripts fail.

Understanding variable data types

When you create a variable, it can hold one of three types of data: text (or *strings,* in programmer-speak), numbers, or Boolean (which is not named after the infamous cube with which you create soup). Here's the skinny on variable type:

- ✔ **String data is composed of characters — letters, numbers, punctuation, and the like.** You can create a string of any length, from a single character to an entire sentence or, for that matter, several sentences. When you use a number in a string, the number cannot be evaluated with a mathematical expression — in other words, Flash can't do the math. Here are a few examples of strings: Bill, Bonnie, 123 Bonnie Lane, and Strings, unlike string cheese, are not sticky.

- ✔ **Number variables can be used to change the characteristics of an object, such as its position, rotation, and size.** When you assign a number to a variable that is evaluated, you specify it as an *expression.* To find out more about expressions, read the "Understanding expressions" section, later in this chapter. Examples of variables you use to evaluate an expression are 27, 621, and 3.14156.

- ✔ **Boolean variables can have only one of two possible values: true or false.**

The neat thing about variables in ActionScript is that they can hold different types of data at different times. In most programming languages, you need to declare the type of data a variable can hold. ActionScript is more forgiving. When you change the type of data a variable contains, Flash deals with it on the fly.

Vive la différence between string data and numeric data

When you use a variable to hold string data, you're using a literal value. A *literal value* comprises alphanumeric characters, including spaces and punctuation. When a string variable contains text data, it's known as a *string literal*. A string variable with numeric data is known as a *numeric literal*.

When you create a variable with numeric data that is used to change the characteristics of an object in your movie, you specify that the value of the variable is an expression. An *expression* is something with which Flash can do the math and use to return an actual value.

Understanding literal values

When you add an input text box to your Web site to collect data, you're collecting literal values. You can also use literal values to display information to people who view your movie. For example, if you create a Flash movie for an e-commerce site, you can use literal values to collect information for a mailing list. You can also use literal values like the viewer's e-mail address to respond to a request for further information.

Suppose that you want to create a variable for the title of this book. In ActionScript, a variable for the title of this book might look like this:

```
title="Flash Web Design For Dummies"
```

Whenever you see quotation marks surrounding a variable's value, it's a dead giveaway that the variable's value is string data.

A numeric literal is also designated with quotation marks around the variable's value. For example, a variable for a street address in ActionScript might look something like this:

```
streetAddress="1620"
```

You can combine variables that contain literal values. Suppose that you have a variable named `streetAddress` and a variable named `streetName`. You can create a new variable named `physicalAddress` that combines these two variables, as shown in Listing 7-1.

Listing 7-1:   Combining Literal Values

```
streetAddress="1620"
streetName="Anywhere Street"
physicalAddress=streetAddress+ " " +streetName
```

Notice that the components of the `physicalAddress` variable are not surrounded by quotes. That's because you want Flash to add the value of `streetAddress` and `streetName` to create the value of the variable `physicalAddress`. In other words, this is an expression in which Flash adds the two literal values together. If you display the value of this variable in a movie, you see `1620 Anywhere Street`.

Notice another literal value between `streetAddress` and `streetName`: a space surrounded by quotation marks. Without the addition of this value, the two variables would run together, and you would have `1620Anywhere Street`.

Before you create ActionScript that asks Flash to do any math, you need to understand what happens when you combine two numeric literals with an expression. Suppose that you have a *numeric literal* variable that is equal to 2 and a second *numeric literal* variable that is equal to 3. When you combine the two variables in an expression, as shown in Listing 7-2, you expect the result to be 5. But the result of this expression is actually 23 because you've asked Flash to evaluate an expression with two *numeric literals,* and it took you literally.

Listing 7-2:   Combining Numeric Literals

```
a="2"
b="3"
c=a+b
```

In the next section, I show you how to create variables with which Flash can do the math. So if you want to find out how to add the variables in Listing 7-2 to return a result of 5, and how to get Flash to do other cool mathematical calculations, please read on.

Understanding expressions

When you create a variable that you want Flash to use to evaluate some property of an object, the value of the variable must be an *expression.* For example, if you want to specify the price of an object, you create a variable such as `Doughnut_price=.50`. In plain English, the variable sets the price of a doughnut at .50 — a bargain at twice the price. The value of the variable isn't surrounded by quotation marks, so you know that it's an expression that Flash can use to evaluate the price of a doughnut. If, at any time, you need to increase the price of the doughnut, you modify the ActionScript and republish the movie.

You can also combine variables that contain expressions. Listing 7-3 shows the same code that's in Listing 7-2, but with two important exceptions: a) The values of the variables a and b aren't surrounded by quotation marks, which means that they're expressions that can be combined in another variable, which is an expression; and b) the value Flash returns for c in this case is 5, the same value my abacus returns. It does add up.

Listing 7-3:   Combining Expressions

```
a=2
b=3
c=a+b
```

Creating mathematical expressions

Sometimes you have to get Flash to do the math. To do so, you must create a mathematical expression or four. If you're not a card-carrying geek, this may seem like a daunting task. However, it's not all that scary; in fact, it's almost as easy as doing grade-school math because you use the standard mathematical operands. You can add math operands to your scripts by manually typing them in a text parameter box, or you can select an operator from the Arithmetic Operators book (which is a sub-book of the Operators book) in the Actions panel. Table 7-1 shows the standard operators you can use in your expressions.

Table 7-1	Arithmetic Operators	
Operand	*Operation Performed*	*Proper Syntax*
+	Adds two numbers	a+b
++	Increases a value by 1	++a or a++
–	Subtracts the second value from the first	a–b
– –	Decreases a value by 1	– –a or a– –
*	Multiplies two values	a*b
/	Divides the first value by the second	x/y
%	Returns the remainder of a division. For example (16 % 3) returns a value of 1	(a%b)

The ++ and -- operands are shortcuts. Whenever you need to increase or decrease (increment or decrement in geek-speak) a value by 1, you can use these shortcuts. However, notice that there are two ways to format these operands; you can put them before or after the variable you are incrementing or decrementing. Where you place the operand is super-important when creating a script, especially when you use these operands in a loop. Listing 7-4 and Listing 7-5 show the different values returned by placing the operand before or after a value being increased or decreased by 1.

Listing 7-4: Pre-increment Syntax of the Operand

```
a = 74;
b = ++a;
```

The code in Listing 7-4 returns a value of 75. You would use this syntax if your script called to increase the value of a by 1 while leaving the value of b unaffected.

Listing 7-5: Post-increment Form of the Operand

```
a = 74;
b = a++;
```

The code in Listing 7-5 returns a value of 74 for b, but returns a value of 75 for a.

If you create a for loop and use the post-increment syntax to increase the value of the variable, the script will fail because the value of the variable would never increase. What you end up doing is creating an endless loop, which causes the Flash Player to crash.

When you create expressions for your ActionScript, you can do so with multiple operations. For example, you can multiply a variable by a randomly generated number and then divide that result by another value. Just remember to separate each operation with parentheses and remember which operators take precedence over the others so the expression generates the expected result. And if you don't know which operator takes precedence over others, read all about it in the next section.

Understanding operator precedence

When you create a complex expression using multiple operations, if you don't take operator precedence into account, you won't get the result you're after. Getting incorrect results will not amuse your Web site visitors, or for that matter, your client. The rules of mathematics insist that certain operations be performed before others. These rules of precedence also apply to the mathematical expressions you create with ActionScript. For example, consider the following expressions:

```
x= 7 + 6 * 10
```

```
x=(7 + 6) * 10
```

The result of the first expression is 67, whereas the second expression yields a result of 130. In the first expression, multiplication takes precedence over addition; in the second equation, the operation in brackets takes precedence over multiplication. A long time ago, I learned how to remember operator precedence by using the acronym BODMAS, brackets, open, division, multiplication, addition, and subtraction. Simply put: Operations in brackets have precedence over division, which has precedence over multiplication, which has precedence over addition, and that leaves the low man on the totem pole, subtraction.

Christening a variable

I start this section with a fact that is blindingly obvious: Every variable needs a name. The variable's name is what you use in your ActionScript to gain access to the variable's data. Naming a variable is easy — much easier than trying to choose a name for your pet iguana. For one thing, you know what the variable is going to do in the movie.

As a pet owner, you can probably Google a good pet name. With variables, no such luck exists, and you can name a variable just about anything you want, as long as you don't give it a name that confuses Flash. The following elements *cannot* be included in a variable name:

- ✔ **Reserved words and commands that Flash may mistake as part of an action:** Don't use `break`, `case`, `continue`, `date`, `default`, `delete`, `else`, `for`, `function`, `if`, `in`, `instanceof`, `new`, `on`, `return`, `switch`, `this`, `typeof`, `var`, `void`, `while`, or `with` as a variable name. You can, however, have one of these reserved words as *part* of a variable name; for example, the name `breakDance` doesn't cause the script to run improperly.

- ✔ **Punctuation:** You also give Flash — and yourself, for that matter — a splitting headache if you use any of the following ActionScript punctuation: `{ }` , `;` . `(` or `)`. If you precede a variable name with two forward slashes (`//`), Flash thinks your variable is a comment.

✔ **Mathematical operators:** If you use +, −, *, or / as part of a variable name, your variable just won't add up because Flash thinks that you're trying to do math.

✔ **Spaces:** No spaces allowed. For example, `bills password` isn't acceptable. If you need to separate two names in a variable, use an underscore, as in `bills_password`, or capitalize the second word in the variable, as in `billsPassword`.

✔ **Numerals:** A variable cannot start with a numeral. A variable name of `7level` doesn't work; `level7` does, though.

When you create a name for a variable, it should be displayed in black in the Actions panel. If you make any sort of mistake in naming the variable, Flash lets you know in a heartbeat by highlighting the variable in red with the message `[The variable name you have entered contains a syntax error]`. As smart as Flash is, it doesn't tell you what the syntax error is. I suggest that you commit the preceding list to memory. It can save you lots of frustration in the future.

Another thing to remember about variable names is case sensitivity. If you create lines of code in Expert mode, Flash is very sensitive to case. If you manually enter the action `geturl` rather than `getURL`, Flash doesn't have a clue as to what you're trying to get done and doesn't execute the action. The same rule follows for variables. They're case sensitive.

If you're working with values on different timelines, you need to add the path to the variable name. For example, if you're working with a variable named `title` in a movie clip named `movie_time` on the main timeline, the full name of the variable is `_root.movie_time.title`.

Another thing to note about variable names is that you can assign the same variable name to a different timeline, and Flash recognizes it as a different variable. For example, if you have another movie clip in which you want to use a variable named `title` and use the same variable name on the root timeline, Flash will differentiate between the two, even though you may not.

Declaring a variable

When you decide to give Flash a memory by creating a variable, you have to declare the variable, which means another trip to ye olde Actions panel. Here's how you declare a variable:

1. **Select the object or keyframe where you first want to declare the variable.**

If you're going to use a variable throughout a movie, it's a good idea to declare it on the first frame in the movie. If, for example, you declare a variable for an input text box, declare the variable in the first frame but don't enter a value for it. When you do this, Flash recognizes the variable but assigns no value to it. The content of the variable is filled when a user enters a value in the input text box.

2. **Choose Window⇨Actions.**

   The Actions panel opens.

3. **Click the Script Assist button, Jenson.**

4. **Choose Statements⇨Variables.**

   The Variables group opens.

5. **Locate the Set Variable action and double-click it.**

   Flash adds the action to the script, and the parameter text boxes appear above the Script pane.

6. **In the Variable field, enter a name for the variable.**

   Choose an easy-to-remember name that describes the data the variable will hold and remember not to break any of the variable-naming conventions. If you don't know how to correctly name a variable — I declare — you've probably jumped directly to this section. Before proceeding to Step 7, please take a moment to read the preceding section, "Christening a variable."

7. **In the Value field, enter the value you're assigning to the variable, as shown in Figure 7-8.**

   If the value will be evaluated, make sure that you select the Expression box.

   If you're declaring a variable for an input text box that will appear later in the movie, leave the Value field empty.

Figure 7-8:
I declare!
I do believe
I see a
variable!

Passing the variable baton to other objects

When you have a variable in a Flash movie, you can pass the baton, so to speak. That is, you can take the content from one variable and pass it to another variable. This process is kind of like going online and using money from your checking account (a variable that stores your money, whose value constantly varies depending on your income and outgo) to make an online payment to a vendor (another variable that stores money, too).

To pass the contents of one variable to another, you simply equate the value of the new variable to the old variable. Figure 7-9 shows a line of code that passes the contents of one variable to another. Notice that the value of the new variable is an expression. If the new variable's value was not an expression, the value of the new variable would be equal to the name you entered in the Value field, not the desired contents of the variable.

Figure 7-9:
One variable passes the baton to another.

You can also create a new variable and set its value equal to the content of two or more variables already used in your movie. If you create a user feedback form with two input text boxes that collect the user's first name (which is assigned to the variable `firstName`) and last name (which is assigned to the variable `lastName`), you can create a new variable called `fullName` that combines `firstName` and `lastName`. Figure 7-10 shows the ActionScript code to create the `fullName` variable. Notice the quotation marks that surround a space between the two variables. This indicates that the information is string data — in other words, text. Without the space, the first name and last name would run together.

Figure 7-10:
You can combine the contents of two or more variables to create a new variable.

Resetting a variable

If you're using a variable several times within your Flash Web site, you may have to reset the variable. For example, if you've created a variable whose contents change based on user input, you need to reset the variable to a null (empty) value; otherwise, the user sees his or her last input when the input text box appears again. To reset an existing variable, follow these steps:

1. **Select the object or keyframe you want to use to reset the variable.**

   If you're working with an input text box, select a keyframe before the input text box appears again or assign the variable to a button that, when clicked, advances the movie to the frame the input text box appears on.

2. **Choose Window⇨Actions.**

   The Actions panel opens.

3. **Choose Actions⇨Statements⇨Variables.**

   The Variables group opens.

4. **Locate the Set Variable action and double-click it.**

   The action appears in the Script pane of the Actions panel, and the parameter text boxes strut their stuff.

5. **In the Variable field, enter the name of the variable you want to reset.**

   Enter the name exactly as it appeared when you first declared the variable. This practice makes matters less confusing for you when you need to edit the movie later, and it makes life much easier if other designers are working with you on the project.

6. **Leave the Value field blank.**

   The content of the variable remains blank until new data is passed to it.

Chapter 8

Creating ActionScript Objects

· ·

· ·

You can use ActionScript to create some very cool and very useful objects for your Flash Web site. If your visitors want to know how much time they've been wiling away at your site, you can add a digital clock so they can keep track of the time. If you want to keep your viewers entertained, you can add background music, complete with a stereo controller. If you want Flash eye candy, the sky is the limit. You can use ActionScript to mask objects and to create drag-and-drop elements. So if you're ready to add some cool and useful stuff to your Flash Web site, hang on; in this chapter I show you how.

To cut some corners, you can download the code and other goodies I use in this chapter from this book's Web site: www.dummies.com/go/flash websites.

Telling Time with a Digital Clock

You can add the time and date to your Flash Web designs by using ActionScript. You can use the various methods of the Date object to retrieve the date and time from the viewer's computer. The information retrieved by the Date object changes as the computer updates the time. In order to retrieve the time or date for the computer visiting your Flash Web site, you must first create an instance of the Date object.

Using the Date object

Creating an instance of the Date object is easy. You can create an instance of the Date object on a keyframe or within a movie clip. When you create ActionScript like this, you manually enter the code. I know, that means you can't use Script Assist. Trust me. If you follow the upcoming steps, you'll create trouble-free ActionScript. Here's how you create an instance of the Date object:

1. **Choose Window⇨Actions.**

   The Actions panel opens.

2. **In the left pane of the Actions panel, click Statements⇨Variables and then double-click** setVariable.

3. **In the Variable field, enter a name for the instance of the** Date **object — for example,** myDate.

4. **In the Value field, type** newDate().

   This creates an instance of the Date object.

5. **Select the Expression check box.**

   After you create an instance of the Date object, you can use the object's methods to retrieve date and time information from the host computer playing your Flash design.

Making the clock tick tock

When you use methods of the Date object to display the date, you display the date in a dynamic text box. You then create a variable with the same name as the dynamic text box variable and set the value of the variable equal to the various methods of the Date object. The following list shows some of the most commonly used Date object methods:

✔ getDate: Returns the current date of the month as a number.

✔ getDay: Returns the current day of the week as a number. The week begins with Sunday, which is designated by the number 0. In order to display the day's name, you create an array with each day of the week. The first element in the array is Sunday, which is array offset 0, the same number the getDay method returns when the day of the week is Sunday. I show you how to do all this a little later in this chapter.

✔ `getMonth`: Returns the current month of the year as a number. January is returned as a `0`, December as an `11`. To display the month's name, you create an array with each month of the year.

✔ `getFullYear`: Returns the current year as a four-digit number, for example, `2006`.

To retrieve the current date from the computer's operating system, you create an instance of the `Date` object as described in the previous section; if you haven't read that section yet, do an about-face and read it *now*. After you create the object, you then create individual variables to retrieve the day, month, date, and year from the host computer's operating system. Again, this means manually entering ActionScript. If you copy the code in Listing 8-1 into the Script pane, you'll be able to display the date at your Flash Web site.

Listing 8-1:   Retrieving the Current Date by Using Methods of the Date Object

```
mydate = new Date();
day = mydate.getDay();
month = mydate.getMonth();
currentdate = mydate.getDate();
year = mydate.getFullYear();
```

The code in Listing 8-1 contains all the variables needed to retrieve the current date from the host computer. To display the date in a dynamic text box with a variable name of `current_date`, you create the script in Listing 8-2. For more information on creating dynamic text boxes, see Chapter 4.

Listing 8-2:   Displaying the Date

```
// Set day array
myday = new Array("Sunday", "Monday", "Tuesday",
          "Wednesday", "Thursday", "Friday", "Saturday");
// create date object and variables for day, month, date,
          and year
mymonth = new Array("January", "February", "March",
          "April", "May", "June", "July", "August",
          "September", "October", "November",
          "December");
mydate = new Date();
day = mydate.getDay();
month = mydate.getMonth();
currentdate = mydate.getDate();
year = mydate.getFullYear();
current_date = myday[day]+", "+mymonth[month]+"
          "+currentdate+", "+year;
```

The two arrays contain the days of the week and months of the year as string objects. The first element of an array is always 0. The getDay and getMonth methods of the Date object return Sunday and January as a 0. The last lines of code combine the elements to display the date in a dynamic text box with the variable name of current_date. The first element of the current_date variable, myday[day], gets the current day of the week from the myday array. The mymonth[month] element of the variable gets the current month from the mymonth array. You retrieve an element from an array by specifying its *offset* (a geek term for showing which number of the array is retrieved) surrounded by square brackets. The variables day and month each return a number that retrieves the proper element from each array.

The first offset (number) from an array is always 0 (zero).

Download the currentDate.as file (the script from Listing 8-2) from the Chapter 8 folder at the Web site associated with this book. Create a keyframe, open the Actions panel, and import this script. Create a dynamic text box and type currentDate in the Var field. When you publish the movie, the text box displays the current date.

Displaying the current time

To retrieve the current time from the host computer playing your Flash Web site, you create an instance of the Date object, as outlined previously. After you create an instance of the Date object, you can use the object's methods to retrieve the current time. The following list shows the most commonly used methods to retrieve the current time from the computer viewing your Flash Web site:

- ✔ getHours: Returns the current hour from the host computer as a whole number. The time returned is based on a 24-hour "military time" clock. Midnight is returned as 0; 11:00 p.m. is returned as 23.

- ✔ getMinutes: Displays the current minute from the host computer's clock as a whole number.

- ✔ getSeconds: Displays the current second from the host computer's clock as a whole number.

After creating an instance of the Date object, you create a variable for each method you want to retrieve. Listing 8-3 shows a script that creates an instance of the Date object and three variables to store the information.

Listing 8-3: Retrieving the Current Time from the Host Computer

```
mydate = new Date();
hours = mydate.getHours();
minutes = mydate.getMinutes();
seconds = mydate.getSeconds();
```

To display the date in a dynamic text box, you have to convert the 24-hour clock to a 12-hour clock, unless, of course, you're creating a Web site for a military organization. Listing 8-4 shows a script that will display the time correctly in a dynamic text box.

The script in Listing 8-4 is available at the Web site associated with this book.

Listing 8-4: Displaying the Time

```
onClipEvent (enterFrame) {
    mydate = new Date();
    hours = mydate.getHours();
    minutes = mydate.getMinutes();
    seconds = mydate.getSeconds();
    // Calculate value of AMorPM variable  before changing
          hours variable to compensate for military time
    if (hours<12) {
        AMorPM = "AM";
    } else {
        AMorPM = "PM";
    }
    // At midnight military time =0
    if (hours<1) {
        hours = 12;
    }
    if (hours>12) {
        hours = hours-12;
    }
    if (minutes<10) {
        minutes = "0"+minutes;
    }
    if (seconds<10) {
        seconds = "0"+seconds;
    }
    current_time = hours+":"+minutes+":"+seconds+"
          "+AMorPM;
}
```

Notice that the code in Listing 8-4 specifies the enterFrame clip event. This code is in a movie clip. Choosing the enterFrame clip event continually updates the time as the host computer's clock ticks away. The lines of code below the `seconds` variable set the display time to a.m. or p.m. and modify the output to a 12-hour clock. These are all conditional statements. If the variable `hours` returns a value less than `1`, it's midnight, and the variable's value is reset to `12`, midnight on a 12-hour clock. If the value of `hours` exceeds `12`, the value is reduced by 12 to display the proper time on a 12-hour clock; for example, 1300 hours is 1:00 p.m. on a 12-hour clock. The last two variables add the string `"0"` to `seconds` or `minutes` if they are less than `10`. The `current_time` variable combines all the variables with the necessary punctuation to properly display the time in a dynamic text box. To create the movie clip, follow these steps:

1. **Choose Insert⇨New Symbol.**

   The New Symbol dialog box appears.

2. **Choose the Movie Clip behavior type and name the symbol.**

   `Digital clock` sounds like a fine name to me.

3. **Select the Text tool.**

4. **Choose Window⇨Properties.**

   The Properties Inspector demands your attention.

5. **Choose Dynamic Text from the Text Type drop-down menu.**

   Choosing Dynamic Text enables you to display the contents of a variable within the text box. In this case, you'll be displaying the current time.

6. **Set the text parameters.**

   I generally choose a legible font like Arial or Times New Roman with a font size between 10 and 20. The font size depends on how much room the clock will take up on your Web site.

7. **Type** current_time **in the Var field.**

   This is the same variable you'll create in the ActionScript code for the movie clip in which the text box is embedded.

8. **Select the dynamic text box.**

9. **Choose Window⇨Align.**

   The Align panel appears.

10. **Center the dynamic text box to the Stage.**

11. **Click the Back button or Current Scene button.**

    The movie clip is added to the document Library.

12. **Choose Window⇨Library.**

    The document Library opens.

13. **Drag the symbol you just created on Stage and position it to suit your design.**

14. **With the symbol still selected, choose Window⇨Actions.**

    The Actions panel stops by for a cameo appearance.

15. **Type the code from Listing 8-4 into the Script pane.**

    Alternatively, choose Import from the Actions panel Options menu and choose the `currentTime.as` file, which you can download from this book's Web site. Your Actions panel should resemble Figure 8-1.

Figure 8-1: To tell the time, you need a lot of Action-Script.

```
▼ Actions - Movie Clip
                                                      ↘ Script Assis
 1  onClipEvent (enterFrame) {
 2      mydate = new Date();
 3      hours = mydate.getHours();
 4      minutes = mydate.getMinutes();
 5      seconds = mydate.getSeconds();
 6      // Calculate value of AMorPM variable  before changing hours
 7      //variable to compensate for military time
 8      if (hours<12) {
 9          AMorPM = "AM";
10      } else {
11          AMorPM = "PM";
12      }
13      // At midnight military time =0
14      if (hours<1) {
15          hours = 12;
16      }
17      if (hours>12) {
18          hours = hours-12;
19      }
20      if (minutes<10) {
21          minutes = "0"+minutes;
22      }
23      if (seconds<10) {
24          seconds = "0"+seconds;
25      }
26      current_time = hours+":"+minutes+":"+seconds+" "+AMorPM;
27  }
28
```
```
Symbol 1
Line 8 of 28, Col 20
```

16. **Press Ctrl+Enter (Windows) or ⌘+Return (Macintosh) to preview the movie.**

Adding Background Music

Many Flash Web sites feature background music. If you or your client thinks background music will kick your site up a notch, the music you choose should have some bearing on the site, and of course you should consider the age of your viewing audience. I mean, let's face it, if baby boomers are your primary audience, hip-hop just won't cut it. You use the `loadMovie` command to get the background music into your Web site.

But wait, there's more. In the upcoming sections, I show you how to control the sound and even provide you with a spiffy sound controller that you can download from the Web. Am I a nice guy or what?

Controlling the volume with a sound controller

No matter how carefully you choose the music, not everyone will like it. For others, it may be too loud; still others want all the volume they can get. The solution is to give the viewer the option to turn the music off — silence is golden — or to adjust the volume. In the following steps, I show you how to program a Flash sound controller with ActionScript. The beauty of this controller is that, after you've programmed it, you can use it in other Flash movies.

Before you begin the steps, open the folder labeled `Sound_controller` on this book's Web site. Download the files from that folder to your computer. Make sure the `soundtrack.swf` file is in the same folder.

1. **Launch Flash and open the** `soundController_begin.fla` **file.**

   Flash opens the file, and you see before you some of my best graphic work. (Well not actually, but it's close.) This Flash document comes with a ready-built sound controller that has two sliders. The slider movie clips, which are nested in the sound controller movie clip, look like the controls you might find on your home stereo system. The _x property of the slider is set equal to a variable, the value of which controls the actual volume and pan. I made the sliders movable objects with `startDrag` and `stopDrag` actions. The motion of the slider is constrained to a range of 100 pixels along the x-axis. The slider is nested within another movie clip and reads the _x property of the movie clip, which is set equal to the value of a variable named `level`. When the slider is all the way to the left, level has a value of 0; to the right, 100. So you've got a sliding scale from 0 to 100, perfect for cranking up the volume or turning it down. The sliders are nested within the main soundtrack control movie clip. The main movie clip is what you'll be creating the ActionScript code for. I've done the other work for you.

2. **Poke around each symbol within the movie clip to see the exact code I created for them; to do this, open the document Library and then double-click the symbol called sound controls.**

You can then poke around with all the individual elements that make up the sound controller. When you get to the individual sliders (which are nested in a movie clip called Level Slider), note the initial position of the bar slider's registration point.

3. **Double-click the sound controls movie clip to open the movie clip in symbol-editing mode.**

   Notice that I created three keyframes for you to work with and several layers that house the symbols used to create the movie clip. There is also an Actions layer, where you create the ActionScript for this little gem.

4. **Click the first keyframe in the Actions layer and then choose Window➪Actions to open the Actions panel.**

   Your first job is to load the soundtrack — a spiffy little tune I created for your listening enjoyment — and create an instance of the sound object. The soundtrack is a published movie with a sound that's set to loop a few thousand times. The first keyframe also initializes the values for the variables.

5. **Click the Script Assist button.**

6. **Click Global Functions➪Browser/Network and then double-click** `loadMovie`**.**

   The `loadMovie` action is added to your script, and the parameter text boxes for the action appear above the Script pane.

7. **In the URL field, type** soundtrack.swf **and, in the field to the right of the location, type** 1**.**

   This line of code loads the `soundtrack.swf` movie into Level 1.

   To use your own soundtracks with this controller, create a movie soundtrack as outlined in "Creating a soundtrack movie," the next section. I aim to please. Name your musical creation `soundtrack.swf` and then publish it. Copy the `soundtrack.swf` file into the same folder as the movie in which you're including the sound controller because this sound controller and your music will play instead of the soundtrack I created.

8. **In the left pane of the Actions panel, click Statements➪Variables and then double-click** `set variable`**.**

   That's right — you're going to create a variable for the sound object.

9. **In the Variable field, type** soundtrack**.**

   You can use any name for this variable, but `soundtrack` is logical, wouldn't you agree?

10. Click inside the Value field and then type new Sound().

This adds an instance of the `Sound` object to your script. Make sure you include a space between `new` and `Sound`; otherwise, you won't be able to control the sound.

11. In the left pane of the Actions panel, click ActionScript Classes 2.0⇨Media⇨Sound⇨Methods and then double-click attachSound.

Above the Script pane, the Object and ID fields open.

12. Type soundtrack **in the Object field and** _level1 **in the ID field.**

13. Click the Expression check box.

The code in Step 12 attaches the soundtrack object into Level 1. The Expression check box is checked because Flash evaluates this information.

14. In the left pane of the Actions panel, click Statements⇨Variables and then double-click set variable.

The next two lines of code you create set the beginning positions of the pan and volume controls. You create two variables that set the start position of each slider. The values of the variables change as your movie viewers drag the sliders to change the characteristics of the soundtrack.

15. Place your cursor in the Variable field, click the Insert a Target Path button, and when the Insert Target Path dialog box opens, choose the Relative mode.

This is a movie clip, and you are addressing a path within the movie clip; therefore, you need to be in Relative mode. If you were addressing a path on the main timeline, you would choose Absolute mode.

16. Click the plus sign (+) to the right of pan_control to expand the path, click sliderBar, and then click OK.

The target path is added to the script, and the dialog box exits, stage right.

17. Type ._x **after** sliderBar.

18. In the Value field, type 50 **and click the Expression check box.**

The line of code you just created sets the position of the slider bar (the movie clip instance named `sliderBar`), which is nested within the movie clip `pan_control`, to x=50. In the next keyframe, you'll use this value to control how the sound is divided between the right and left speakers, or for you left-handed readers, between the left and right speakers.

19. Repeat Steps 14–18 to create a variable that sets the _x property of the volume control slider bar movie clip, set its value equal to 75, and then click the Expression check box.

Your finished code for the first keyframe should look like Figure 8-2. This line of code sets the position of the slider bar for the sound control to 75. In other words, the sound will play at 75 percent volume when the movie begins. Now it's time to create the code for the second keyframe.

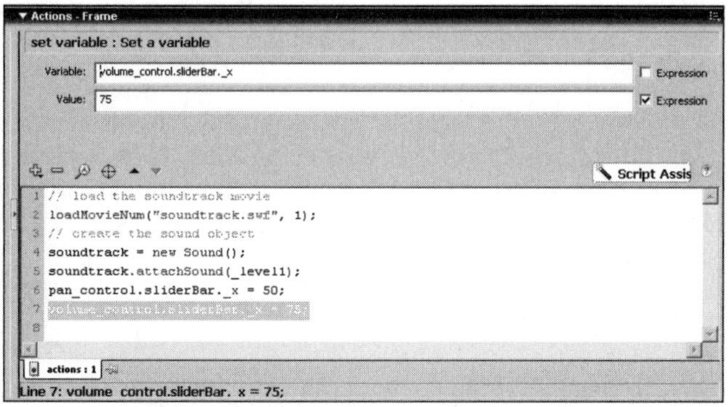

Figure 8-2: This code sets the initial position of the sound controls.

And now you create the ActionScript code for the second keyframe:

1. Click the second keyframe and, in the left pane of the Actions panel, click Statements⇨Variables and then double-click `set variable`.

In this keyframe, you'll create two variables that record the current values of the volume control and pan control.

2. In the Variable field, type pan; **in the Value field, type** 100-(pan_control.level*2).

Be sure to click the Expression box.

3. In the left pane of the Actions panel, click Statements⇨Variables and then double-click `set variable`.

Ah yes, another variable.

4. In the Variable field, type vol; **in the Value field, type** volume_control.level.

Be sure to click the Expression box. This variable records the current _x property of the volume control slider, which will be a value between 1 and 100.

5. **In the left pane of the Actions panel, click ActionScript 2.0 Classes⇨ Media⇨Sound⇨Methods and then double-click** setPan.

Above the Script pane, the Object and Parameters text boxes appear.

6. **In the Object field, type** soundtrack **and then, in the Parameters field, type** pan.

This tells Flash to use the current value of the variable pan to set the panning between speakers.

7. **Repeat Steps 5 and 6, but this time, use the** setVolume **method of the** sound **object, and type** soundtrack **for the Object and** vol **in the Parameters field.**

This line of code sets the volume by measuring the current value of the volume bar slider, which, as you may remember, is its x position. Your completed line of code for this keyframe should look like Figure 8-3. This keyframe's code sets the volume and pan properties of the sound based on the current position of the slider bars. But, of course, the position of the slider bars is subject to change at the whim of the viewer; hence the need for the third keyframe.

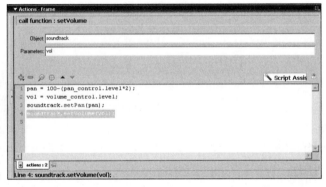

Figure 8-3:
Play it loud,
play it soft;
play it left,
play it right.

8. **Click the third keyframe, and in the Actions panel, click Global Functions⇨Timeline Control and then double-click** goto. **Accept the default parameters but type** 2 **in the Frame parameter text box.**

And that's all there is to setting the sound controls. By bouncing back and forth between the second and third keyframes, Flash is constantly evaluating the position of each slider control and using the _x property of each to set the volume and distribute the sound between the Web site visitor's speakers. Of course, there are two other controls to consider, the Stop and Reset buttons. These are invisible buttons, which I've already coded for you. If you're curious, the Stop button uses the unloadMovie action to clear out level_1, and the Reset button uses the loadMovie action to reload the soundtrack into level 1 and advance to frame 2, where the current positions of the sliders are recorded by the variables you created. Kind of like a traffic circle, this script goes round and round.

9. **Press Ctrl+Enter (Windows) or ⌘+Return (Macintosh) to preview the movie in another window.**

   As soon as the movie starts, the soundtrack plays. Click and drag the slider bars to change the panning and volume of the sound. The beauty of this little gem is the fact that it's modular. You can use this movie clip in any Flash movie you create. Simply open this file and open the document Library. Click the button that looks like a pushpin to *pin* the document Library (keep the Library open even when you open a different document), open the Flash document you want to use the controller in, and then drag the sound control movie clip into the current document's Library or position it as desired on Stage. As long as you have a movie named soundtrack.swf with a looping soundtrack in the same directory, the sound will play when the movie is loaded.

Creating a soundtrack movie

Follow these steps to create your own soundtrack movie:

1. **Create a new movie with a size of 1 pixel by 1 pixel.**

   I know; it's a small movie. But that's okay because you won't see anything when the published movie is loaded, but you should hear music playing.

2. **Import the desired soundtrack into the document Library.**

   You can import any sound format recognized by Flash. Most music is copyrighted. If you're using music from your personal music collection or that of your client, make sure you receive a license to use the work in your Flash Web design. Actually, it's pretty easy to find royalty-free loops on the Web or make your own using an application such as Acid Music (Windows) or Garage Band (Macintosh).

3. **Click the first frame in the movie.**

4. **Open the Properties Inspector.**

5. **Click the triangle to the right of the Sound field and select the sound you just imported.**

6. **In the Loops field, enter a high value, such as** 900.

A high value here makes sure that your soundtrack plays repeatedly while the movie plays. What? You say your viewer's might not want to listen to 900 repetitions of your soundtrack? Well, you did include a stop button in your sound controller, didn't you?

7. **Publish the movie and follow the steps in the previous section to load the soundtrack into a movie.**

Creating a Preloader

You create a preloader when you think your Flash movie may break the bandwidth bank. When that happens, your movie stops while other content loads. Neither your viewer nor your client will be amused if this happens. Your first step to avoid this unhappy situation is to test and see whether the movie actually needs a preloader. This determines which frame your movie stops on to wait for additional content to stream into the Flash Player. If you decide you need a preloader, you use the `if` action to create a conditional statement that tests to see whether a specific number of frames has been loaded. To create the preloader, you create a scene with a preload loop, which is a set of frames that plays over and over again until the designated number of frames has loaded. When the proper number of frames has downloaded, the main movie begins playing. In plain English, the statement says, "If the designated number of frames has loaded, go to the main movie."

I generally prefer to build a preload loop after the rest of the movie has been created. That technique does two things: First, you know whether or not you actually need a preload loop; second, you know exactly how many frames you're working with.

Using the Bandwith profiler

If you've been working with Flash for a bit, you know that it does a wonderful job of compressing movies into a compact package. However, sometimes the files can get large, especially if you have lots of bitmap images in your movie. If you've been taking the advice of this book, you've created an interface into which other content loads. However, in spite of the petite interface, some of your content may cause bandwidth problems. In reality, what happens is that if your movie exceeds a user's bandwidth (the number of kilobytes per second that she can download at her connection speed), the movie stops playing while it waits for additional frames to load. With a preloader, you prevent *bandwidth interruptus* (a condition I just invented) by loading all the essential elements while the preload loop plays. To see whether you need a preloader for your movie, you use the Bandwidth Profiler as follows:

1. **Choose Control⇨Test Movie.**

   Flash publishes the movie and plays it in another window.

2. **Choose View⇨Download Settings and select a connection speed from the menu.**

   I generally test my movies at the 28.8 setting. Testing at this setting ensures that even viewers with slow dialup connections — remember those? — can view your movie without interruption. If you're relatively sure that your viewing audience accesses the Internet at a different connection speed, change to the setting nearest to that connection speed.

   You can also create a custom setting if your viewers access the Internet with a cable modem or ISDN. Choose View⇨Download Settings⇨ Customize and modify any or all the user settings to suit your needs.

3. **Choose View⇨Bandwidth Profiler.**

   While you're looking at this menu section, make sure that you also have the Streaming Graph option selected.

4. **Choose View⇨Simulate Download.**

   Flash begins playing the movie as it will load at the connection speed you selected in Step 2. As the movie plays, a green bar scrolls across the timeline at the top of the window, showing the movie's downloading progress. A downward-pointing arrow indicates the frame being played. Watch the arrow as the movie plays. If it catches up with the scrolling green bar and stops, that's a bad thing. It means that your movie will be interrupted while additional frames load. If this happens, you need a preloader.

Scripting a one-act preloader

After you decide that a viewer's bandwidth may not be up to speed, you build a preloader and then create the ActionScript to make it work. The most primitive preloader is shown in this set of steps. The preloader displays Loading, which can get rather hypnotic when it plays over and over and over and over and over — yawn, stretch — until the movie loads.

To script the preloader, download the preloader.fla file from the Web site associated with this book and then follow these steps:

1. **Launch Flash, choose File⇨Open, navigate to the folder where you copied the** `preloader.fla` **file, and then open the file.**

   Flash opens the file, and you see the main scene of the movie. I've already created the content and a preloader scene for you.

2. **Click the Edit Scene button near the upper-right corner of the workspace and choose Preloader from the drop-down menu.**

   The Preloader scene opens. Notice that three layers of content are already set up. The first two layers contain the elements that keep your viewers entertained while the site loads. The third layer — conveniently labeled Actions — is where you write your ActionScript.

3. **Click the first frame in the Actions layer to select it.**

4. **Choose Window⇨Properties.**

   The Properties Inspector opens.

5. **In the <Frame Label> field, type** preloadLoop **and press Enter or Return.**

   Flash labels the frame.

6. **Select the eleventh frame on the Actions layer and convert it to a keyframe by pressing F6.**

7. **Choose Window⇨Actions.**

   The Actions panel opens.

8. **Click Statements⇨Conditions/Loops and then double-click the** `if` **action.**

   The action appears in the Script pane, and the Condition parameter text box opens.

9. **Place your cursor inside the Conditions field and type** _framesloaded >=.

   This might remind you of your high school math class. It's your basic greater-than-or-equal-to math operand. Don't move that cursor yet.

10. **Type the number of the frame that you determined is causing the movie to stop.**

    Remember to add 12 frames for the number of frames in the preloader. The statement you just created is checking to see if the number of frames loaded is greater than or equal to the number of frames you determined need to load in order for the movie to play in its entirety. Now you need to tell Flash what will happen when this condition is true.

11. **Click Global Functions⇨Timeline Control and then double-click** `goto`.

    Flash adds the `goto` action and the parameter text boxes appear.

12. **To finish the code for this keyframe, click the triangle to the right of each field in the parameters text area and do the following:**

    • **Scene:** Choose Mainmovie from the drop-down menu.

    • **Type:** Choose Frame Label from the drop-down menu.

    • **Label:** Choose beginmovie from the drop-down menu.

    Your Actions panel should look like the one shown in Figure 8-4.

Figure 8-4:
The preload loop plays while enough frames download to play the movie without stopping.

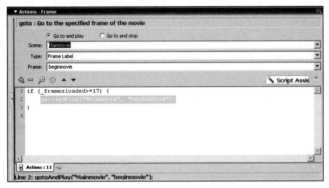

13. **To finish creating the preloader, select frame 12 and press F6 to convert it to a keyframe.**

14. **Choose Window⇨Actions.**

    The Actions panel opens.

15. **Click Global Functions⇨Timeline Control and then double-click** goto.

    The action appears in the Script pane of the Actions panel, and the parameter text boxes for this action appear.

16. **Accept the default Go To and Play option, click the triangle to the right of each parameter field, and do the following:**

    • **Scene:** Choose Preloader from the drop-down menu.

    • **Type:** Choose Frame Label from the drop-down menu.

    • **Label:** Choose preloadLoop from the drop-down menu.

17. **To test the preloader, choose Control⇨Test Movie. Flash publishes the movie and plays it in another window.**

    Whoa! What happened to the preloader? The preloader appeared only momentarily because the movie loaded at light speed from your hard drive. To test the preloader, you need to stream the movie as it would download from the Internet.

18. **Choose View⊏>Simulate Download.**

If you followed these steps correctly, you see *Loading* flashing on the screen, followed by three small dots. When the suspect frame is loaded, the movie begins.

The heart of the preloader is frame 11. The conditional statement tests to see if enough frames of the movie have loaded for it to play without interruption. If they haven't, the next frame of the Preloader scene plays, which sends the preloader back to the frame labeled `preloadLoop` and starts the cycle again. If the number of frames you determined need to load for the movie to play non-stop have indeed loaded, the next action on frame 11 is executed — the movie begins.

In this movie, all of the frames need to load in order for the movie to play without interruption. If you test a movie as outlined in the previous section and notice that the movie begins playing before the green bar reaches the last frame, you can modify your conditional statement to reflect that. For example, the code

```
if (_framesloaded>=50) {
```

executes the next action as soon as frame 50 is loaded, which, if you follow my example, plays the first frame of the movie's main scene.

Hiding Objects with an ActionScript Mask

Many previous versions of Flash allowed you to create a mask layer. The shape you put on the mask layer reveals objects on masked layers beneath it. You can add a degree of interest to the mask by creating a rudimentary motion tween animation. Flash MX introduced an action that enables you to use a movie clip with animation to mask another movie clip. It's a cool action for any Web site that needs a little panache, so I'm including it here. If you create a random animation in the movie clip that masks another other movie clip, you can create Flash eye candy that will interest even the most jaded Web surfer.

To create an ActionScript mask:

1. **Create a movie clip symbol that you want to use as a mask.**

You can animate the movie clip if desired by using motion tweening, frame-by-frame animation, or ActionScript that generates random motion.

2. **Create a movie clip for the object that will be masked.**

   This movie clip can be animated as well. However you'll get your best results if you mask a static image such as a vector graphic or a bitmap.

3. **Open the document Library and drag an instance of the movie clip you want to mask on Stage.**

4. **Drag an instance of the movie clip that will serve as the mask on Stage.**

5. **With the mask movie clip still selected, choose Window⇨Properties.**

   The Properties Inspector opens.

6. **Enter a name for the movie clip in the <Instance Name> field and close the Properties Inspector.**

7. **Select the movie clip that will be masked.**

8. **Choose Window⇨Actions.**

   The Actions panel opens.

9. **Click the Script Assist button.**

10. **Click ActionScript 2.0 Classes⇨Movie⇨Movie Clip⇨Methods and then double-click** setMask.

    Two parameter text boxes appear above the Script pane.

11. **In the Object field type** this.

    The object is what is being masked. Because the ActionScript is being applied to the object being masked, the this alias can be used. If the ActionScript is assigned to a button, the absolute path to the movie clip needs to be entered in this field.

12. **Place your cursor in the Mask Movie Clip field and click the Insert Target Path button to open the Insert Target Path dialog box.**

13. **Click the button that represents the movie clip you are using as a mask, click the Absolute radio button, and then click OK to close the dialog box.**

    When the movie is published, the animated movie clip mask will reveal the masked object. Figure 8-5 shows four frames of a movie clip mask in action.

Figure 8-5:
You can create dazzling eye candy by using the setMask action.

You can also create an ActionScript mask within a movie clip symbol. You do this by nesting the movie clip and the movie clip that will serve as a mask within a third movie clip. Then it's a simple matter of applying the ActionScript and choosing the right path, as shown in the following steps:

1. **Create the movie clip that will serve as the mask, as outlined previously.**

2. **Create a movie clip symbol for the object you want to mask, as outlined previously.**

3. **Choose Insert⇨New Symbol.**

   The Create New Symbol dialog box appears.

4. **Name the symbol, choose the Movie Clip behavior type, and then click OK to enter symbol-editing mode.**

5. **Choose Window⇨Library to open the document Library.**

6. **Drag an instance of the movie clip symbol you want to mask on Stage.**

   Use the Align panel to center the movie clip to the Stage.

Color Plate 1: Optimizing images for your Web site in Photoshop.

Color Plate 2: Optimizing images for your Web site in Macromedia Fireworks.

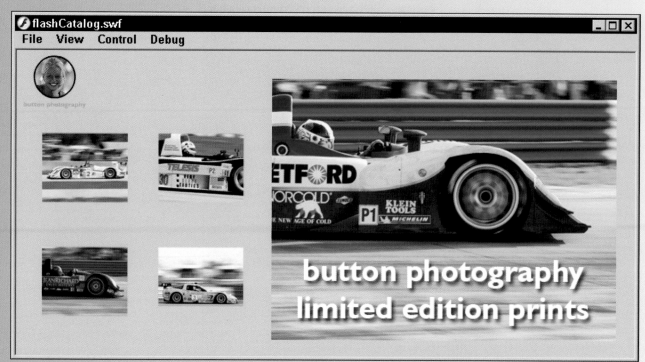

Color Plate 3: Creating a Flash catalog.

Color Plate 4: Adding ActionScript code to transform a catalog into a shopping cart.

Color Plate 5: Adding a moving text marquee to a Flash Web design.

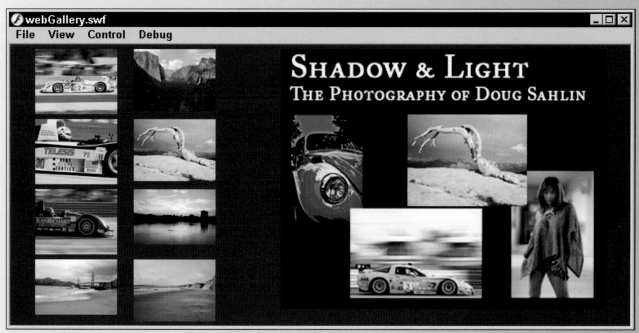

Color Plate 6: Loading the welcome banner into a Flash XML-powered Web gallery.

Color Plate 7: Loading an image and adding text when a button is clicked.

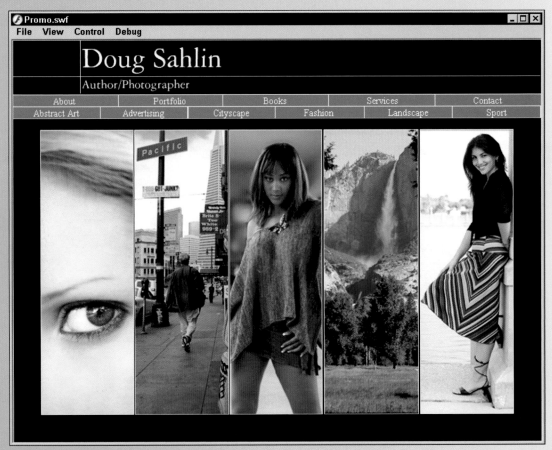

Color Plate 8: Creating an interface with a navigation menu into which other content loads.

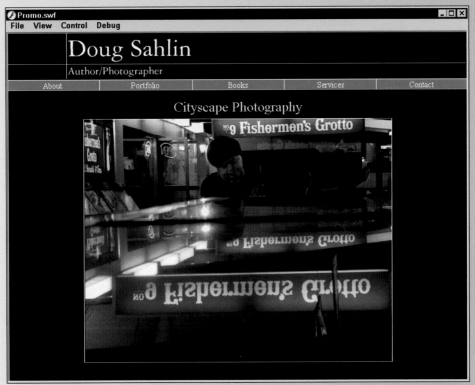

Color Plate 9: Loading external content into the interface when a button is clicked.

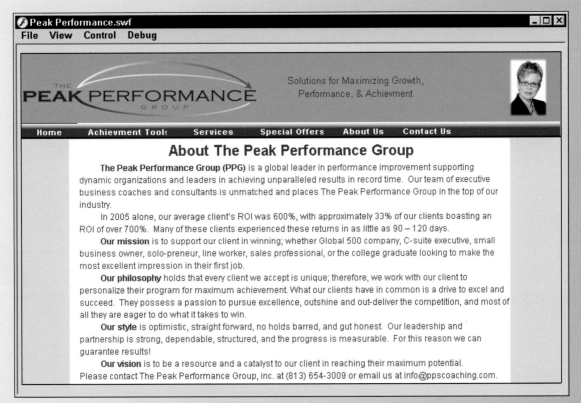

Color Plate 10: Adding text to the Web site.

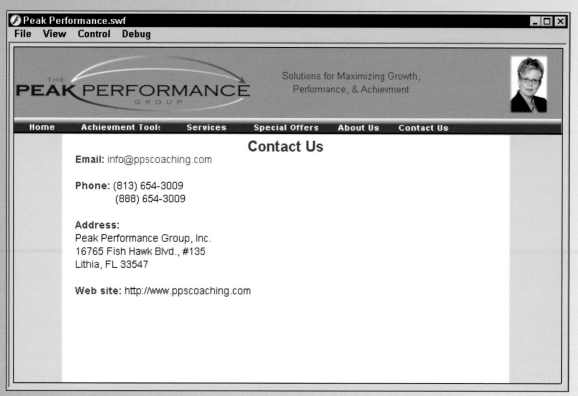

Color Plate 11: Adding text with hyperlinks.

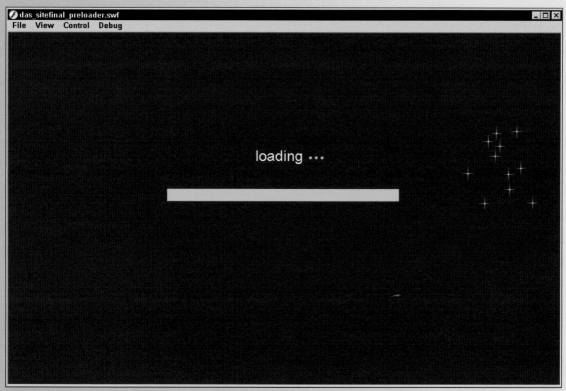

Color Plate 12: Creating a preloader.

Color Plate 13: Creating a Web design with a sound controller, digital clock, and animated background.

Color Plate 14: Adding a drag-and-drop menu to the site.

Color Plate 15: Creating a Flash Web site with eye candy such as moving banners.

Color Plate 16: Loading new content when a button is clicked.

7. **Drag an instance of the movie clip that you'll use as a mask from the document Library to the Stage and align it to the center of the Stage.**

8. **With the movie clip still selected, choose Window⇨Properties.**

   The Properties Inspector opens.

9. **Type** mask **in the <Instance Name> field and then close the Properties Inspector.**

10. **Select the movie clip that will be masked and then choose Window⇨Actions.**

    The Actions panel opens.

11. **Choose ActionScript 2.0 Classes⇨Movie⇨Movie Clip⇨Methods and then double-click** setMask.

    Two parameter text boxes appear above the Script pane.

12. **In the Object field, type** this.

    The object you are masking is the selected object; therefore, you can refer to it by the this alias.

13. **Place your cursor inside the Parameters field and then click the Insert a Target Path button.**

    The Insert Target Path dialog box opens.

14. **Click the Relative radio button and then click the button labeled "mask." Click OK to close the dialog box.**

15. **Click the Back button to exit symbol-editing mode.**

When you create an ActionScript mask in a movie clip symbol, you can use it anywhere in the document. You can have two or three instances of the ActionScript mask playing at one time, or you can create several movie clips in which you use ActionScript to mask different objects. You can resize the movie clips as needed. Consider the effect you can achieve by having multiple instances of an animated mask movie clip on Stage, each clip a different size.

Creating Drag-and-Drop Elements

Drag-and-drop objects are useful critters. In Flash, you use drag-and-drop objects in games, in e-commerce sites, or as the basis for a drag-and-drop menu.

To create a drag-and-drop object, you use ActionScript. When you create a drag-and-drop object, it begins life as a movie clip. You can create two types of drag-and-drop objects: one that displays the hand cursor when a user rolls her mouse over it, and one that can be dragged and dropped but doesn't change the user's cursor. Both types work the same, but I prefer the type that changes the user's cursor; that way, she knows that she has something she can interact with. To make this little jewel, you nest an invisible button in the movie clip.

Creating an element that can be dragged

To create an element that can be dragged, simply create a movie clip. The movie clip can have one frame or as many frames as you want. If you want to show an animation in a movie clip that can be dragged, use as many frames as you need. After the movie clip is created, you use the startDrag action to enable dragging and use the stopDrag action to disable dragging. My favorite method of creating a drag-and-drop object is to nest an invisible button within the movie clip, like this:

1. **Drag an instance of the movie clip you want to convert into a drag-and-drop object from the document Library to the Stage.**

   The movie clip can be a multi-frame animation or a single-frame movie clip with just a graphic.

2. **Double-click the movie clip instance to enter symbol-editing mode.**

   Flash opens the movie clip in another window.

3. **Create a new layer and label it** Invisible Button.

   You can call the layer anything you want, but Invisible Button is logical, and it will make it easier for you to figure out what you created the layer for when you edit the movie in a month or two.

4. **Select the first frame on the Invisible Button layer.**

5. **Drag an instance of an invisible button from the document Library.**

   If you have no invisible button in your Library, create one by using the steps outlined in Chapter 5.

6. **Resize and align the button as needed.**

   The size and positioning of the button depends on the type of drag-and-drop object you're creating. For example, if you're creating a drag-and-drop menu with a tab in its upper-left corner, you resize the button so that it's slightly bigger than the tab and positioned directly over the tab.

7. Click the Back button to return to movie-editing mode.

The invisible button is safely nested within the object. To make a drop-dead gorgeous — or mildly provocative, depending on your taste and that of your client — drag-and-drop object, you use the startDrag action.

Using the startDrag action

You use the startDrag action to convert an instance of a movie clip into an object that can be dragged. The action has parameters that you can use to limit the range in which the object can be dragged. To use the startDrag action, follow these steps:

1. Select an instance of the movie clip to which you want to assign the action.

If you don't have an instance of the movie clip on Stage, select it from the document Library, drag it on Stage, and then position it.

2. Double-click the movie clip.

Flash enters symbol-editing mode.

3. Select the invisible button.

If your movie clip doesn't have an invisible button nested in it, follow the steps in the preceding section to add an invisible button on its own layer.

4. Choose Window⇨Actions.

The Actions panel opens.

5. Click the Script Assist button.

We can all use assistance every now and again. Flash Web designers are no exception.

6. Click ActionScript 2.0 Classes⇨Movie⇨Movie Clip⇨Methods and then double-click startDrag.

The action is added to the script, and the parameter text boxes appear, as shown in Figure 8-6.

7. Click inside the Object field and type this.

The this alias refers to this movie clip; you know, the thing you want to drag.

Figure 8-6:
This action
enables
your Web
site visitors
to drag the
object.

8. **Type** true **or** false **inside the [Lock Center] text field.**

If you type **true**, this option locks the center of the object to the coordinates of the mouse. If you type **false**, the coordinates where you initially
clicked the object are locked to the coordinates of the mouse. If you
enter a value in this field, *do not* uncheck the Expression check box.
Otherwise, Flash will think true or false is a string value, and the script
will fail.

9. **In the [Left], [Right], [Top], and [Bottom] fields, enter values to define
the area in which the object can be dragged.**

To constrain motion relative to the object's position on Stage, you must
subtract half of the width of the object from the width of the movie, half
of the height of the object from the height of the movie, and use this
values for [Right] and [Bottom]. For the Left value, type half of the
object's width, and for the Top value, type half of the object's height.
To constrain where the user can drag the movie clip to a specific area of
the Stage, type any values greater than the [Left] or [Top] dimensions
of your movie, and less than [Right] and [Bottom] dimensions of your
movie. For example, if you want to constrain dragging horizontally along
a 200-pixel range, type **[Left]=0** + half of the object's width, **[Right]=200 –**
half of the object's width, **[Top]=0** + half of the object's height, and
[Bottom]=0 + half the object's height. This option constrains motion relative to the document; in other words, to the 0,0 *x* and *y* coordinates,
which is the upper-left corner of the Stage.

10. **Click the line of code that reads** on (release) {.

The default event handler executes the startDrag action when the
mouse is released. Isn't that useless? Well, they had to have some kind
of default.

11. **Click the Press check box and deselect the Release check box as shown in Figure 8-7.**

Figure 8-7:
Pressing
event, this.

The ActionScript changes to reveal the new event. Now the action will occur when the mouse button is pressed, just what the doctor ordered.

Using the stopDrag action

After you assign the `startDrag` action to an object, it sticks like glue to the mouse, faithfully following it like a puppy tethered to a leash (and never once stopping to lift its leg on a virtual tree). However, as with your puppy, you have to let go of the object at some point. If you don't, the object becomes — ahem — kind of a drag. To put an end to this potentially boorish behavior, you use the `stopDrag` action. As a rule, you assign this action at the same time you assign the `startDrag` action; you just use a different event handler to tell Flash which event must occur for the object to give up its fatal attraction to the mouse cursor. To assign the `stopDrag` action to an object, follow these steps:

1. **Double-click the movie-clip to which you need to add the** `stopDrag` **action.**

   The movie clip appears in symbol-editing mode.

2. **Select the invisible button.**

   You apply the `stopDrag` action to the invisible button.

3. **Choose Window⇨Actions.**

   The Actions panel opens.

4. Click the Script Assist button.

It's always there to lend you a helping hand.

5. Click ActionScript 2.0 Classes⇨Movie⇨Movie Clip⇨Methods and then double-click stopDrag.

The action is added to the script with the default on (release) event handler.

6. Accept the default on (release) **event handler.**

Your script for the object should resemble Figure 8-8.

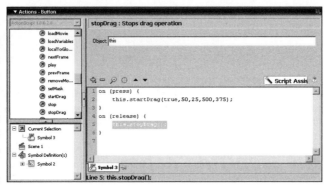

Figure 8-8:
The stopDrag action is the ActionScript equivalent of "Whoa, Nellie."

Chapter 9

Going Visual

Many designers think that just because they use Flash to create a Web site, it's cool by default. Well, coolness is subjective, and if the site isn't cool by default, it's de fault of de designer, not of Flash. In the hands of a competent designer with a creative mind, Flash definitely has more than enough features to make a site cool. In this chapter, I show you a few things you can add to your Flash Web site to kick the coolness level up a notch or so. It's almost as easy as that TV chef sprinkling oregano on your design and then saying, "Bam!"

The code examples I use in this chapter can be downloaded from the Web site associated with this book. You can find it at www.dummies.com/go/flashwebsites.

Adding Tool Tips to Your Web Site

If you add a lot of bells and whistles to your designs, it may be difficult for some viewers to figure out exactly what each element of your design does. You can alleviate some of the confusion by creating tool tips that appear when the cursor rolls over certain elements in your design. Another good use for tool tips is to reinforce information. Can you say *redundant?* For example, you can add a tool tip that tells the viewer what they'll see when a button is clicked, as shown in Figure 9-1, even though it's obvious that clicking the button will give you information about the agents.

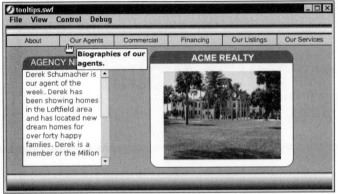

Figure 9-1:
You can create a tool tip to tell a site visitor what happens next.

Creating the tool tips

The tool tip itself is actually a plain-Jane movie clip. You can get as creative as you want when designing the graphics for the tool tip. For example, you can create a rounded rectangle with a triangle at the top that points to the object the user's mouse is over. To create tool tips for a design, follow these steps:

1. **Create the basic shape for the tool tip by using any of the drawing tools.**

   Do not create a new symbol. You want to create the shape and then convert it to a symbol so you can specify the registration point.

2. **Choose Modify⇨Convert to Symbol.**

   The Convert to Symbol dialog box appears, as shown in Figure 9-2.

Figure 9-2:
X marks the spot for the tool tip's registration point.

3. **Specify the registration point for the symbol.**

   For most tool tips, you'll choose the upper-left corner, which is the 0 coordinate for both the *x*- and *y*-axis.

4. **Name the symbol, choose the Movie Clip behavior type, and click OK.**

   You just created a symbol.

5. **Choose Edit⇨Edit Selected to work in symbol-editing mode.**

6. **Add the tool tip text and any other elements needed for your design.**

7. **Click the Back or current scene button to exit symbol-editing mode.**

8. **Delete the symbol instance.**

   The master symbol is stored in the document Library. You duplicate it to create the other tool tips for your design.

9. **Choose Window⇨Library.**

   The document Library opens.

10. **Right-click (Windows) or Control-click (Macintosh) the symbol and choose Duplicate from the context menu.**

    The Duplicate Symbol dialog box appears.

11. **Type a name for the duplicated symbol and then click OK.**

    A carbon copy of the original symbol is created.

12. **Repeat Steps 10 and 11 as needed to create additional tool tips for your design.**

    When you duplicate each symbol, give it a name that reflects the tool tip's function. After you create the duplicates, edit them to change the text.

After you create enough duplicates for all of the tool tips needed for your design, you're ready to create instances of them on Stage. When the movie loads, you don't want the tool tips to be visible, so you place them off Stage. After positioning the tool tips, you create the necessary ActionScript for each button to make the applicable tool tip appear when a user hovers the cursor over a button. To position the tool tips, follow these steps:

1. **Choose Window⇨Library.**

   The document Library opens.

2. **Select all of the tool tips.**

   Select the first tool tip and then Shift-click the remaining tool tips.

3. **Drag the tool tips to a position off Stage.**

4. **With the tool tips still selected, choose Window⇨Properties.**

   The Properties Inspector opens.

5. **Write down the values shown in the X: and Y: fields.**

   You'll need these values when you create the ActionScript to return the tool tips after the user's mouse rolls off the button.

6. **Choose Modify⇨Timeline⇨Distribute to Layers.**

   A new layer is created for each tool tip. Each layer is labeled with the corresponding tool tip's name, as shown in Figure 9-3. By distributing each tool tip to its own layer, you can easily select each tool tip, even though they are in identical positions.

Figure 9-3:
You distribute each tool tip to its own layer so you can work with them individually.

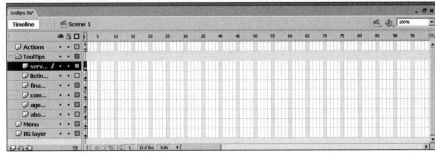

If you're creating a design that involves many objects, create a layer folder to store the tool tips in. After you create the tool tips, you can close the folder so it takes up only one position on the timeline. The tool tips in Figure 9-3 are stored in a folder labeled ToolTips.

7. **Select a tool tip and then choose Window⇨Properties to open the Properties Inspector.**

   To select an individual tool tip, lock and hide the other tool tip layers. Then you'll be able to select the tool tip by clicking its layer, as shown in Figure 9-4.

8. **Enter a name for the tool tip in the <Instance Name> field.**

9. **Repeat Steps 7 and 8 to name the other tool tips in your design.**

After you've christened your tool tips, you're ready to create the ActionScript that makes the tool tips appear. You could create the same script for each object that uses a tool tip. However, that can get rather tedious if you have several tool tips. The easier solution is to create one function to display the tool tips and another to hide them.

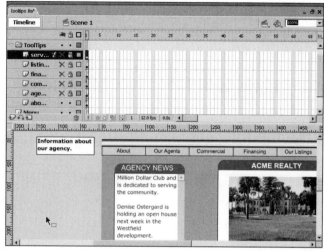

Figure 9-4:
Lock and hide the tool tip layers so you can edit an individual tool tip.

Creating the tool tip functions

The functions you create to display and then hide the tool tips simplify your ActionScript workflow. The function that displays each tool tip changes the tool tip's _x and _y properties to the current x and y coordinates of the mouse, allowing for a bit of room if the user rolls over the top of the button. The function that hides each tool tip returns the tool tip to the _x and _y positions you jotted down when you added the tool tips to your document. If you didn't jot down this information, select all of the tool tips and record their *x* and *y* coordinates from within the Properties Inspector, as noted in Step 5 of the previous section. To create the tool tip functions:

1. **Select the top timeline layer and then click the Insert a Layer button; name the layer** Actions.

2. **Select the first frame on the Actions layer and then choose Window⇨Actions.**

   The Actions panel opens.

3. **In the left pane of the Actions panel, click Statements⇨User-Defined Functions and then double-click** function.

   The action is added to the Script pane, and the parameters text boxes shown in Figure 9-5 appear.

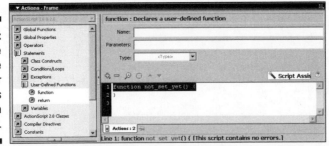

Figure 9-5:
These
are the
parameter
text boxes
for a
function.

4. **In the Name field, type a name for the function.**

Tooltips would be a wise choice.

5. **In the Parameters field, type** mc.

This designates that the function is applied to movie clips. Leave the
Type field blank.

6. **Click Global Functions⇨Miscellaneous Functions and then double-
click** evaluate.

The Expression field appears above the Script pane.

7. **In the Expression field, type** _root[mc]._x=_xmouse.

This line of code sets the _x property of the movie clip called by the
function equal to the current _x position of the mouse.

8. **Click Global Functions⇨Miscellaneous Functions and then double-
click** evaluate.

The Expression field appears above the Script pane.

9. **In the Expression field, type** root[mc]._y=_ymouse.

The function you just created displays the tool tip. Now you need to
create a function to hide the tool tip.

To create a function that hides the tool tips, follow these steps:

1. **Select the last line of code (the solitary curly brace) you just created.**

2. **In the left pane of the Actions panel, click Statements⇨User-Defined
Functions and then double-click** function.

That's right — this is a functional kind of script.

3. **In the Name field, type a name for the function.**

4. **In the Parameters field, type** mc.

5. **In the left pane of the Actions panel, click Global Functions⇨ Miscellaneous Functions and then double-click** evaluate.

The Expression field appears above the Script pane.

6. **In the Expression field, enter** _root[mc]._x= **followed by the *x* value you recorded from the Properties Inspector when you added the tool tips to your design.**

7. **Repeat Steps 5 and 6 to create an expression for the** _y **property of the movie clip.**

Listing 9-1 shows two functions that show and hide tool tips.

Listing 9-1:   Creating Functions to Show and Hide Tool Tips

```
function showTip(mc) {
    _root[mc]._x=_xmouse+5;
    _root[mc]._y=_ymouse+5;
}
function hideTip(mc) {
    _root[mc]._x=-150;
    _root[mc]._y=-5;
}
```

Notice that a value of 5 was added to the _xmouse and _ymouse properties in the code in Listing 9-1 that displays the tool tips. This was to allow a bit of space so the item the user's mouse hovers over is still visible.

After you create the functions, you create the code that displays or hides the movie clips, depending on where the user's mouse is in relation to the button.

Programming the buttons

You've done the grunt work by creating the functions. Now all you need to do is create the ActionScript for each button, which calls the proper function when a user's mouse rolls over or rolls out of the button target area.

If you want a tool tip to appear when a user's mouse is over a graphic, you must nest the graphic in a movie clip with an invisible button.

Here's how you program the buttons:

1. **Select a button and choose Window⇨Actions.**

The Actions panel opens.

2. **In the left pane of the Actions panel, click Deprecated⇨Actions and then double-click** `call function`.

   That's right, a deprecated action. Sometimes the oldies are still goodies. Three parameter text boxes appear above the Script pane.

3. **In the Object field, type _root.**

   This tells the Flash Player that the function will be applied to an object on the root timeline.

4. **In the Method field, enter the name of the function you created to display the tool tip.**

   For my example, I would enter **showTip**.

5. **In the Parameters field, enter the instance name of the tool tip you want to appear.**

   The instance name must be surrounded by quotation marks, as shown in Listing 9-2.

6. **Click the first line of code and select the Roll Over check box, making sure you deselect the default Release event.**

   The button is now programmed to call the function that makes the tool tip appear when a user's mouse rolls over the button target area.

7. **Click the last line of code (the curly brace) and repeat Steps 2 through 6 to call the function that hides the tool tip.**

   For the event, choose Roll Out. Listing 9-2 shows a typical ActionScript to display and hide a tool tip.

Listing 9-2:   Calling the Functions

```
on (rollOver) {
    _root.showTip("about");
}
on (rollOut) {
    _root.hideTip("about");
}
```

Creating a Moving Navigation Menu

If you've ever seen a Flash Web site with a navigation menu that moves from left to right in a seemingly endless loop, with the first item of the menu reappearing after the last, you know how cool this effect is. The code to create this effect is relatively simple. You begin by creating a navigation bar, as outlined in Chapter 5, and then create a duplicate nav bar and align them end to end. A bit of ActionScript completes the wizardry.

Creating an endless menu

An endless menu is an enigma that food connoisseurs with bottomless pits for stomachs have yet to find. When it comes to Flash, an endless menu is an enigma to your Web site visitors, but after reading this section, it will no longer be an enigma to you. Actually, an endless menu is kind of like a double-decker sandwich, but instead of being stacked one on top of the other, the menus are stacked side by side. That is, unless you decide to create a vertical endless menu, which is kind of like an endless submarine sandwich — diver down. Use the following steps to solve the endless menu enigma.

Instead of reinventing the wheel, I've already created the beginnings of a moving navigation bar. Download the `movingNavBar.fla` file you'll find in this chapter's folder at this book's Web site.

1. **Launch Flash and open the `movingNavBar.fla` file.**

   The project is partially completed. You have a basic interface and a nav bar, as shown in Figure 9-6.

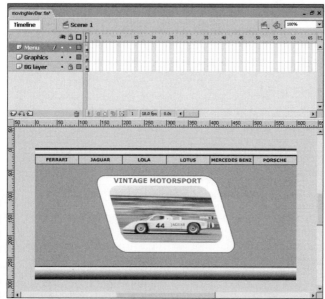

Figure 9-6: Your first step is to create a nav bar.

2. **Select all of the buttons and then choose Modify⇨Convert to Symbol.**

   The Convert to Symbol dialog box appears (see Figure 9-7).

3. **Name the symbol, choose the Movie Clip behavior type, click the center-left square in the Registration section, and then click OK.**

   The buttons are converted to a movie clip symbol, and the symbol is added to the document Library.

4. **Select the symbol you just created and then choose Edit⇨Edit Selected.**

   You are now working in symbol-editing mode.

5. **Select all of the buttons and then choose Edit⇨Copy.**

   The buttons are copied to the clipboard.

6. **Choose Edit⇨Paste in Place.**

   You now have a carbon copy of each button in the nav bar. Now you need to align the first button so that it appears after the last button on the nav bar you copied. The document is 600 pixels wide, as is the nav bar. To move the selected buttons, you change the x value in the Properties Inspector.

7. **With the buttons still selected, choose Window⇨Properties to open the Properties Inspector.**

8. **In the X: field, enter a value of** 600.

   The buttons are perfectly aligned.

9. **Click the Back button to exit symbol-editing mode.**

   When you return to movie-editing mode, the symbol is still selected.

Now you've got an enigmatic menu with end-to-end buttons. You're probably wondering how to make it endless. Read on.

Putting the menu in motion

An endless menu that doesn't move? Hey, like, isn't that an oxymoron or something? Indeed it is, but putting the menu into motion isn't rocket science. But it does require ActionScript. After you put my menu in motion, you'll know how to do the same with endless menus of your own design. (Hmm . . . I wonder if you could create an endless sushi bar by using this technique.) Here's how you put your endless menu into motion:

1. **Choose Window⇨Actions.**

   The Actions panel opens.

2. **In the left pane of the Actions panel, click Statements⇨Conditions/Loops and then double-click** if.

3. **In the Condition field, type** this **and leave your cursor at the end.**

4. **In the left pane of the Actions panel, click ActionScript 2.0 Objects⇨Movie⇨Movie Clip⇨Methods and then double-click** hitTest.

5. **Position your cursor between the parentheses and type the following:**
   _root._xmouse, _root._ymouse, true.

   The condition you just created tests to see whether the mouse has hit the nav bar.

6. **In the left pane of the Actions panel, click Global Functions⇨Miscellaneous Functions and then double-click** evaluate.

7. **In the Expression field, type** this._x-=0.

   You may recognize this as a decremental expression. If the mouse hits the nav bar, the x position of the nav bar decrements by a value of 0. In other words, there is no motion. To set the nav bar in motion, you need to use the else action.

8. **In the left pane of the Actions panel, click Statements⇨Conditions/Loops and then double-click** else.

9. **In the left pane of the Actions panel, click Global Functions⇨Miscellaneous Functions and then double-click** evaluate.

10. **In the Expression field, type** this._x-=5.

    This expression decrements the *x* position of the nav bar by a value of 5 pixels. But if the nav bar continues to move, eventually it will scroll past the end of the movie. To prevent against this, you create another conditional statement using the if action. The nav bar is 600 pixels long, and you tacked a 600-pixel duplicate to the back end. The first button on the nav bar is at *x*-coordinate 0. When the nav bar moves

600 pixels to the left, the nav bar you copied to the back end is fully displayed. Therefore, you set the _x property of the nav bar to 0 as soon as it exceeds –600. This is how the nav bar appears to continuously reappear.

11. **In the left pane of the Actions panel, click Statements⇨Conditions/ Loops and then double-click** if.

12. **In the Condition field, type** this._x<=-600.

13. **In the left pane of the Actions panel, click Global Functions⇨ Miscellaneous Functions and then double-click** evaluate.

14. **In the Expression field, type** this._x=0.

    As soon as the movie clip's _x property is less than or equal to –600, the property is reset to 0 and the nav bar appears as though it never ends.

15. **Select the first line of code that reads** onClipEvent (load) {.

16. **Select the Enter Frame clip event.**

    Your code for the nav bar should look like Listing 9-3.

17. **Choose Control⇨Test Movie.**

    After the movie publishes, it is displayed in another window. If you followed the steps exactly, the nav bar should begin moving to the left. Move your mouse over the nav bar and it stops.

Listing 9-3:   Creating ActionScript for a Moving Nav Bar

```
onClipEvent (enterFrame) {
    if (this.hitTest(_root._xmouse, _root._ymouse, true)) {
        this._x-=0;
    } else {
        this._x-=5;
    }
    if (this._x<=-600) {
        this._x=0;
    }
}
```

This technique can also be used when the width of the nav bar exceeds the width of the movie. For example, if you create a document that is 600 pixels wide, and you have eight buttons that are 100 pixels long, you change the values accordingly. When you duplicate the buttons and paste them onto the back end of the original nav bar, you change the value in the X: field in the Properties Inspector to **800**. When the nav bar's _x property is less than or equal to –800, you reset the property value to 0. For another interesting variation, you can create a vertical nav bar and have it continuously scroll from top to bottom by decrementing the nav bar's _y property.

Creating a Flash Photo Gallery

Flash has the ability to read data from XML documents. You can use this feature to your advantage when you need to create a photo gallery. Instead of reinventing the wheel by recoding and republishing your Web design every time your client changes the images, you simply update the XML document, which is a heck of a lot quicker than recoding and republishing the Flash design. Shhh . . . don't tell your client.

Preparing images for the gallery

In your favorite image editing program, you resize the images to suit the design. The gallery you're going to be creating is for landscape images. The thumbnails are 100 pixels wide. The main images are 380 pixels wide. If you use an application like Macromedia Fireworks or Adobe Photoshop, you can take advantage of batch processing to resize the images. I also create an image that appears when the gallery first loads. This can be a collage with text, such as the one shown in Figure 9-8.

To examine a completed Flash Web photo gallery, download the Flash Web Gallery folder from the Chapter 9 folder at this book's Web site.

Figure 9-8: Hit 'em with your best shot when the gallery loads.

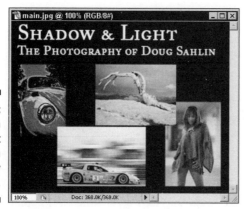

Laying out the gallery

When you create a Flash Web gallery, you can load it into an interface as outlined in Chapter 3. When you load a Flash movie into an interface, you need to size the movie so that it fits within the document, taking into account the Web site banner and navigation menu. For the purpose of this exercise, assume that the banner is 50 pixels high and the navigation menu is 20 pixels high. To lay out the gallery, follow these steps:

1. **Create a new document and size it to 760 pixels wide by 350 pixels high.**

   When you load this into a target movie clip positioned at X=0, Y=70, in a document that is 760 pixels by 420 pixels — the default size for a maximized Web browser on an 800 x 600 desktop — the published movie fills the maximized browser. If you're loading content into another movie, make sure you match the frame rate of the document into which you're loading the photo gallery.

2. **Choose Insert⇨New Symbol.**

   The New Symbol dialog box appears.

3. **Choose the Movie Clip behavior type and name the symbol.**

   Thumbnail_loader is a good name.

4. **Click OK.**

   This transports you to symbol-editing mode. Do not add any graphics. You're creating a target movie clip into which the gallery thumbnails load.

5. **Click the Back or current scene button.**

   The movie clip is added to the document Library.

6. **Create a new layer and name it** Thumbnail.

7. **Create an instance of the** `Thumbnail_loader` **movie clip.**

8. **Choose Window⇨Properties.**

   The Properties Inspector opens.

9. **Type** 30 **in the X field and** 5 **in Y field.**

   This aligns the target movie clip near the upper-left corner of the movie.

10. **Type** thumbnails **in the <Instance Name> field.**

    You'll be addressing the movie clip with ActionScript, hence the need for an instance name.

11. **Lock the Thumbnail layer by clicking the dot to the right of the layer name and below the lock icon.**

12. **Create a new layer and name it** Main Image.

13. **Repeat Steps 2 through 5 to create a new target movie clip called** Images.

14. **Create an instance of the movie clip on the Main Image layer.**

15. **Type** 330 **in the X text field and** 30 **in the Y text field.**

    This aligns the movie clip near the upper-left corner of the movie.

16. **Choose Window⇨Properties.**

    The Properties Inspector opens.

17. **Type** main **in the instance name text box.**

    You'll be loading the large images into this target movie clip.

18. **Lock the layer.**

    Locking the Thumbnail and Main Image layers prevents you from accidentally moving the target movie clips while editing other parts of your movie.

19. **Create a new layer and name it** Text Title.

20. **Select the Text tool.**

21. **Select Dynamic Text from the Type drop-down menu and then set the text parameters.**

    For the purpose of this exercise, use the Verdana text type and choose a font size of 16. Choose a text color that contrasts well with your background.

22. **Choose Window⇨Properties.**

    The Properties Inspector opens.

23. **Type** 330 **in the X text field and** 307 **in the Y text field.**

    This aligns the dynamic text box beneath the spot where the images will appear.

24. **Type** title **in the <Instance Name> field, as shown in Figure 9-9.**

    This figure also shows the rest of the layout. I know, it doesn't look like much now, but wait 'til you see it with thumbnails and images. It's sweet.

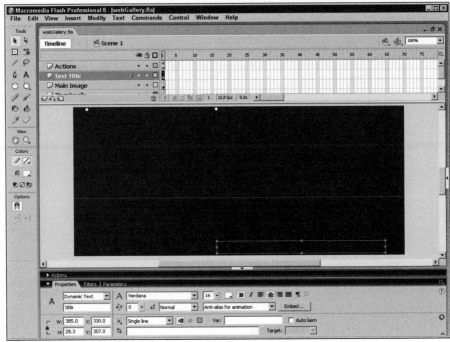

Figure 9-9:
The Web
gallery, laid
out for all
to see.

Creating the XML document

The beauty of this Flash photo gallery is that you don't have to rewrite ActionScript and republish the movie every time you want to change images in the gallery. *XML* stands for *eXtensible Markup Language*. In essence, it's a language used by Web designers that enables them to create their own objects. You can use information from an XML document in a Flash movie. In this case, the XML document tells Flash the name and location of the thumbnails and images as well as the title of the photo. Follow these steps to create the XML document:

1. **Open your favorite word processor.**

   If you're on a Windows machine, Notepad works great for this.

2. **Type** <photo_gallery>.

   Make sure you include the underscore; otherwise, the XML document will not load properly into Flash. In essence, you're loading a variable into Flash, and variable names cannot have spaces.

3. **Create a new line and type** <image **followed by the other attributes for your image.**

In XML lingo, `image` is an object. For the photo gallery, you have three attributes of the `image` object: `title`, `main`, and `thumb`. The attributes specify the information that will be relayed to Flash via the XML document — in this case, the image title, the path and name of the main image, and the path and name of the thumbnail image.

For the first image in the sample gallery, the line of XML code reads:

```
<image title="Audi R8 at speed"
       main="images/img_1.jpg"
       thumb="thumbnails/img_1.jpg"/>
```

Notice there are three attributes: `image title`; `main`, which specifies the path to and the filename of the main image; and `thumb`, which specifies the path to and filename of the thumbnail image.

4. **Repeat Step 3 for each image in your photo gallery. Press Enter or Return after creating each line of code.**

   This keeps each line of code on a separate line.

5. **Create a new line and type** </photo_gallery>.

   Your finished XML document should resemble Figure 9-10.

Figure 9-10: Creating the XML code that will tell your Flash Web gallery where to find the images.

6. **Save the document as** `xmlgallery.xml`.

Scripting the gallery

Now comes the fun part: creating the ActionScript. Actually, there's quite a bit of ActionScript. Even though Script Assist is the painless way to create ActionScript, I manually coded the gallery. The easiest way to learn how to create the code for a Web photo gallery is to load the code I've already created. But don't worry, I won't leave you in the dark. I tell you what each line of code does in the upcoming sections.

I've exported the code for the Web gallery. It's a document named `webgallery.as`, which you'll find in the Flash Web Gallery folder in the Chapter 9 folder at this book's Web site. After you've downloaded the file, follow these steps to create the ActionScript that powers your photo gallery:

1. **Create a new layer and name it** Actions.

   You do create your ActionScript code on a separate layer, don't you? If you don't, I recommend you start right now. Picture a 60-frame movie with 6 or 7 layers sprinkled with 10 or 15 ActionScript snippets on keyframes. It would be a lot easier to find your code if it's on its own layer, wouldn't it?

2. **Select the first frame in the Actions layer and then choose Window⇨Actions.**

   The Actions panel opens.

3. **Click the Actions panel Options icon and choose Import Script from the drop-down menu.**

   The Open dialog box appears.

4. **Navigate to the Flash Web Gallery folder you downloaded to your computer and then choose** `webgallery.as`.

5. **Click Open to import the code.**

   Your Actions panel should resemble Figure 9-11.

Figure 9-11: Importing the code for the Web photo gallery.

```
1  loadMovie("images/main.jpg", "_root.main");
2  myGallery = new XML();
3  myGallery.ignoreWhite = true;
4  myGallery.onLoad = function(success) {
5      numimages = this.firstChild.childNodes.length;
6      spacing = 85;
7
8          for (i=0; i<numimages; i++) {
9          this.picHolder = this.firstChild.childNodes[i];
10         this.thumbHolder = thumbnails.createEmptyMovieClip("thumbnail"+i, i);
11
12         this.thumbHolder._y = i*spacing;
13         this.thumbLoader = this.thumbHolder.createEmptyMovieClip("thumbnail_image'
14         this.thumbLoader.loadMovie(this.picHolder.attributes.thumb);
15         this.thumbHolder.title = this.picHolder.attributes.title;
16         this.thumbHolder.main = this.picHolder.attributes.main;
17         if (i>3){
18             this.thumbHolder._x=120;
19             this.thumbHolder._y = this.thumbHolder._y-340;
20         }
21
22         this.thumbHolder.onRelease = function() {
23             main.loadMovie(this.main);
24             title.text = this.title;
25
26         );
27     }
28
29 );
30 myGallery.load("xmlgallery.xml");
```

Dissecting the code

Now that you've got all that code in your Actions panel, you're probably thinking, "Do what?" Don't worry. In this section, I show you what each line of code means. After you know what the code does, you'll know how to modify it for your own Flash Web galleries.

Listing 9-4 shows every line of code needed to make the Flash photo gallery do its thing. Listing 9-5 shows the first few lines of code. In Listing 9-6, you see the remainder of the code for the Flash photo gallery. I give more detailed explanations for each following the listings.

Listing 9-4:   Code for the ActionScript Photo Gallery

```
loadMovie("images/main.jpg", "_root.main");
myGallery = new XML();
myGallery.ignoreWhite = true;
myGallery.onLoad = function(success) {
    numimages = this.firstChild.childNodes.length;
    spacing = 85;
        for (i=0; i<numimages; i++) {
    this.picHolder = this.firstChild.childNodes[i];
        this.thumbHolder =
         thumbnails.createEmptyMovieClip("thumbnail"+i,
         i);

        this.thumbHolder._y = i*spacing;
        this.thumbLoader =
         this.thumbHolder.createEmptyMovieClip("thumbnai
         l_image", 0);

        this.thumbLoader.loadMovie(this.picHolder.attri
        butes.thumb);
        this.thumbHolder.title =
         this.picHolder.attributes.title;
        this.thumbHolder.main =
         this.picHolder.attributes.main;
        if (i>3){
                this.thumbHolder._x=120;
                this.thumbHolder._y =
        this.thumbHolder._y-340;
        }

        this.thumbHolder.onRelease = function() {
            main.loadMovie(this.main);
            title.text = this.title;

        };
    }

};
myGallery.load("xmlgallery.xml");
```

Listing 9-5:   Creating an Instance of the XML Object

```
loadMovie("images/main.jpg", "_root.main");
myGallery = new XML();
myGallery.ignoreWhite = true;
```

The first line of code loads the image that viewers see when the gallery loads. The image is loaded into the movie clip target that you've given the instance name of main. The next line of code creates an instance of the XML ActionScript object, which is housed in the variable myGallery. The next line of code sets the ignoreWhite property of the XML object to true. In essence, what this does is ignore white space between individual object nodes, which can cause errors when the XML document loads.

Listing 9-6:   A Function Here and a Lot of Script There

```
myGallery.onLoad = function(success) {
    numimages = this.firstChild.childNodes.length;
    spacing = 85;
        for (i=0; i<numimages; i++) {
    this.picHolder = this.firstChild.childNodes[i];
        this.thumbHolder =
        thumbnails.createEmptyMovieClip("thumbnail"+i,
        i);

        this.thumbHolder._y = i*spacing;
        this.thumbLoader =
        this.thumbHolder.createEmptyMovieClip("thumbnai
        l_image", 0);

        this.thumbLoader.loadMovie(this.picHolder.attri
        butes.thumb);
        this.thumbHolder.title =
        this.picHolder.attributes.title;
        this.thumbHolder.main =
        this.picHolder.attributes.main;
        if (i>3){
                this.thumbHolder._x=120;
                this.thumbHolder._y =
        this.thumbHolder._y-340;
        }

        this.thumbHolder.onRelease = function() {
            main.loadMovie(this.main);
            title.text = this.title;

        };
    }

};
myGallery.load("xmlgallery.xml");
```

The first line of code in Listing 9-6 is the function that occurs when the XML document successfully loads. The variable numimages records the number of images by extracting the information from the XML document. The variable spacing is used to set the spacing between thumbnails. The next line of code creates a loop that extracts the information from the XML document. The picholder variable is a reference that stores the attributes from each object in the XML document. The other reference, thumbHolder, does a number of things. First and foremost, it creates an empty movie clip. Each empty movie clip is spaced with the line

```
this.thumbHolder._y = i*spacing;
```

This changes the movie clip's Y position by the iteration of the loop (i) multiplied by the variable spacing. The first iteration of a loop is always 0; therefore, the spacing is not changed. In each additional iteration of the loop, the Y position (the _y property of the empty movie clip) is increased by 85 pixels. The conditional statement that begins with if i>3 creates the next column. When i is greater than 3, the X position (_x property of the empty movie clip) is changed to 120 and the Y position is decreased by 340, which creates the next column.

The empty movie clips are populated with thumbnail images with the line of code that reads

```
this.thumbLoader.loadMovie(this.picHolder.attributes.thumb
    );
```

In essence, this line uses the loadMovie action to load one of the thumbnail images. If you remember, the thumb attribute of each object in the XML document references the path to and filename of the thumbnail image. The this.thumbHolder.title and this.thumbHolder.main variables extract the title and main image that match the thumbnail by plucking these attributes from the XML document.

After the thumbnails are populated, a function takes care of loading the main image and creating the title text. The line of code that begins with this.thumbHolder (onRelease) is a function that loads the image, which is represented as main in the XML document, into the main target movie clip. The title attribute from the XML document is loaded into the dynamic text box with the instance name of title. The function executes when visitors to your photo gallery release the mouse button after clicking the applicable thumbnail. The last line of code loads the XML document, which makes everything happen.

I know the code looks complex, but if you experiment with it, you'll be able to modify the code for your own Flash photo gallery.

To see the finished photo gallery in action, press Ctrl+Enter (Windows) or ⌘+Return (Macintosh). Click the thumbnails to see the individual images load. The text also changes to reflect the title of the image. The finished Flash photo gallery from the example is shown in Figure 9-12.

Figure 9-12: Click a thumbnail to load a full-size image.

Importing Full-Motion Video — A Moving Tale

Flash photo galleries are just the thing for photographers. But what if your client is a videographer or simply has some cool video he wants to display on his Flash Web site? You can take care of either eventuality with Flash. Full-motion video in Flash is pretty awesome. You tailor the video for your client's Flash Web site and the type of equipment used by the client's audience. You can also add playback controllers to the video.

Encoding the video in Flash

When you need to add a video to a Flash movie, you can do so quickly by encoding the video within Flash. When you encode a video in Flash, you can choose whether the video will work with the Flash 7 Player or Flash 8 Player, as well as the data rate. Here's how you encode a video in Flash:

1. **Create a new document.**

   If you're loading video into another Flash movie, size the new document to match the size of the video. Make sure you match the frame rate of the main movie.

If you're adding a skin to your video that features external playback controls, add 35 pixels to the height of the document to accommodate the external controls.

When creating an interface into which you're going to load video content, choose a frame rate for the interface that matches the frame rate of the video you intend to display in the interface. In the case of full-motion video, that's either 15, 18, or 30 frames per second, the lowest values being for DSL users. If part of your intended audience will be accessing the Internet with dialup modems, you should create a 12 fps variation as well.

2. Choose Import➪Import Video.

The Import Video dialog box, shown in Figure 9-13, appears.

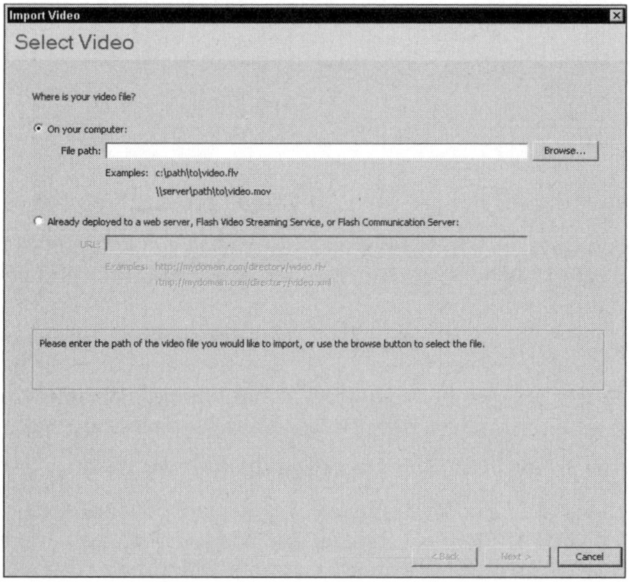

Figure 9-13:
You can import video into your Flash document.

3. Click Browse.

The Open dialog box appears.

4. Select the video you want to import and then click Open.

The path to and filename of the video appear in the File Path field.

5. Click Next.

The Deployment section of the Import Video dialog box appears, as shown in Figure 9-14.

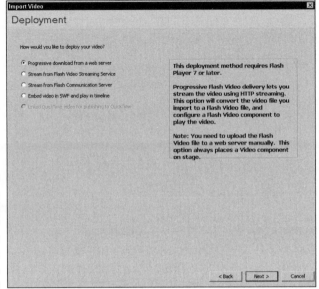

Figure 9-14:
You choose
the manner
in which the
video is
deployed.

6. **Accept the default Progressive Download from a Web Server option.**

Unless you have a client who owns several oil wells and is rich enough to afford Flash Video Streaming Service or Flash Communication Server, the default is fine.

7. **Click Next.**

The Encoding section of the Import Video dialog box appears, as shown in Figure 9-15.

8. **Choose an option from the Encoding drop-down menu.**

Your choices are Low, Medium, and High quality for the Flash 7 or Flash 8 Player. If your audience accesses the Internet with a dialup modem, choose Low; with a DSL connection, choose Medium; with a fast cable connection, choose High. If you're certain your audience has the Flash 8 Player, choose Flash 8 player. The encoding for the Flash 8 Player is the latest and greatest. If high quality with fast streaming is your main concern, choose one of the Flash 8 options.

If you choose one of the Flash 8 options, you can hedge your bets by telling your audience that they need the Flash 8 Player to view the video and providing a link to where they can download the application, which, at the time of writing, is www.macromedia.com/shockwave/download/download.cgi?P1_Prod_Version=ShockwaveFlash.

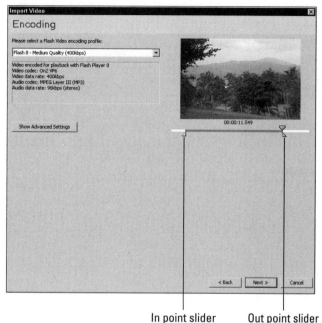

Figure 9-15:
You choose
the encoder
for your
Flash video.

In point slider   Out point slider

9. **Drag the In Point slider to determine which frame of the source video will be the starting point of your Flash video.**

10. **Drag the Out Point slider to determine which frame of the source video will be the ending frame of your Flash video.**

11. **Click Next.**

    The Skinning section of the Import Video dialog box appears. This section enables you to choose a skin and controls for the video, as shown in Figure 9-16.

12. **Choose a skin from the Skin drop-down list.**

    When you choose a skin, the dialog box changes to show the skin you selected. My advice is to preview several skins until you see one you like. When choosing a skin, you also choose how much control you give your viewers. You can supply them with all of the controls, playback controls with a volume mute, or a controller with playback seek and volume mute, or you can choose None to give the viewer no controls to play with.

    The minimum width of the skin is listed after you choose it. If the minimum width is larger than the width of your video, choose a skin that doesn't have as many controls.

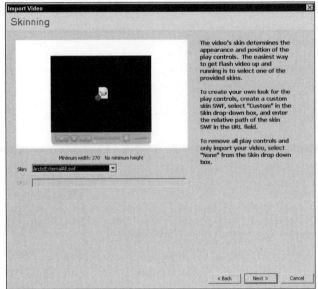

Figure 9-16:
Skin 'em if
you got 'em.

13. **Click Next.**

The Finish Video Import dialog box, shown in Figure 9-17, appears. This lists all of the options specified in other sections of the Import Video dialog box.

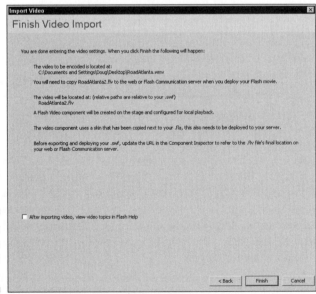

Figure 9-17:
You have
to finish
sometime.

14. **Click Finish to encode the video.**

    Alternatively, you can click the Back button to navigate to a section and make a change. After you click Finish, the Flash Video Encoding Progress dialog box, shown in Figure 9-18, appears. This useful critter tells you how long it will take to encode your video. If the remaining time is longer than a minute, relax and fix yourself a cup of tea. After the video is encoded, an FLV file appears in the folder in which you saved the FLA file. An FLV playback component appears in the document Library. You can modify the parameters of the component as outlined in the "Modifying video playback control parameters" section, later in this chapter.

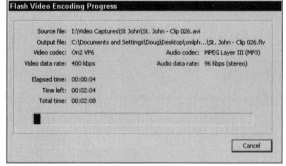

15. **Choose Control⇨Test Movie to preview your video.**

    Figure 9-19 shows a Flash video with an external controller being previewed.

When you encode video from within Flash, the video encoder creates an FLV (FLash Video) file with the same name as the source video, plus the SWF movie for the video skin you selected. These files need to be uploaded to your Web server along with the published SWF movie.

Linking encoded video to a Flash document

If you use the Flash 8 video encoder to batch process multiple video files for use in your Flash Web site as outlined in Chapter 2, you must manually add the video skin (the video controllers) to a document and then specify the link to the FLV file. You do that like this:

1. **Create a new document.**

2. **Modify the default document size to match that of the encoded video that will be linked to the document.**

   If you're using a video skin with external controls, add 35 pixels to the height of the document to accommodate the external controls. Make sure you match the document frame rate to that of the video that will be linked to the document.

3. **Choose Window⇨Components.**

   The Components panel opens, as shown in Figure 9-20.

Figure 9-19:
Previewing
the encoded
video.

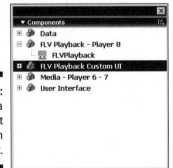

Figure 9-20:
Adding a
component
to a Flash
document.

4. **Select the FLV Playback component, drag it on Stage, and align it to the center of the Stage.**

5. **Choose Window⇨Properties.**

   The Properties Inspector opens.

6. **Click the Parameters tab.**

   The Properties Inspector reconfigures, as shown in Figure 9-21.

Figure 9-21:
Configuring
the
component
parameters.

7. **Click the Content Path parameter field and then click the button that looks like a magnifying glass.**

   The Content Path dialog box opens, as shown in Figure 9-22.

Figure 9-22:
Inserting the
path to your
video
content.

8. **Click the Folder icon and select the desired video clip.**

9. **Click OK to link the video with the controller.**

10. **Choose Control⇨Test.**

    The video plays in an external window, as shown in Figure 9-23.

When you upload the published SWF movie to your Web server, you'll also have to upload the accompanying FLV movie and the SWF movie for the video skin you selected. The video skin file will be called something like `ArticExternalAll.swf`.

Figure 9-23:
Previewing
your
handiwork.

Modifying video playback control parameters

After you add the FLV Playback component to a file, as outlined in the previous section, Flash takes a lot of things for granted. In other words, the component has defaults for each parameter, excepting of course the Content Path parameter, for which you fill in the blank. After you add content to the FLV Playback component, you can modify the parameters to suit your project. Most of the parameters are Boolean values: true or false. If the value is true, the parameter happens. For example, the default parameter for AutoPlay is true, which means the video plays after the Flash movie loads. Changing the parameter to false pauses the video on the first frame. You specify false if you want the viewer of your Flash Web site to use the skin controls to begin playing the video. Modifying the video playback parameters is a piece of cake:

1. **Select the FLV Playback component.**

2. **Choose Window⇨Properties.**

   The Properties Inspector opens.

3. **Modify the desired parameters.**

   To find out more about a component's parameters, click the icon that looks like a question mark in the Properties Inspector and then choose Help on This Component from the drop-down menu.

Adding Pop-ups

Okay, so you hate pop-ups. So do I. But some clients absolutely insist on having them. As they say, the client is always the client. But the client doth put the bread on the table. So when the client speaks, you listen. And what do you do when the client says he wants the pop-up to thwart the most per-sistent pop-up blocker in the world? You say no problem. And it is no prob-lem when you use ActionScript in Flash. Here's how to add a pop-up to your Flash Web site:

1. **Choose Insert⇨New Symbol.**

   The Insert New Symbol dialog box appears.

2. **Choose the Button type, name the symbol, and then click OK.**

   You are in symbol-editing mode.

3. **Create a button similar to the button shown in Figure 9-24.**

   This is the button your viewers will use to close the pop-up window. After creating the button, click the Back or current scene button to exit symbol-editing mode and add the button to the document Library.

Figure 9-24:
Creating
the Close
Window
button.

4. **Choose Insert⇨New Symbol.**

   The Insert New Symbol dialog box appears.

5. **Choose the Movie Clip type, name the symbol, and then click OK.**

   You are magically transported to symbol-editing mode.

6. **For the purpose of this exercise, create a movie clip similar to the button in Figure 9-25.**

   This is the pop-up window your viewers will see when the Web site loads. Of course, you'll come up with your own pop-up designs based on your client's needs. Notice that the button symbol is nested within the movie clip.

7. **Click the Back or current scene button to exit symbol-editing mode and add the symbol to the document Library.**

Figure 9-25:
Creating the
pop-up.

8. **Choose Window⊅Library.**

   The document Library opens.

9. **Right-click (Windows) or Control-click (Macintosh) the symbol and choose Linkage from the context menu.**

   The Linkage Properties dialog box appears.

10. **Type a name in the Identifier text field.**

    Make sure the name has no spaces.

11. **Check the Export for ActionScript and Export in First Frame check boxes, as shown in Figure 9-26.**

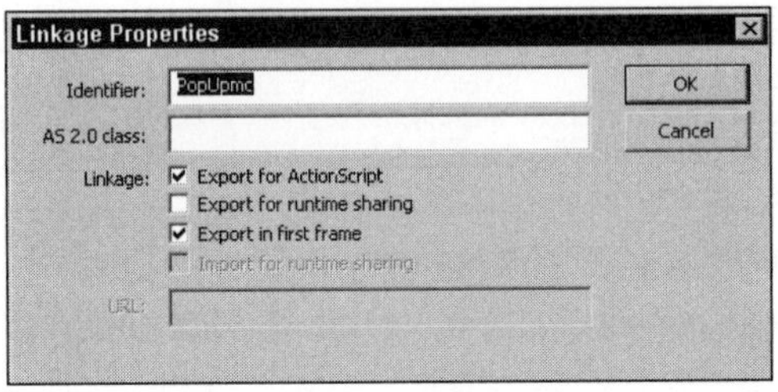

Figure 9-26:
Giving the
symbol an
identity
crisis.

12. **Click OK to exit the Linkage Properties dialog box.**

    The symbol now has an identity that can be referred to by ActionScript.

13. **Click the first frame in your movie and then choose Window⊅Actions.**

    The Actions panel opens. The reason for choosing the first frame is that you want the pop-up to appear when the movie loads. If you were loading a complex interface over the course of 20 frames, you'd put the ActionScript that opens the pop-up on the 20th frame.

14. Click the Script Assist button.

Ah yes, a little help from your friend.

15. In the left pane of the Actions panel, click ActionScript 2.0 Classes⇨ Movie⇨Movie Clip⇨Methods and then double-click attachMovie.

The attachMovie action is added to your script, and several parameter text boxes appear.

16. Type the following information in the text boxes:

- *Object:* Type **this**.

- *Linkage Name:* Type the Identifier you specified in the Linkage Properties dialog box. Be sure to uncheck the Expression check box.

- *New Name:* Type **window**. Be sure to uncheck the Expression check box.

- *Depth:* Type **1**.

The Script pane should resemble Figure 9-27.

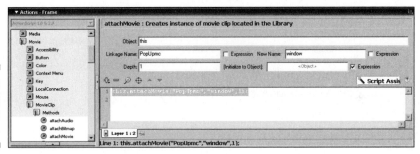

Figure 9-27: Attaching the pop-up movie clip.

17. In the left pane of the Actions panel, click Statements⇨Variables⇨set variable.

The set variable action is added to the script, and two parameter text boxes appear.

18. In the Variable text box, type window._x.

This line of code sets the _x property for the attached pop-up. Do not click the Expression check box.

19. In the Value text box, type 250 **and then click the Expression check box, as shown in Figure 9-28.**

This sets the position in which the pop-up will appear.

20. Repeat Steps 17 through 19, only this time name the variable window._y and set the value of the variable to 150.

That's right, you're setting the Y position of the pop-up window.

Now all you're left to do is program the button that closes the pop-up window. After all, you don't want the thing hanging out in the breeze and blocking the rest of your gorgeous Flash Web design. To program the Close Window button, follow these steps:

1. Choose Window⇨Library.

The document Library opens.

2. Double-click the pop-up window symbol.

The symbol appears in symbol-editing mode.

3. Select the button.

4. Choose Window⇨Actions.

The Actions panel opens.

5. In the left pane of the Actions panel, click ActionScript 2.0 Classes⇨Movie⇨Movie Clip⇨Methods and then double-click removeMovieClip.

The action is added to your script, and a single parameter text box appears.

6. Type this **in the Object text box and then type "window" (the new name that you gave the movie clip when you used the** attachMovie **action to make the pop-up appear) in the Parameters text box, as shown in Figure 9-29.**

Make sure you have quotes around the word *window.* Otherwise, Flash will think this is an expression to be evaluated instead of a reference to an object. If you didn't follow my sage advice and use *window* for the new name, type whatever name happened to strike your fancy.

Figure 9-29:
Removing
the
attached
movie clip.

7. **Click the Back or current scene button to exit symbol-editing mode.**

8. **Choose Control⇨Test Movie.**

   The pop-up window appears. If it doesn't, check your ActionScript —
   you goofed somewhere. Figure 9-30 shows an example of a pop-up
   window on a Flash Web site.

9. **Click the Close Window button.**

   Say, "So long, pop-up."

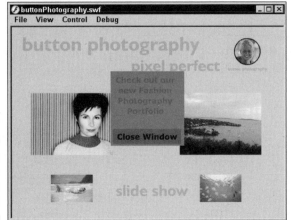

Figure 9-30:
Pop-up
goes the
window.

Chapter 10

Going Commercial

- -

- -

Some Web designers think that if a site has to be commercial, Flash is out of the question. To that, I politely reply, "Bunk." Flash has variables, therefore it gives you the capability to send and receive information. You can use the superior graphic capabilities of Flash to create compelling forms, online catalogs, and much more. In this chapter, I show you how to go commercial, whether for yourself or for a client. I show you how to create forms in Flash and how to create a printable page, an online catalog, and a shopping cart.

I put the example files for this chapter in the Chapter 10 folder on the Web site associated with this book. When you need to download a file to follow along, point your browser to www.dummies.com/go/flashwebsites to find the file.

Creating Flashy Forms

Standard HTML forms are not very artistic. In fact, they're downright boring. If you need to add Flash forms to your Web site, you can use your creative genius and the Flash tools to create an interesting form. When you create a Flash form, you use input text boxes to receive information from site visitors. Each input text box is assigned a variable name. When the user completes the form and clicks the Submit button, the information is transmitted to the recipient via the Web server's mail-forwarding scripts. Each Web hosting service uses a different script to forward mail. Check with the server that will host your design for specific information. In the sections that follow, you find out how to transmit the results to a Web server's mail-forwarding CGI script.

Creating form elements

To create the form elements, you use the Text tool. Create a separate input text box for each form element. Each input text box has a variable assigned to it, which as you may remember from Chapter 4 is the Var field found in the Properties Inspector, when you set the parameters for the text box. When the user inputs information into the text box, Flash stores the data until the user clicks the Submit button. Then the magic of ActionScript sends the information via the Web. Figure 10-1 shows input text box parameters being modified in the Properties Inspector.

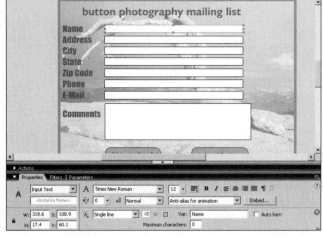

Figure 10-1:
You create the form elements with the Text tool.

When you create input text boxes, you can specify whether a single line of text, multiple lines of text, or password text is accepted by the variable. You can also limit the number of characters that will be stored by the variable. For more information on creating input text boxes, refer to Chapter 4. Figure 10-2 shows a finished Flash form complete with Add to Mailing List and Reset Form buttons.

Scripting the form

When you create the ActionScript for a form, you're sending the information from the variables in the input text boxes to a mail-forwarding script. To make a mail-forwarding script work in Flash, you have to figure out what information the mail-forwarding script needs and then send that information via variables. You also have to write some script to reset the form. After all, you want all of the people viewing your Flash Web site to submit their information, don't you? The only way to do this is to reset the form. That way, another user of the same computer can use your form immediately after his friend or significant other has submitted information via your form.

Figure 10-2:
You can use input text boxes and other elements to create an aesthetically pleasing form for your designs.

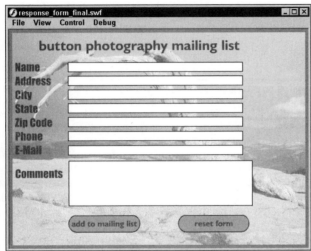

Creating ActionScript for the Reset button

When you create a form for a Flash movie and users input information into the form, you can give them the option to erase all of the information in the form and start over. This option comes in handy if more than one user views your design from the same computer. After one user fills in the form and submits the information, a different user can clear the form by clicking the Reset button and then submit his or her information. When you create the code for a Reset button, you are resetting the variable for each input text box to null, in other words, a variable with no data. To reset a variable, follow these steps:

1. **Choose Window⇨Actions.**

   The Actions panel opens.

2. **Click Statements⇨Variables and then double-click** set variable.

3. **In the Variable field, enter the name of the variable you want to reset.**

4. **Leave the Value field blank.**

   Listing 10-1 shows ActionScript to reset several variables when a button is clicked.

Listing 10-1:   Code for a Reset Button

```
on (release) {
    name = "";
    address = "";
    city = "";
    state = "";
    zip = "";
    phone = "";
    e_mail = "";
}
```

Creating ActionScript for the Submit button

Creating the input text boxes and buttons is the easy part of creating a Flash form. The difficult part comes when you need to submit the information to the designated recipient at a Web site. Each Web server uses different scripts to forward form results. Check with the support staff of the Web hosting service where your design will be uploaded for specific information. In this section, you see how to interpret an HTML mail-forwarding script and use that information to transmit the data from your Flash form to the intended recipient. Listing 10-2 shows a typical CGI mail-forwarding script.

Listing 10-2:   An HTML Mail-Forwarding Script

```
<form action="http://scripts.myserver.com/cgi-
        bin/mailto.exe"
method="POST" onSubmit="return
FrontPage_Form1_Validator(this)"name="FrontPage_Form1">
<input type="hidden" name="sendto"
        value="webmaster@dasdesigns.net">
<input type="hidden" name="server"
        value="smtp.myserver.com">
<input type="hidden" name="subject" value="Form Processed
        Email Response">
<input type="hidden" name="resulturl"
        value="http://www.dasdesigns.net/thanks.htm">
<input type="hidden" name="VTI-GROUP" value="0">
```

The code may look a little daunting. When you analyze a script like this, you're looking for the information that is required to forward the information to a recipient. When you create a variable, you need to enter a value and a name for the variable. If you analyze the script, you notice several instances where the script asks for a value. With each value is also a name. This is the information you need to create the ActionScript to submit the form results to the intended recipient. The script in Listing 10-2 requires five values. When you create the ActionScript for the Submit button, you create a variable for each name in the CGI script and set the variable value equal to the value in the script.

To code a Submit button for the CGI script shown in Listing 10-2, follow these steps:

1. **Select the button that will submit the information.**

2. **Choose Window⇨Actions.**

   The Actions panel opens.

3. **Click the Script Assist button.**

   Like a good neighbor, Script Assist is there.

4. **Click Statements⇨Variables and then double-click** set variable.

   Two parameter text boxes appear above the Script pane.

5. **In the Variable field, enter the first name from the CGI mail-forwarding script.**

   If you were coding a Submit button for the example in Listing 10-2, enter **sendto**. This is the recipient. All mail-forwarding scripts require a recipient.

6. **In the Value field, enter the value for the** sendto **variable, which would be the recipient's e-mail address.**

   Following the scenario for Listing 10-2, you would enter **webmaster@dasdesigns.net**.

7. **Repeat Steps 3 through 6 for the other required names in the CGI script.**

8. **Choose Global Functions⇨Browser\Network and then double-click** getURL.

   Three parameter text boxes appear above the Script pane.

9. **In the URL field, enter the path to the mail-forwarding script in your Web hosting service's CGI bin.**

   For example, **http://scripts.myserver.com/cgi-bin/mailto.exe**. Check with your Web hosting service for the path to the mail-forwarding script.

10. **Click the Variables down arrow and choose Send Using GET.**

    This instructs the Flash Player to get the data from the variables in the movie and send them to the specified URL.

After the document is published as a Flash movie and is uploaded to the Internet, when a user fills out the form and clicks the Submit button, the information is forwarded to the specified recipient. Listing 10-3 shows the ActionScript for the script shown in Listing 10-2. Mail-forwarding scripts differ. Contact the service that will be hosting your Flash Web site for a copy of the script.

Listing 10-3:   Creating ActionScript for a Submit Button

```
on (release) {
    sendto = "das001@earthlink.net";
    server = "smtp.myserver.com";
    subject = "Form Processed Email Response";
    resulturl = "http://www.mywebsite.com/thanks.htm";
    getURL("http://scripts.mywebserver.com/cgi-
            bin/mailto.exe", "", "GET");
```

Creating a Printable Page

If you create an e-commerce Flash Web site, you can include a printable page, which is actually a frame from a Flash movie. The contents of the frame can be a spec sheet, a catalog product, or a form that the user can print, fill out, and then mail. When you create a printable frame, you specify the print area and then create the ActionScript for a button that, when clicked, prints the page on the user's default printer.

If you create the page by using vector graphics, it will print out just fine, even when increased to the size of the printer paper. However, if you use bitmap graphics on the page, the image may be pixilated when increased to the size of the printer paper. If you're creating a frame with bitmap graphics and intend for it to be a printable frame, import the bitmap image into the document with a resolution of 150 dpi or better. The resulting Flash file will be slightly larger, but your viewers will get a more faithful rendition of the image when they print it.

When you create a printable frame, put it in a two-frame movie clip with a button that, when clicked by a viewer, summons the movie clip with the image the viewer wants a hard copy of. To create a printable frame, follow these steps:

1. **Choose Insert⇨New Symbol.**

   The Create New Symbol dialog box appears.

2. **Name the symbol and choose the Movie Clip type.**

3. **Select the first frame and either import the artwork you want to give viewers the capability of printing or open the document Library and drag an instance of an existing symbol into the movie clip.**

4. **Add a button symbol to the frame. Create a two-layer button and include the word *Print* on the second layer.**

   All of your Flash Web site visitors will know exactly what it's for.

5. **Select the first keyframe and then choose Window⇨Properties.**

   The Properties Inspector opens.

6. **Enter #p in the Frame field.**

   This syntax tells the Flash Player that the frame is printable. If you create the ActionScript to print the frame as-is, Flash prints everything, including the button. To restrict printing to a given area, follow the remaining steps.

7. **Select the next frame in the movie clip and convert it to a keyframe by pressing F6.**

8. **Choose Window⇨Properties to open the Properties Inspector.**

9. **In the <Frame Label> field, enter b#.**

   This nomenclature tells Flash that the contents of the frame act as a bounding box, restricting the print area.

10. **Click the Onion Skin button near the bottom of the timeline.**

    By enabling Onion Skins, you can see the content of the printable frame.

11. **Select the Rectangle tool and create a rectangle with no fill that surrounds the area you want to give viewers the capability of printing.**

12. **Click the printable frame and then choose Window⇨Actions.**

    The Actions panel opens.

13. **Click Global Functions⇨Timeline Control and then double-click stop.**

14. **Select the button and, in the left pane of the Actions panel, click Global Functions⇨Printing Functions and then double-click Print.**

    Three parameters boxes appear above the Script pane, as shown in Figure 10-3.

15. **Click the Print down arrow and choose the applicable parameter.**

    If you're printing a page with graphics created with the Flash tools, choose As Vectors. If you're printing a page that contains photorealistic images, choose As Bitmaps.

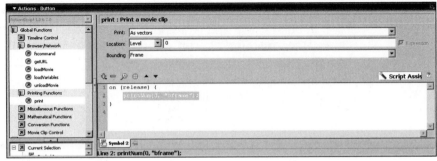

Figure 10-3:
Even a print
command
needs
parameters.

16. **Accept the default Location option of Level and the default level of 0.**

17. **Click the Bounding down arrow and choose Frame.**

18. **Click the Back or current scene button to exit symbol-editing mode.**

19. **Add an instance of the movie clip where you want users to be able to print the frame.**

That's all you need to do to create a printable frame. When the movie is published and the button is clicked, the frame prints on the viewer's default printer.

Designing a Flash Catalog

If you need to design a movie for a client that sells merchandise online, you can create a very effective display by creating a movie clip for each product in your customer's catalog. Instead of setting up an extensive timeline that advances to a different frame each time a button is clicked, you create ActionScript linkage for each product movie clip and then use the attachMovie method of the Movie Clip object to attach the movie clip to a target movie clip. In the following exercise, you flesh out a photographer's online print gallery.

To follow along with this exercise, copy the flashCatalog.fla file to your hard drive from the Web site associated with this book.

Use the flashCatalog.fla file to create a Flash catalog:

1. **Launch Flash and open the** flashCatalog.fla **file.**

    You already have several buttons set up on Stage and a target movie clip. This is an online catalog for a photographer who is selling prints.

When a button is clicked, the full-sized photo appears in a target movie clip. You'll do the grunt work for one photo and one button.

2. Choose Window⇨Library.

The document Library opens.

3. Right-click (Windows) or Control-click (Macintosh) the Library object named image_01 **and then choose Linkage from the context menu.**

The Linkage Properties dialog box opens.

4. Click Export for ActionScript.

Flash automatically assigns the name image_01 as an ActionScript identifier, as shown in Figure 10-4.

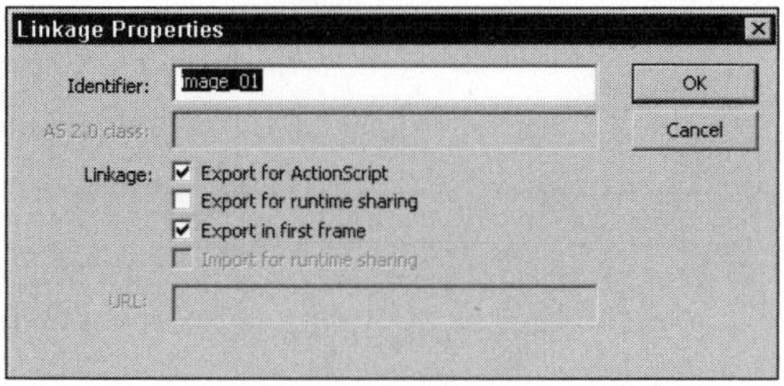

Figure 10-4:
You can
create
ActionScript
linkage for a
movie clip.

5. Click OK to close the dialog box and assign the identifier to the movie clip.

6. Click the first button on left side of the Stage and then choose Window⇨Actions.

The Actions panel opens.

7. Click the Script Assist button if the Script Assist feature is not already enabled.

8. Click ActionScript 2.0 Classes⇨Movie⇨Movie Clip⇨Methods and then double-click attachMovie.

Five parameter text boxes appear above the Script pane.

9. Place your cursor in the Object field and then click the Insert a Target Path button.

The Insert Target Path dialog box appears. Make sure you click the Absolute radio button.

10. Click the button labeled targetMC.

This is the instance name of the target movie clip near the center of the movie, which I've labeled for your convenience.

11. **Click OK to add the target path to the script and close the dialog box.**

    Now that you've assigned the target path, you need to fill in the parameters. The `attachMovie` method has five parameters, three of which you'll be using to attach the `image_01` movie clip to the target window. The first parameter is the linkage identifier, the second parameter is the new name of the attached movie clip, and the third parameter you'll use is the depth. The depth is the level you attach the movie clip to. The base movie is `_level0`. You'll be attaching the movie clip to `_level1`, so the depth is `1`.

12. **In the Linkage Name field, type image_01 and click the Expression check box to deselect the option.**

13. **In the New Name field, type product and click the Expression check box to deselect the option.**

14. **In the Depth field, type 1.**

    Your Actions panel should look like Figure 10-5.

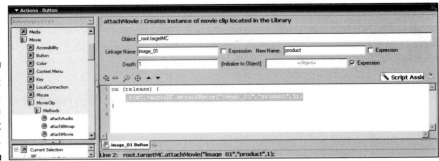

Figure 10-5: Attaching a movie clip to a target movie clip.

15. **Choose Control➪Test Movie.**

    Flash publishes the movie and plays it in another window. When the movie loads, a splash screen appears, which is another movie clip that is attached to the `targetMC` movie clip. Figure 10-6 shows the catalog when first loaded.

16. **Click any of the buttons to display a different photo in the target window.**

    Figure 10-7 shows a movie clip that loaded when the corresponding button was clicked.

Figure 10-6:
A splash
screen
appears
when the
catalog
loads.

Figure 10-7:
Attaching a
movie clip
when a
button is
clicked.

By using the same methods presented in this exercise, you can create a one-frame movie and display many different products. If your client has an extensive product catalog, break the catalog into categories and create a separate movie for each catalog. Create a product category menu by using one of the techniques presented earlier in this book and then use the `loadMovie` action to load a category movie on demand.

Creating an E-Commerce Shopping Cart

It seems like everyone has something to sell, and most people want to sell it online. However, the high cost of a secure Web hosting service scares most people away from the idea of online sales. PayPal is an excellent solution for anyone who wants to dip her feet in the water and see what kind of a splash she can make in e-commerce. It's easy to set up a PayPal account, and the selling fees are very reasonable. And you can use a bit of ActionScript in Flash to enable people to buy from your online catalog.

Download the file `shoppingCart.fla` to your computer from this chapter's folder at this book's Web site.

Here's how you can create a PayPal shopping cart:

1. **Open the file** `shoppingCart.fla`.

   This may look familiar to you. It's the online catalog you worked on in the last section, but with a couple of new buttons, as shown in Figure 10-8. Also note the input text boxes beside each button, which enable Web site viewers to enter the number of images they wish to purchase. Each text box has a unique variable name (the `Var` property in the Properties Inspector).

2. **Select the first shopping cart button and choose Window⇨Actions.**

   The Actions panel opens. The ActionScript to make the shopping cart communicate with the PayPal secure server is similar to the script you saw in the section on creating a Flash form. Again, you use variables for each attribute that PayPal needs to process the transaction.

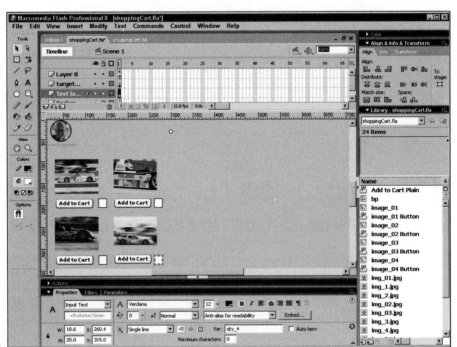

Figure 10-8:
You're
gonna sell
some
photos.

3. **Click the Script Assist button.**

Yes, I get by with a little help from my friend.

4. **In the left pane of the Actions panel, click Statements⇨Variables and then double-click** set variable.

Two parameter text boxes appear above the Script pane.

5. **Type** business **the Variable text field and then type your e-mail address in the Value text field.**

When you set up a PayPal account, the account is identified by your e-mail address. Simple, isn't it?

Do not click the Expression check box for this variable.

6. **Repeat Steps 4 and 5 to set the following variables:**

   - item_name: This is the name of the item you are selling.

   - item_number: This identifies the number of the item you are selling. For example, if you're selling several photographs, you'd identify the photograph number and then the size of the photograph. When you receive notification from PayPal that someone has placed an order, this information enables you to send the proper product.

   - amount: The price of the product.

   - currency_code: The currency code for the country in which you live. For the USA, the code is USD.

     Do not click the Expression check box for any of the previous variables.

7. **Create another variable.**

Type **quantity** in the Variable text box and then type **qty_1** in the Value text box. Make sure you click the Expression check box for this variable. The value for this variable, qty_1, is the Var value for the input text box next to this button. When the Web site visitor enters a value in this field and clicks the Add to Cart button, the quantity variable is set equal to this amount. PayPal uses the quantity variable along with the others to ring up the transaction. The Var values for the other Input text boxes will be different. In this shopping cart they would be qty_2, qty_3, and so on. When you set the value for the quantity variable in the other Add to Cart buttons, you use the applicable value to equate the quantity entered in the input text box with the variable.

8. **In the left pane of the Actions panel, choose Global Functions⇨ Browser/Network and then double-click** getURL.

Three parameters boxes appear above the Script pane.

9. **Type** https://www.paypal.com/cart/add= + 'quantity' **in the URL text field.**

Okay, this may look scary, but really it isn't. It's a secure Web address at PayPal. The /cart part of the link opens the shopping cart for the business specified in the business variable. The /add part tells PayPal this item is being added to a shopping cart. The = + "quantity" part of the link adds the value from the quantity variable to the shopping cart for the item being specified.

10. **Click the Window down arrow and choose _blank from the drop-down menu.**

    This tells the Flash Player to open the Web page in a new window.

11. **Click the Variables down arrow and choose Send Using GET from the drop-down menu.**

    This instructs the Flash Player to send the value of each variable to the PayPal Web page, while getting the information stored in each variable. The parameters boxes for the getURL action should look like Figure 10-9.

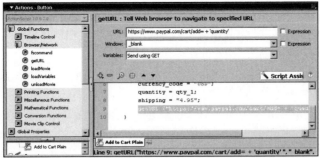

Figure 10-9:
Get URL, whoever he is.

12. **To program the rest of the buttons, all you need to do is right-click (Windows) or Control-click (Macintosh) and choose Copy from the context menu. Select the next button, open the Actions panel, right-click (Windows) or Control-click (Macintosh), and then choose Paste from the drop-down menu. Change the values to suit the item being sold, and remember to change the value of the** quantity **variable to match the input text box next to the button.**

    The ActionScript for a button is shown in Figure 10-10.

13. **After programming each button, choose Control⇨Test Movie. Flash plays the movie in another window. Click one of the thumbnail images to display a full-sized image, as shown in Figure 10-11.**

14. **Enter a value in one of the input text boxes and then click the applicable Add to Cart button.**

    The sale is registered on the PayPal secure server in another window. Figure 10-12 shows the PayPal shopping cart after a couple of items have been selected for sale.

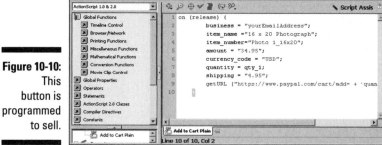

Figure 10-10:
This button is programmed to sell.

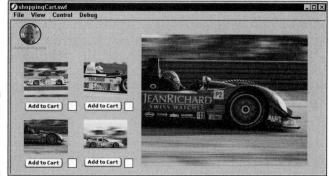

Figure 10-11:
E-commerce is alive and well.

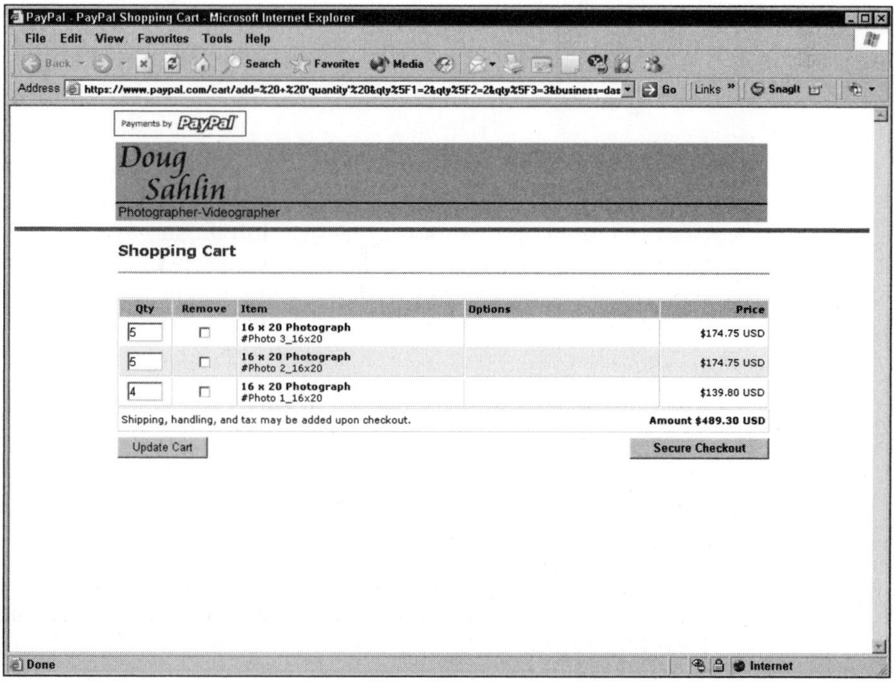

Figure 10-12:
Cha-ching!

Chapter 11

Creating Flash Eye Candy

. . . .

. . . .

*I*t's the subtle, and sometimes not-so-subtle, things that make people want to visit a Web site over and over and over again. Sometimes you have to add the little extras that set your design apart from the competition. But you have to add those little extras like you add seasonings to food: Add them one at a time and then test the results. If you throw everything but the kitchen sink at your Web site's viewers, your site will be way over the top. In this chapter, I present recipes for little goodies you can add to kick your site up another notch. Bam!

Some of my examples involve downloading files that I have already created for you. You can find these files at www.dummies.com/go/flashwebsites.

Creating a Mouse Chaser

Have you ever visited a Flash site where the designer created a cool little graphic that you could drag around by the scruff of the neck while the movie loaded? This is an effective bit of eye candy that you can easily create. Begin by creating an interesting movie clip with some groovy effects, nest an invisible button inside it, and then use the startDrag and stopDrag actions to create a toy that will keep your viewers amused while your preloader is running. In this exercise, I've already created the movie clip with the invisible button; all you have to do is program the button. Such a deal.

To follow along with this exercise, download the file mouse_chaser_begin. fla from this chapter's folder at the Web site associated with this book.

 1. **Launch Flash and open the** mouse_chaser_begin.fla **file.**

    How convenient, the movie clip with its invisible button is ready and waiting for you on Stage.

 2. **Select the movie clip and then choose Window➪Properties.**

    The Properties Inspector opens.

 3. **Type mouseChaser in the <instance name> field.**

    The final choice of the name is up to you, but mouseChaser is, as Mr. Spock would say, logical.

 4. **Double-click the movie clip you just christened** mouseChaser **and select the invisible button.**

    In symbol-editing mode, it's actually visible in a haunting shade of light blue.

 5. **Choose Window➪Actions.**

    The Actions panel opens.

 6. **Click the Script Assist button if you're not already working in Script Assist mode.**

 7. **Click ActionScript 2.0 Classes➪Movie➪MovieClip and then double-click** startDrag.

    The action is added to the script, and you get parameter text boxes.

 8. **Place your cursor inside the Target parameter text box and then click the Insert a Target Path button.**

    The Insert Target Path dialog box opens.

 9. **Click the Absolute radio button, click the button labeled mouseChaser — or whatever you called it — and then click OK.**

    The dialog box closes, and the target path is added to the script.

10. **In the Lock to Center field, type** true.

    When the movie plays, the mouseChaser clip latches on to the cursor's center, no matter where the movie clip is initially placed on Stage.

11. **Click the first line of script and then click Press.**

    Make sure you deselect the default Release event. By selecting the Press event, the movie clip develops its magnetic attraction to the user's cursor when the invisible button is dragged.

12. **Click the last line of script.**

    You know, that funny curly brace symbol.

13. **Click ActionScript 2.0 Classes➪Movie➪MovieClip and then double-click** stopDrag. **Accept the default Release event.**

Yup, that's right, the mouse chaser gives up the ghost when the user releases the mouse button. Your finished ActionScript should resemble Figure 11-1.

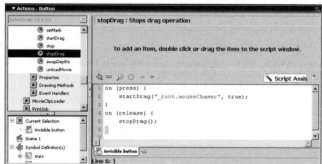

Figure 11-1: With this ActionScript, a movie clip stays stuck to a mouse like white on rice.

14. **Click the Back or current scene button to exit symbol-editing mode.**

The mouse chaser is programmed and ready to go for a wild ride.

15. **Choose Control➪Test Movie.**

Flash publishes the movie and plays it in another window. Go ahead, click the movie clip and start dragging it by the scruff of the neck. Release the mouse button and the stars just sit there twinkling. Fun, isn't it?

Creating a Custom Cursor

Another useful object you can add to your Flash movies is a custom cursor. The custom cursor can be any graphic that you convert to a symbol; for example, a customer's logo or a specialized cursor to suit a game you've created. In this section, I show you how to create a custom cursor that replaces the standard — may I say boring? — pointing-hand cursor.

To follow along with this exercise, locate the file custom_cursor_begin. fla in this chapter's folder at the Web site associated with this book. Then just follow these simple steps:

1. **Launch Flash and open the** custom_cursor_begin.fla **file.**

Flash opens the file, and you see two buttons. The buttons are already programmed to randomly display an image every time either button is clicked. You'll be creating a clever cursor that is completely clickable.

2. **Choose Insert⇨New Symbol.**

   The Symbol Properties dialog box opens.

3. **Accept the default Movie Clip behavior type, type** cursor **in the Name field, and click OK.**

   You are now in symbol-editing mode.

4. **Choose Window⇨Library.**

   The document Library opens.

5. **Double-click the Symbols folder, locate the symbol called** *logo,* **and then click and drag it on Stage.**

   An instance of the logo symbol appears in the movie clip.

6. **Using the Align panel, center the logo on Stage.**

7. **Click the Back or current scene button to return to movie-editing mode.**

   The cursor movie clip is added to the document Library.

8. **In the Timeline window, click the first frame of the cursor layer.**

   The frame is selected. Notice that the cursor layer is on top of the other layers. This is so the cursor is visible no matter what object you drag it over.

9. **In the document Library, locate the cursor symbol you just created and drag an instance of it on Stage.**

   Drop it anywhere you please, Louise. As soon as the published movie is played, the custom cursor symbol develops a magnetic attraction for the user's mouse.

10. **Choose Window⇨Actions.**

    The Actions panel opens. If you're not already in Script Assist mode, click the Script Assist button.

11. **In the left pane of the panel, click ActionScript 2.0 Classes⇨Movie⇨ Mouse⇨Methods and then double-click** hide.

    The Mouse.hide line of script does exactly that — it hides the default mouse cursor.

12. **In the left pane of the Actions panel, click ActionScript 2.0 Classes⇨ Movie⇨MovieClip⇨Methods and then double-click** startDrag.

    As if you didn't already know, Flash adds the action to your script, and look, you have parameters to deal with (see Figure 11-2).

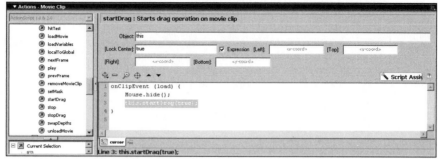

Figure 11-2:
Don't know
what I'm
gonna do,
'cause this
code's
gonna make
my custom
cursor stick
like glue.

13. Position your cursor in the Object field and type this.

The object the ActionScript is addressing is the cursor; therefore, the this alias is just what you need.

14. In the Lock Center field, type true.

This informs the Flash Player that you want the movie clip locked to the center of the mouse. When the movie is published, the cursor movie clip sticks like glue to wherever the user moves her cursor and functions just like the boring cursor it is replacing.

15. Choose Control⇨Test Movie.

Flash publishes the movie and plays it in another window. Start moving your mouse, and the cursor movie clip follows. Click one of the slide show buttons and you'll see that the custom cursor works just like the one you've hidden. Trés cool.

If you create a custom cursor for a movie that has multiple levels, create a separate movie with just the custom cursor in it and publish it as a Flash movie (SWF format). In the first frame of the movie you created the cursor for, use the loadMovie action and load the cursor movie in level 99, the highest level you can load into the base movie. Then the cursor appears on top of every object in every movie that you load into the base movie.

Building a Moving Backdrop

Another interesting effect you can add to your designs is a moving backdrop. In these steps, I show you how ActionScript generates random duplicates of a small sphere to simulate a star field. Unfortunately, the number of steps involved in creating this effect is quite high. Rather than have you read a lengthy tutorial, the steps that follow dissect the ActionScript used to create the effect.

ON THE WEB

To create a star field backdrop, copy to your hard drive the `randomStars.fla` file found in this chapter's folder at this book's Web site.

To see the star field backdrop effect in action, just do this:

1. **Launch Flash and open the** `randomStars.fla` **file.**

2. **Choose Control⇨Test Movie.**

   Flash publishes the file and plays it in another window (see Figure 11-3).

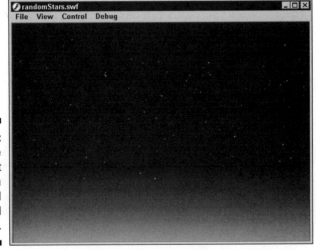

Figure 11-3:
You can use ActionScript to create a star field background like this one.

As the movie plays, you see what appears to be an ever-changing field of stars. In reality, it's only one movie clip duplicated over 100 times. The entire file is only 689 bytes, dainty by any Web designer's standards. You can use this file or a similar one of your own creation for an interesting backdrop. To see how the effect is created, close the window and follow these steps:

1. **Click the small white dot in the upper-left corner of the movie and choose Edit⇨Edit Selected.**

   Flash enters symbol-editing mode.

2. **Choose Window⇨Actions.**

   The Actions panel opens.

3. **Click the small white dot just above the center of the Stage.**

   This is a small circle nested in the movie clip. Listing 11-1 shows the ActionScript that sets the initial position of the movie clip.

Listing 11-1: Initializing the Movie Clip

```
onClipEvent (load) {
    this._x=Math.random()*540;
    this._y=Math.random()*280;
    this._xscale=Math.random()*100;
    this._yscale=this._xscale;
    this._alpha=Math.random() * 100;
    if (this._alpha<50) {
        this._alpha=50;
    }
}
```

When the movie clip first loads, its _x and _y properties are set to random positions.

The ActionScript in lines 2 and 3 changes the _x and _y properties of the movie clip by multiplying a number by the random function of the Math object, which randomly generates a number between 0 and 1. The value of 540 for the _x property was chosen to keep the movie clip within the boundary of the movie. The value of 280 for the _y property was chosen to keep the stars above the orange part of the background, which, by the way, is a gradient blend created with the Color Mixer.

Line 2 generates a number between 0 and 540 for the _x property.

Line 3 generates a random number between 0 and 280 for the _y property.

Line 4 generates a random value for the _xscale of the movie clip, and Line 5 sets the _yscale equal to the _xscale so the movie clip resizes proportionately.

Line 6 varies the opacity of the movie clip. The conditional statement sets the _alpha property equal to 50 if the random value generated drops below 50. This statement was entered to prevent the movie clip from blending into the background. The desired effect is to simulate twinkling stars; an alpha value less than 50 would cause the stars to all but disappear.

To see the code used to create the rest of the effect, click the first keyframe. If you still have the Actions panel open, you see the code in Listing 11-2.

Listing 11-2: Creating the Stars

```
k = 0;
i = Math.random()*200;
while (k<i) {
    duplicateMovieClip("circle", "circle"+k, k);
    k = ++k;
}
```

Line 1 of the code declares a variable named k and sets it equal to 0.

Line 2 initializes a variable named i and sets its value equal to a random number between 1 and 200.

Lines 3 and 4 of the code initialize a while loop. While the value of k is less than the value of i, the movie clip is duplicated. The movie clip is duplicated each time it loads, and new random values are generated, which simulates the appearance of a star on another part of the Stage.

Line 5 increments the value of k by 1.

The loop continues creating duplicate stars until the value of k exceeds i. After the loop finishes, the movie clip plays frame 2, which has a goto action that returns it to frame 1, whereupon the whole process repeats itself, and a new field of stars is generated.

However, one additional item on the second frame pauses the movie so the viewer can see the stars.

1. **Click the small white dot below the center of the Stage.**

   This is a user-defined component that contains nothing but ActionScript. The component pauses the movie. You *could* pause the movie by adding a few frames between the keyframes. However, if you ever needed to change the effect, you'd have to add or delete frames. Also, with a given number of frames, the effect would be too predictable. The user-defined component is a timer that pauses the movie for a different amount of time every time the frame plays.

2. **With the component still selected, click the arrow to the left of Properties to open the Properties Inspector.**

   The component has only one parameter: Seconds. The ActionScript in the component will pause the movie for a random amount of time up to the value entered in the Seconds field.

3. **To see how the component works, click the number (.6) to the right of Seconds and enter a higher value.**

4. **Choose Control⇨Test Movie.**

   After Flash publishes the file, you'll see that the stars don't change as quickly.

5. **Enter a smaller value in the Seconds field, and a new star field is generated more quickly.**

You can create a similar effect by re-creating the code in your own movie, or you can modify this movie to suit your needs by creating a different background or by creating a new movie clip symbol with a different graphic than a circle. Edit the starfield movie clip and swap the circle movie clip for your own symbol.

Creating a Ticker Tape Marquee

Did you ever see a scrolling marquee above the entrance to a movie theater? Well, that's the effect I show you how to create in this section. To create a scrolling marquee, you use arrays and dynamic text boxes to create a ticker display. You also find out in this section how to display text one letter at a time by adding characters from an array element to the display in the dynamic text box.

To follow along with this section, first download the `scrollTick.fla` file from this chapter's folder at the Web site associated with this book and then just follow along with these steps:

1. **Launch Flash and open the `scrollTick.fla` file.**

   Notice that this document has a text box and a custom scroll bar. If you want to learn more about the ActionScript that makes the scroll bar tick, double-click the symbol and then select each part of the symbol with the Actions panel open. The auto-scrolling marquee appears in the white space below the banner, as shown in Figure 11-4.

   The text box is actually nested in a movie clip. When you nest ActionScript and other components in a movie clip, you can use the movie clip in any of your designs by opening the file, pinning the document Library, and dragging an instance of the movie clip into the current document Library.

Figure 11-4:
The scrolling ticker appears below the banner.

2. **Double-click the movie clip to display it in symbol-editing mode.**

   After the movie clip is displayed in symbol-editing mode, notice that you have six keyframes on the Actions layer. Select the first keyframe and open the Actions panel to display this code:

```
// initialize labels and counter
k = 0;
tickText = "";
tickerList = new Array();
tickerList[0] = "Welcome to Pepper Cay... your
        vacation paradise... ";
tickerList[1] = "White water rafting trips... ";
tickerList[2] = "Fishing for marlin and kingfish... ";
tickerList[3] = "Experienced guides available... ";
tickerList[4] = "Create your own adventure in
        paradise... ";
endLine = tickerList.length;
```

   The code in this keyframe initializes the array and three variables:

   - k is a counter.

   - endLine returns the number of elements (length) of the array, which in this case is 5. The value of endLine could have been set equal to 5; however, that would limit you to using this movie clip only with an array with 5 elements. If you modify this movie clip for use in another design, you can add as many array elements as needed, and the endLine variable will always return the number of elements in the array.

   - tickText is the same variable assigned to the dynamic text box that displays the elements of the array.

   Another thing to notice is the manner in which the array has been created; each element is created separately. You can accomplish the same thing by creating a variable named tickerList and then entering each array element in quotes and separating them with commas. This particular method was chosen for this effect because it's easier to see each array element's *offset* (the number in brackets). In ActionScript, the offset of the first element of an array is always 0. You'll be referring to each array element by its offset to complete the project.

3. **Select the second keyframe.**

   In the Actions panel, you see a single line of code that initializes a variable named lineNum and sets its value equal to 0. This is the offset of the first element in the tickerList array. This frame has been labeled newLine.

4. **Select the third keyframe, which has been labeled lineLoop.**

   In the Actions panel, notice that two lines of code have been created. Two new variables have been declared, as shown here:

```
len = tickerList[lineNum].length;
i = 0;
```

The variable `len` returns the length of an individual array element. When the code is first executed, the variable returns the length of the element in the `tickerList` array at offset 0, the initial value of the variable `lineNum`. The variable `i` is another counter.

5. **Select the fourth keyframe, which has been labeled** `msgLoop`.

   In the Actions panel, notice that a conditional statement has been started for you. You'll be creating the action that executes when the value of `k` is less than 65.

6. **In the Actions panel Script pane, select the first line of code.**

7. **In the left pane of the Actions panel, click Statements⇨Variables and then double-click** `setVariable`.

8. **In the Variable field, type** tickText.

9. **In the Value field, type** tickText+tickerList[lineNum].charAt(i).

   This line of code begins displaying text. It takes the initial value of `tickText`, an empty string variable, and sets it equal to itself plus the first character of the first element in the array. The `.charAt(i)` part of the code returns the string value of the character at this position in the string. The variable `i` increments by a value of 1 by virtue of the loop you'll examine in Step 14. This determines which character is displayed. When the code first executes, it returns the first character ($i = 0$) of the first element (the initial value of `lineNum` is 0) from the `tickerList` array. The `.charAt` element of the code is a property of the `String` object.

10. **In the left pane of the Actions panel, click Statements⇨Conditions/Loops and then double-click** `else`.

    You'll now create the code that executes when the value of `k` exceeds 65. When `k` reaches 65, the dynamic text box cannot accept any additional characters. In order for the ticker to display the next character, one character must be removed from the string in `tickText`. In other words, the number of characters in `tickText` must be reduced to 64 before the next character can be displayed. To achieve this, you use the `substring` method of the `String` object. You'll use this method to return the 1st through 65th characters of the `tickText` string, which in essence removes the first character.

11. **In the left pane of the Actions panel, choose Statements⇨Variables and then double-click** `set variable`.

12. **In the Variable field, type** tickText.

13. **In the Value field, type the following:**

```
TickText.substring(1,65)+tickerList[lineNum].charAt(i)
```

This line of code returns a substring of the 1st through 65th characters of tickText and adds the next character to the string. Remember, the first character of a string is position 0. The rest of the code has been written for you.

14. **Select the fifth keyframe and open the Actions panel to view the following code:**

```
i = ++i;
k = ++k;
if (i<len) {
    gotoAndPlay("msgLoop");
}
```

The first two lines of this code increment the value of the variables i and k by 1. The third line of code is a conditional statement that evaluates the value of the variable len, which is the length of an array element. As long as the value of i is less than the length of the array element, the movie clip loops to the frame labeled msgLoop, and another letter from the array element is added. When the value of i becomes greater than len, frame 6 plays.

15. **Select the sixth keyframe and notice the following code in the Actions panel:**

```
lineNum = ++lineNum;
if (lineNum==endLine) {
    gotoAndPlay("newLine");
} else {
    gotoAndPlay("lineLoop");
}
```

The code in this keyframe increments the value of lineNum by 1. When the value of lineNum is equal to endLine, the movie clip goes to the frame labeled newLine, which sets the value of lineNum equal to 0 and begins displaying the characters from the first array element. Otherwise, the movie loops to the frame labeled lineLoop, which sets the value of i equal to 0 to display the first character from the next array element.

16. **Click the Back or current scene button to exit symbol-editing mode and then choose Control⇨Test Movie.**

The movie plays and the text advances one letter at a time across the marquee until the text box is filled, whereupon the next letters advance one at a time.

Several things happen in this movie clip:

After the variables are declared and the array is set, the first element in the array is displayed one letter at a time by evaluating the charAt() property of the string data (the text) in the array.

When the last letter of the string in the first element of the array is displayed, as determined by the conditional statement, the next element in the array is selected. The conditional statement in frame 4 evaluates the length of the variable (tickText) storing the string data. When it exceeds the specified value, the substring property of the String object takes the first character away from the string.

When the last element in the array is displayed, the code loops back to newLine, which resets to the first element in the array, and letters from that element are added to continue the ticker.

You can use this movie clip in one of your own designs. All you need to do is change the size of the text box to suit your movie. You can also modify the color, size, and font by selecting the text box and modifying the parameters in the Properties Inspector. When you change the size of the text box, or any of the text parameters, you'll have to experiment to get the proper value for k and the ending value of the substring. If you choose a smaller font size, you'll have to increase the value of k, otherwise the code will start dropping letters before the end of the text box is reached. Change both values in the fourth keyframe until the text advances properly, as shown in Listing 11-3.

Listing 11-3: Modifying the Code for a Different Text Size

```
if (k<85) {
    tickText = tickText+tickerList[lineNum].charAt(i);
} else {
    tickText =
            tickText.substring(1,85)+tickerList[lineNum].ch
            arAt(i);
}
```

The values you use will vary depending upon the font size and size of the text box. Each font has different kerning characteristics, which will enter into the value you end up using.

To create a programmable marquee ticker that you can add to any Flash Web site you design, copy the file marqueeComponent.fla to your hard drive and then follow these steps:

1. **Launch Flash and open the file** marqueeComponent.fla.

   In the document Library, you'll find a single component.

2. **Drag the component on Stage and center it to the top of the document.**

3. **Open the Properties Inspector and then click the Parameter tab.**

4. **Click the magnifying glass to open the Values panel.**

   Three values have already been entered.

5. **Click a value and type your own text. To add additional values, click the button that looks like a plus sign and type some text.**

6. **Click OK to apply the modifications.**

7. **Choose Control⇨Test Movie to preview the movie in another window.**

The String object has one property and many methods you can use to evaluate string data. In this chapter, you've been exposed to the charAt() and substring methods. A detailed discussion of each string method is beyond the scope of this book, but I urge you to experiment with these methods. To understand what each method does, open the Actions panel, click the Reference icon, choose ActionScript 2.0 Classes➪Core➪String➪Methods, and then click each method for an explanation of what the method does. For a detailed explanation, right-click (Windows) or Control-click (Macintosh) a method and then choose View Help from the context menu.

Creating Flying Text

If you've been reading from the start of the chapter, you have some cool tools to add to your Flash Web design arsenal. If you haven't, well shame on you. The printers used a lot of good paper to display this text for your reading and informational pleasure. But if the only cool effect you want to add to your Flash Web design is flying text, and that's the reason you haven't read the rest of the chapter, you are forgiven. Creating flying text is actually very easy; much easier than the other techniques in this chapter. So then, if you want to kick your text banners up another notch, read on:

1. **Create a new Flash document and accept the default document size and frame rate.**

2. **Select the Text tool and choose Window➪Properties.**

    The Properties Inspector opens.

3. **Format your text.**

    For the purpose of this exercise, choose the Arial font, boldface the text, choose a font size of 45, and choose red for the text color.

4. **Type the word Text in the upper-left corner of your document.**

5. **With the text still selected, press F8.**

    The Convert to Symbol dialog box appears.

6. **Choose the Movie Clip behavior type, name the symbol, and click OK.**

    The Convert to Symbol dialog box closes, and a new symbol is born.

7. **Right-click (Windows) or Control-click (Macintosh) and then choose Edit in Place from the context menu.**

    The reason you want to edit this puppy in place is so you can move the letters about on Stage and know exactly where within the movie the letters are.

8. **Press Ctrl+B (Windows) or ⌘+B (Macintosh) twice to break the text apart into individual shapes.**

9. **With the text shapes still selected, right-click (Windows) or Control-click (Macintosh) and then choose Distribute to Layers from the Context menu.**

   This command creates a new layer for each selected item, as shown in Figure 11-5.

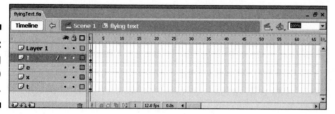

Figure 11-5: Distributing the text to layers.

10. **Select Layer 1 and delete it.**

    Layer 1 is no longer needed because the objects are already on their own layers. Less is more.

11. **Select each letter and then press Ctrl+B (Windows) or ⌘+B (Macintosh).**

    This step converts each letter to a shape. If you made a typo, you won't be able to correct it because the letters are no longer editable as text.

12. **Convert each letter to a graphic symbol by selecting each letter individually and then pressing F8.**

    This opens the Convert to Symbol dialog box. Choose the Graphic behavior type for each letter and give each letter a unique name. I always use the actual letter as the symbol name. When you have a duplicated letter, such as in our example, append the symbol name with a number. For example, t2, t3, and so on.

13. **Select the sixth frame in the top layer and then Shift-click the sixth frame in the bottom layer.**

    This selects the sixth frame in each layer. Choosing only six frames produces a rather quick animation — each letter flies for half a second because the default frame rate is 12 frames per second. If you prefer your flying text on the lethargic side, select a frame farther down the timeline. For example, if you convert the 12th frame in each layer to a keyframe, each letter dances for a full second at the default frame rate.

14. **Press F6 to convert the frames to keyframes.**

15. **Click one of the in-between frames on the top layer and then Shift-click the same frame on the bottom layer.**

16. **Right-click (Windows) or Control-click (Macintosh) and choose Create Motion Tween from the context menu.**

    Your timeline should resemble Figure 11-6.

Figure 11-6:
This is
what makes
the letters
fly, Guy.

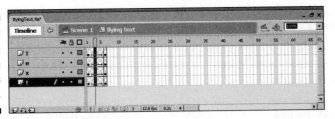

17. **Select the first frame on each letter and then use the Move tool to reposition the letters below their original positions and to the far right side of the Stage.**

18. **With the letters still selected, choose Modify➪Transform➪Flip Horizontal.**

19. **With the letters still selected, select the Free Transform tool and then enlarge and skew the letters.**

    Enlarge the letters about 15 percent and skew them as much as you wish. Experimentation and creative playtime is the key to nailing the parameters you like best.

20. **With the letters still selected, choose Window➪Properties.**

    The Properties Inspector makes a grand entrance.

21. **Click the Color down arrow and then choose Tint from the drop-down menu.**

    This applies the Tint color style to each symbol, which enables you to change the color of each letter at the start of the animation.

22. **Click the Tint color swatch and then click the background of your movie.**

    This samples the background color of the movie as the tint color.

23. **Enter 100 in the Tint percent column.**

    This tints the text to 100 percent of the background color, which in essence renders the text invisible. The end result is to make the text appear as though it materializes from thin air.

    The previous steps will make the text fly into position. However, they'd all fly in at the same time and the animation would play over and over and over again; not exactly what you want for a banner. The following steps show you how to fly the text in one letter at a time.

24. **Click the first and last keyframes of the second layer and drag the text one frame to the right.**

25. Repeat Step 24 for the other layers in your animation, moving each consecutive layer one frame to the right of the preceding layer.

Now you have the letters flying in, staggered by one frame. However, you need to add frames to each layer except the last so that the letters will be visible during the entire animation.

26. Select the frame after the last keyframe on the next-to-last layer and then Shift-click the corresponding frame on the top layer.

27. Press F5 to add frames to each layer.

28. Right-click (Windows) or Control-click (Macintosh) the top layer and then choose Insert Layer from the Context menu.

Flash adds a new layer at the top of the stack.

29. Name the new layer Actions.

Whenever you add ActionScript to a movie or movie clip, you should always put it on a separate layer. This makes it easier for you to debug your ActionScript because it's all on a separate layer.

30. Select the last frame on the Actions layer and press F6 to convert it to a keyframe.

Your timeline should resemble Figure 11-7.

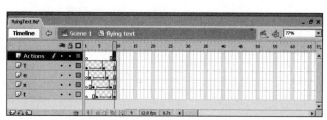

Figure 11-7:
Your
timeline
is now
arranged for
flying text.

31. Select the last keyframe on the Actions layer and then choose Window➪Actions.

The Actions panel opens. If you're not already in Script Assist mode, click the Script Assist button.

32. In the left pane of the Actions panel, choose Global Functions➪ Timeline Control and then double-click stop.

If you don't stop the animation, your viewers and their pets may get motion sickness.

33. Choose Control⇨Test Movie.

The text flies in from stage right, as shown in Figure 11-8.

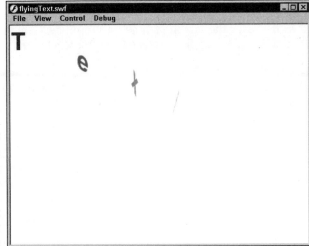

Figure 11-8:
It flies
through the
movie with
the greatest
of ease.

Part IV
Sharing Your Site with the World

The 5th Wave   By Rich Tennant

"Oh, Arthur is very careful about security on the Web. He never goes online in the same room on consecutive days."

In this part . . .

1 show you how to finalize your Web design by optimizing it. Optimizing a site makes it load faster, which is a good thing. To accomplish this task, I show you how to get rid of unused Library items and list other things you can do to optimize your site.

In this part, I also show you how to debug your ActionScript. This is not a huge part of the book, but it is a very important part. It would be a shame to create a cool site, only to have it fall flat on its face because it takes too long to load or has a hiccup or four in the ActionScript.

After showing you how to tend to those sundry items, I explain how to publish the site, which is also important because, if you don't publish your Flash Web site and upload it to your Web server, no one except you will ever see it.

Chapter 12

Optimizing Your Site

*A*fter you get all of your ducks in a row, you may think all you have to do is publish your Flash Web site and upload it to a Web hosting service for the entire world to see. But before you can publish each document for your Flash Web site, you have to optimize the documents. You also have to ascertain that all of your ActionScript executes flawlessly. If you don't, you (or your client) will wind up with a lot of egg on your face. And if your blunder embarrasses your client, your reputation will go downhill faster than a Sumo wrestler on a bobsled. And that's pretty fast. In this chapter, I show you some things you can do to optimize your site and at the same time debug it. If you've constructed your site as recommended in this book, you'll have to perform this on the interface and on each document that will be published as a movie and loaded into the interface.

Optimizing Your Site

When you publish a movie for your Flash Web site, Flash combines all of its elements into a single SWF movie. When your Web site viewers access the HTML document into which the Web site SWF movie is embedded, the SWF movie streams frame-by-frame into the user's browser and begins to play as soon as enough data has downloaded to play the first frame of the movie. As the designer of the Flash Web site, you should strive to keep your content as compact as possible. You can do a lot of this beforehand by optimizing all Web site images in an image editing application. You can also optimize images by specifying export settings from within Flash, which I show you how to do in Chapter 13.

However, there are some other things you can do to further optimize your movie before you publish it, as shown in the following list:

- ✔ **Whenever possible, group graphic objects.** Grouped items are treated as a single item by the Flash Player and will therefore download quicker.

- ✔ **Whenever possible, convert graphic objects to symbols.** When you create instances of symbols in your Flash documents, the Flash Player refers to the document Library to create the symbol, resulting in a smaller file size for the published movie. You may not be able to do this during the final stages of a Web site project, but you should keep this in mind while creating each document for your Flash Web site.

- ✔ **Whenever possible, use tweening instead of frame-by-frame animations.** Tweened animations result in skinny file sizes. If your Web site has movie clips with frame-by-frame animations, if possible, convert them to tweened animations.

- ✔ **Optimize all bitmap (photo realistic) objects.** You can optimize each bitmap by selecting it in the document Library, right-clicking (Windows) or Control-clicking (Macintosh), and then choosing Properties from the context menu to open the Properties dialog box. As a rule, you can apply more compression to small bitmaps that are displayed for a short period of time. You can also set image quality for all bitmaps in the document by using the Publish Settings dialog box, as shown in Chapter 13. However, I recommend you use an image editing application such as Macromedia Fireworks or Adobe Photoshop to optimize your Web site images.

- ✔ **Don't embed fonts unless it's absolutely necessary.** Embedding fonts increases the document's file size. If you stick with system fonts (serif or sans), your Flash Web site will display properly on most systems and with most popular browsers. If your client says she just *has* to have fancy fonts for ornamental elements, such as headers, convert the characters into vector graphics by using the Break Apart command (Ctrl+B [Windows] or ⌘+B [Macintosh]).

  Remember that you need to apply the Break Apart command twice to text objects; the first time you apply the command, the text object is converted into individual characters, and the second time, the characters are converted into vector graphics.

- ✔ **Limit your use of components.** Components can increase the size of the published movie, so the fewer the better.

- ✔ **Whenever possible, use the default movie frame rate of 12 fps.** A higher frame rate results in smoother playback but increases the file size. The only time you should disregard this sage advice is when you're displaying full-motion video in your Web site. Then, your frame rate should be 15 or 18 fps for people who will be accessing your Flash Web site with a dialup modem, and 30 fps for people who will be accessing the site with a broadband connection.

✔ **When creating graphic symbols for your Flash Web sites, don't use multi-colored gradients unless you absolutely have to.** They look really cool, but they can horribly bloat the file size of the published movie.

The last thing you should do before publishing a Flash movie is to delete any unused objects from the document Library — this is the equivalent of putting your Flash movie on a diet:

1. **Choose Window⇨Library.**

   The document Library opens.

2. **Click the Options icon in the right corner of the document Library and then choose Select Unused Items.**

   Flash highlights unused items, as shown in Figure 12-1.

Figure 12-1: Like a librarian, Flash is smart enough to select unused Library items.

3. **Press Delete or drag the items to the trash can icon.**

   Flash cleans house in the document Library.

Test Each Web Site Movie

When you planned your Flash Web site — you did plan the site, didn't you? — you gauged several factors: the intended viewing audience's Internet connection speed, the computer equipment likely to be used, the desktop size, and so on. If you haven't done this ahead of time, your best efforts will go to waste if the movie exceeds the viewing audience's available bandwidth.

As you create each document for your Web site, you should always have the final phase of the project in mind. In other words: test, test, and then test some more. You should test your production any time you make a major change. For example, when you create ActionScript for a button to play a frame of a movie clip or to load external content, make sure that the button functions perfectly before you do anything else to the movie. Testing while you're building the Web site can save you hours of headaches during the final phases of your work. If you have a complex Flash Web site that loads different movies into an interface and one item in one movie isn't functioning perfectly, the problem could be almost anywhere. It could turn into a logistical nightmare.

When you create a Flash Web site, your first line of defense for catching any potential problems is the Test Movie command. Invoking this command publishes your document as an SWF movie and opens it in another window. When you preview a movie in this manner, it plays using the same Flash Player plug-in used to view Flash movies in a browser; however, when you use the Test Movie command, you have more options in the form of menu commands that appear after you invoke the command. You can examine your movie in detail to see the amount of data present on each frame of the movie, to simulate how the movie will download when streaming into a browser at different connection speeds, and so on. You also test a movie to determine whether you need a preloader, as outlined in Chapter 8.

Here's how you test a movie:

1. **Choose Control➪Test Movie.**

   The movie opens in another window.

2. **Choose View➪Bandwidth Profiler.**

   Flash displays a graph that shows you the size of the movie and the amount of data on each frame of the movie, as shown in Figure 12-2.

3. **Test everything in the document.**

   That means you need to click each button — just like your Web site visitors will — to make sure the proper information loads.

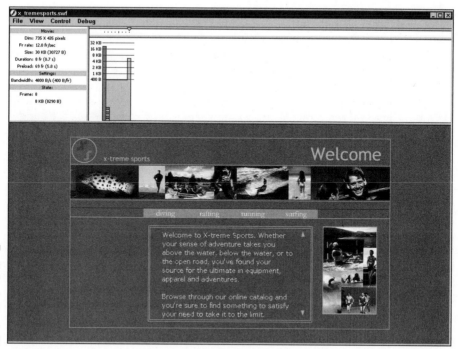

Figure 12-2:
Putting your
Web site to
the acid
test.

When you test a movie with the Test Movie command, you can uncover any potential flaws in your production. However, you do not simulate your intended audience's experience. You can preview the movie in your system's default browser by choosing Publish Preview⇨HTML or by pressing F12.

Debugging the Site

When you design a Flash Web site, you need to ensure that your interface, and every movie that loads into it, plays flawlessly and that your ActionScript executes without a hitch. If you can see what's going on in each Flash movie as it is playing, you stand a better chance of exterminating the bugs before you publish the Web site and upload it to a Web hosting service. Failure to eliminate every bug in your Flash Web site will not gain you any favor with your client or your client's intended audience, which will dwindle rapidly after encountering a bug or four. For this sundry task, you use a device with the ubiquitous name of Debugger:

1. **Choose Control⇨Debug Movie from the menu.**

   This publishes the movie in another window and displays the Debugger window, as shown in Figure 12-3.

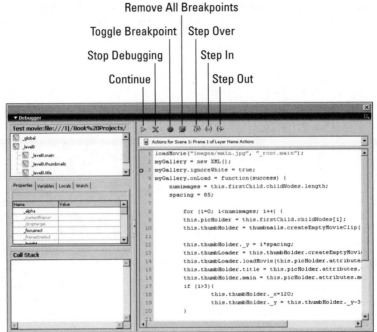

Figure 12-3:
Flash's bug
extermina-
tion service
at work.

2. **Click the Continue button (it looks like a Play button) in the Debugger to begin playing and debugging your movie.**

   The status bar at the top of the Debugger window tells you the location of the movie you are debugging. The window below the status bar displays all of the movie clips in your movie, including those external movies that load into your interface when you click a button. Notice the tabs just below the movie clip list in the Debugger window. These tabs are populated with values after you click the Continue button, which begins playing the movie. These allow you to further analyze individual elements in your movie to detect any glitches:

   • **Properties:** This tab allows you to view the properties and the values of properties of a selected movie clip and change them as the movie runs. To do this, click a movie clip in the top display list; the Properties tab values update. Double-click any of the active values in this tab and enter a different value to preview the effect it will have on your movie.

   • **Variables:** This tab allows you to view the variables and the values of variables used in a selected movie clip. Click the Variables tab to view variables associated with the currently selected item from the display list. The variables update as the movie plays. To see the effect a different value will have, double-click a variable value in this tab and then enter a new value.

If the properties and variables are not visible, click the divider bar above Call Stack and drag down to reveal them.

- **Locals:** This tab displays the local variables used in the movie and the value of each variable.

- **Watch:** This tab allows you to monitor selected variables closely. When you first launch the Debugger, no variables are on the Watch list. You can add variables to this list by selecting them in the Variables tab and then choosing Add Watch from the Debugger Options menu. Alternatively, you can select the variable, right-click (Windows) or Control-click (Macintosh), and choose Watch from the context menu. In the Variables tab, a blue dot appears to the left of a watched variable.

To remove a variable from the Watch list, select the variable in the Watch list and choose Remove Watch from the Debugger Options menu. Alternatively, you can select the variable in the Watch list, right-click (Windows) or Control-click (Macintosh), and choose Remove from the context menu.

Adding Breakpoints

In Figure 12-3, notice the button in the Debugger window that looks like a stop button. This toggles a breakpoint. Breakpoints are not part of the infamous breakdance; they enable you to pause a script at a given point so you can see what's happening. Why would you want to pause a script? Well, if it's a long script, you can take a short break, stretch, and grab a coffee. But seriously, if your script contains lots of variables, conditional statements, property changes, or — yikes — math, you can pause the movie when the script reaches one of the aforementioned breakpoints to make sure the script is working the way you planned. Without the breakpoint, the movie continues playing and you have no idea whether the complex ActionScript is doing its thing or letting you down.

You set breakpoints in the Actions panel and control them in the Debugger. You can also set breakpoints in the Debugger. However, the logical course of action is to set the breakpoint in the Actions panel. To set a breakpoint on a line of code in the Actions panel, do the following:

1. **If line numbers are not currently displayed in the script pane, choose View Line Numbers from the Actions panel Options menu.**

2. **If you're currently in Script Assist mode, click the Script Assist button to disable this feature.**

   You have more debugging options when you're not in Script Assist mode.

3. **Select a line of code on which you want to insert a breakpoint.**

4. **Click the Debug Options icon (which looks like a stethoscope) in the Actions panel to reveal a pop-up menu.**

5. **Select Set Breakpoint from the pop-up menu.**

   A red dot appears to the left of a line to which you've added a breakpoint, as shown in Figure 12-4.

   Note that you can also remove breakpoints by using this pop-up menu. To remove a breakpoint, select a breakpoint line and then select Remove Breakpoints from the pop-up menu.

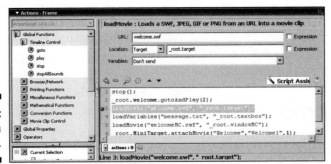

Figure 12-4: You've got a breakpoint.

You can also set a breakpoint by clicking to the left of a code line number.

6. **Choose Control⇨Debug Movie.**

   The Debugger appears immediately after Flash publishes the movie in another window. In the right window of the Debugger, an alert appears that reads, "The Flash Player is paused so that breakpoints may be adjusted. Click Continue to start the movie."

7. **Click the Continue button.**

   Flash begins playing the movie, and the movie stops at the first breakpoint you specified in the Actions panel.

8. **Use the various windows of the Debugger to analyze properties, vari-able values, and so on.**

   Figure 12-5 shows a movie halted at a breakpoint. However, no proper-ties are displayed because a variable has not yet been selected.

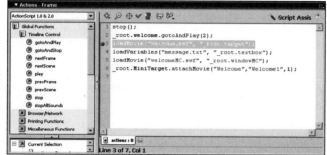

Figure 12-5: Stop in the name of debug!

9. **After analyzing the script at the breakpoint, click the Continue button. To add another breakpoint in the Debugger window, select a line of code and click the Toggle Breakpoint button.**

   You can remove all breakpoints by clicking the Remove All Breakpoints button. To skip over a breakpoint, click the Step Over button.

When you add breakpoints in the Debugger, they are active only for the cur-rent debugging session. This is also true when you remove breakpoints. When you exit movie-testing mode and return to the authoring workspace, the breakpoints are restored to what you set in the Actions panel. The only way to completely remove a breakpoint is to select the line of code that con-tains the breakpoint in the Actions panel, click the Debug Options icon, and then choose Remove Breakpoint from the pop-up menu.

As you click the Continue button to navigate through breakpoints in the Debugger, the current breakpoint icon (red stop sign) contains an arrow to indicate that it is the current breakpoint.

To remove all breakpoints from a movie, open the Actions panel, and with Script Assist disabled, click the Debug Options icon and choose Remove All Breakpoints.

Chapter 13

Publishing the Site

● ●

In This Chapter

▶ Specifying publish settings

▶ Optimizing images

▶ Optimizing sounds

▶ Publishing your site

● ●

*A*fter you test your site and stomp on all those nasty little bugs, your next step is to publish the site. The cool thing about Flash is that when you publish a site, you don't need a printing press. You set everything up in the Publish Settings dialog box. You can then publish the site either from within the Publish Settings dialog box or by using a menu command. In this chapter, I show you everything you need to know to publish the documents that make up your Flash Web site.

Setting Publish Settings

Before you publish your Web site, you use the Publish Settings dialog box to set the parameters for the published file. If your Web site comprises several Flash movies, you use the same publish settings for each movie. The Publish Settings dialog box enables you to publish your movies in many different file formats in addition to the Flash SWF format. However, this isn't necessary when you're publishing a Web site. Therefore, all you need are the Flash and HTML tabs to get the job done. After all, as cool as your Flash site is, it still needs to be embedded in an HTML document. The following steps give you an overview of how to set publish settings for your Flash movie:

1. **Choose File⇨Publish Settings.**

   The Publish Settings dialog box appears, as shown in Figure 13-1. By default, it opens to the Formats section.

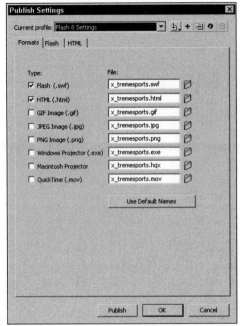

Figure 13-1:
Choosing
publishing
formats.

2. **Click the Flash and HTML check boxes.**

   Those are all you need to publish a Flash Web site.

3. **Click additional tabs to finish setting publish settings as outlined in the upcoming sections.**

Specifying Flash settings

You set all the parameters for the Flash movie in the Flash tab. From within this tab, you choose which version of the Flash Player your movie is compatible with as well as other options, as follows:

1. **Choose File⇨Publish Settings.**

2. **Click the Flash tab.**

   The Flash section of the Publish Settings dialog box appears, as shown in Figure 13-2.

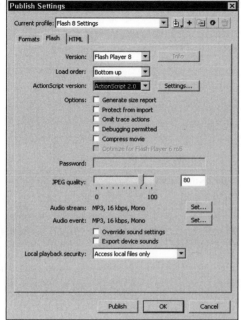

Figure 13-2:
Publishing
your site for
a specific
version of
the Flash
Player.

3. **Set your Flash publication options.**

The Flash tab offers a lot of options. Here's an overview:

✔ **Version:** Choose the version of the Flash Player with which your movie is to be compatible. You can choose from versions 1 through 8. Note that if your movie contains ActionScript from a particular version of Flash and you publish the movie for an earlier version of the Flash Player, your movie might not play as desired. As a rule, I set up everything for the previous version of the Flash Player (which, as of this writing, is version 7) unless I'm sure beyond a shadow of a doubt that all of the intended audience for the site will have Flash Player 8.

If you must publish your movie with the latest version of the Flash Player, you can display a warning that tells viewers that they need the Flash Player 8 to view the site and then include a link to the page where they can download the current version of the Flash Player 8, which, as of this writing, is

```
www.macromedia.com/shockwave/download/download.cgi?P1_
        Prod_Version=ShockwaveFlash
```

✔ **Load Order:** You can specify the order in which the Flash Player loads the layers of your movie by selecting one of the following options from the Load Order drop-down menu. If playback on the Web is slow, Flash will start to display individual layers in the order specified.

- *Bottom Up:* This option loads the movie in a browser from the bottom layer to the top layer.

- *Top Down:* This option downloads and displays the top layer first and then continues down the list to the bottom layer.

✔ **ActionScript Version:** Choose ActionScript 2.0 for a movie you created in Flash Professional 8.

✔ **Options:** The Options section includes the following check boxes:

- *Generate Size Report:* When you publish your movie, this option generates a text file that supplies you with a detailed report about the size of each frame and other miscellaneous information about your movie.

- *Protect from Import:* This option prevents viewers from importing the SWF file into Flash and converting it into a source file, which is essentially stealing.

- *Omit Trace Actions:* This option deletes any Trace actions in your movie when you publish the file, which prevents the Output window from appearing when your published movie is viewed.

- *Debugging Permitted:* This option allows you to debug your movie from a remote location after supplying a password.

  The Password field becomes available if you select the Debugging Permitted option. Type the password that will enable you and, if you're very brave, your client to debug the site remotely.

- *Compress Movie:* Use this option to compress your movie with the SWF compression methods. Note that this option has the most noticeable effect when you publish a movie for the Flash 7 or 8 Player.

✔ **JPEG Quality:** You can adjust the JPEG quality for every image in your Flash movie by using the JPEG Quality slider or by entering a value from 0 (low quality) through 100 (high quality) in the text field. Note that this setting will not override any changes you've made to a bitmap's properties in the document Library.

I advise you to set the JPEG quality for the individual images in an image application, such as Macromedia Fireworks or Adobe Photoshop, and then in the Flash Publish Settings dialog box, set the JPEG quality to 100 so that Flash will not further compress the images.

✔ **Audio Stream or Audio Event:** Use either of these options if your sound is streaming or occurs with an event. When you click Set, the Sound Settings dialog box shown in Figure 13-3 appears, offering you the following options:

- *Compression:* You can set the sound compression parameters for MP3 (the default), ADPCM, Speech, or Raw Format, or you can disable sound altogether.

- *Bit Rate:* Choose from the following bit rates: 8 Kbps, 16 Kbps, 20 Kbps, 24 Kbps, 32 Kbps, 48 Kbps, 56 Kbps, 64 Kbps, 80 Kbps, 112 Kbps, 128 Kbps, and 160 Kbps. Higher settings result in better sound quality at the expense of a larger file size.

- *Quality:* You can choose from Fast, Medium, and Best. This setting determines how long it takes Flash to compress sound files. If you choose Medium or Best, the audio portions of your movie sound better, but Flash takes longer to publish the movie.

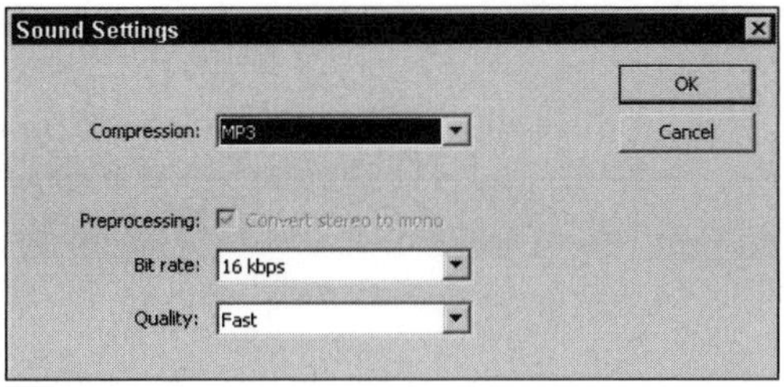

Figure 13-3:
You can
modify
sound
settings
of the
published
file.

✔ **Override Sound Settings:** This setting overrides all settings you specified in the sound's Properties dialog box from within the document Library. As a rule, I never choose this option because I change a sound's properties in the document Library for a good reason. For example, when I have a musical soundtrack, I choose a higher data rate so the music sounds better. When I'm setting properties for a button sound, I specify a lower data rate.

✔ **Export Device Sounds:** This option exports sounds that are suitable for devices such as cell phones and PDAs. This option is used when you publish using one of the Flash Lite player options. As such, the export Device Sounds option is never used for a Flash Web site.

✔ **Local Playback Security:** This is a new option for Flash 8 Professional that lets you decide whether the SWF file can exchange information with local files and networks or external networks. Because your published movie will be on a server, choose the default Access Local Files only option.

If you've optimized your sounds in an application, such as Sony Sound Forge or Adobe Audition, do not change the sound settings within the Publish Settings dialog box.

Specifying HTML settings

Every Flash movie, no matter how big or how small, must be embedded in an HTML document if it's to be viewed in a Web browser. The Web browser then calls up the friendly Flash Player plug-in, and the movie plays. And yes, Virginia, there is an HTML tab in which you specify the settings.

If you're publishing a Flash movie that will load into an interface, you need to publish an HTML document only for the Flash document you created for the interface. All other Flash movies need be published using only the Flash tab in the Publish Settings dialog box.

To set the HTML settings for the document in which your Flash Web site is embedded, follow these steps:

1. **Choose File⇨Publish Settings.**

2. **Click the HTML tab.**

   The HTML section of the Publish Settings dialog box appears, as shown in Figure 13-4.

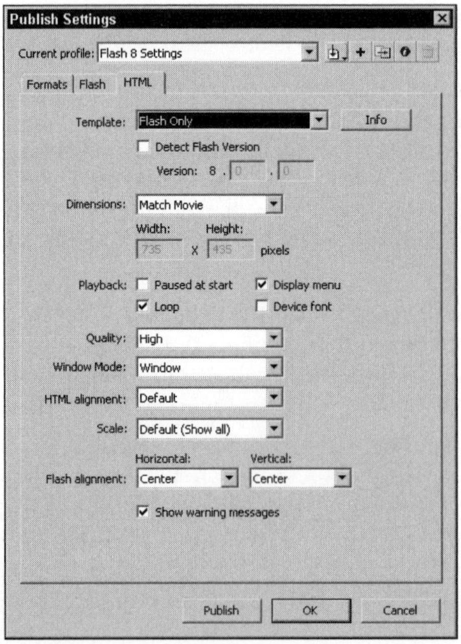

Figure 13-4:
Specifying
HTML
settings.

3. Specify the HTML settings for your Web site.

The HTML tab has even more options than the Flash tab. Here are some guidelines for adjusting your HTML settings:

✔ **Template:** Choose Flash Player Only. This is all you need for a Flash Web site.

✔ **Detect Flash Version:** Click this check box to embed code in the HTML document to detect which version of the Flash Player the user has installed on his or her system. When you choose this option, text boxes appear that enable you to choose the minor version of the Flash Player you specified within the Flash tab. For example, the current version of the Flash 8 player is 8.00.00.

✔ **Dimensions:** This option enables you to specify the movie's dimensions within the browser. The following selections are available in the Dimensions pop-up menu:

  • *Match Movie:* This selection matches the dimensions of the published movie to the size you specified when creating the FLA document. I recommend you stick with this setting.

  • *Pixels:* This allows you to type in values within a range of 1 to 28,800 pixels for width and height.

  • *Percent:* This setting allows you to type in values within a range of 1 to 100 for width and height.

✔ **Playback:** This section offers several playback choices for your movie:

  • *Paused at Start:* This option allows your viewer to begin the movie by clicking a button you've programmed to play the movie. This option is useful if you want to display certain information on the first frame of the movie that you want users to read before the movie plays.

  • *Display Menu:* Choose this option to give the viewer access to the full Flash context menu. If you deselect this option, viewers will not be able to choose playback options from the context menu.

  • *Loop:* Select this option if you want the movie to start over again when it has reached its last frame.

  • *Device Font:* This option enables Windows viewers to speed playback on their systems by substituting device fonts (sans or serif) whenever a Flash movie uses system-installed fonts from the viewer's computer.

✔ **Quality:** This enables you to dictate the quality setting used by the Flash Player to play your movie. If your viewing audience accesses the Internet with slow connection speeds or older computers, choosing a lower setting can speed up the playback of your movie. These choices will control smoothing of images and anti-aliasing of text and images in the Flash movie. The Quality setting balances image quality with play-back speed when the published movie is viewed. The following settings are available:

- *Low:* Flash disables anti-aliasing.

- *Auto Low:* Flash begins playing back the movie with anti-aliasing off. If the Flash Player decides that the viewer's system and Internet connection can support anti-aliasing without affecting movie playback, the player enables anti-aliasing.

- *Auto High:* The Flash Player enables anti-aliasing when the movie starts playing and disables it if playback issues occur.

- *Medium:* With this setting, you are at the 50-50 mark; the Flash Player handles minor anti-aliasing but does not smooth bitmaps.

- *High:* With this setting, the Flash Player applies anti-aliasing to all graphics except animated bitmaps.

- *Best:* This option causes the Flash Player to apply anti-aliasing to all objects as the movie plays.

✔ **Window Mode:** The following settings are available for Window Mode:

- *Window:* This is the regular default window mode that plays the movie in a rectangular window within the browser window.

- *Opaque Windowless:* This option causes the Flash Player to hide all elements that exist on the HTML page except the Flash movie.

- *Transparent Windowless Effect:* This option causes the Flash Player to display any elements on the Web page that exist beneath areas of the Flash movie where there are no graphics. This option works for Windows Internet Explorer only and may cause playback issues.

✔ **HTML Alignment:** The alignment selected will be added to the HTML template. Choose from the standard HTML settings of Default, Left, Right, Top, and Bottom.

✔ **Scale:** This option gives you four choices:

- *Default (Show All):* This option defaults to the user's browser settings.

- *No Border:* This option scales the Flash movie to the specified area and shows no border. The movie is scaled proportionate to the original dimensions; however, parts of the movie will not be dis-played if you specify a scale or dimension that exceeds the user's desktop size.

- *Exact Fit:* This scales the movie to fit the available browser area. Note that distortion occurs if the browser area is not proportion-ate to the dimensions of the movie.

- *No Scale:* This option does not allow the user to scale the movie.

- ✔ **Flash Alignment:** From the Horizontal pop-up menu, you can choose Left, Center, or Right. From the Vertical pop-up menu, you can choose Top, Center, or Bottom.

- ✔ **Show Warning Messages:** When you select this option, any problems or conflicts that occur when you publish your file will be brought to your attention. For instance, if you choose this option, a warning will appear if you specify a faulty tag setting, such as alternate text for an image that doesn't exist.

Publishing Your Site

Geez, after all the hubbub leading up to publishing the site, you'd think a brass band would play and fireworks would go off when you publish the site. Not a chance. Publishing the site is almost an anti-climax. To publish your site, do one of the following:

- ✔ Choose File⇨Publish.
- ✔ After setting Publish Settings in the Publish Settings dialog box, click the Publish button.

After doing either of the above, an SWF file and an HTML file are created. These files are in the same folder as the FLA document you used to create the movie you just published. To complete the cycle, you'll have to upload the files to your Web server. You can upload files by using an FTP client such as CuteFTP. Contact your Web hosting service for specific information on uploading files to their server.

When Flash publishes the HTML document, the Flash file is located in the default browser position, which is the left side of the browser window. To center the Flash SWF movie in the HTML document, edit the HTML file in an HTML editor, use the `<div align="center">` tag before the `<object>` tag, and use the `</div>` tag after the `<object>` tag. The following code is an example of centering a Flash SWF movie in an HTML document:

```
<div align="center">
  <object classid="clsid:d27cdb6e-ae6d-11cf-
          96b8-444553540000"
          codebase="http://fpdownload.macromedia.com/pub/
          shockwave/cabs/flash/swflash.cab#version=7,0,0,
          0" width="550" height="420" id="redcoats"
          align="middle">
    <param name="allowScriptAccess" value="sameDomain" />
    <param name="movie" value="redcoats.swf" />
    <param name="quality" value="high" />
    <param name="bgcolor" value="#e51c24" />
```

```
    <embed src="redcoats.swf" quality="high"
        bgcolor="#e51c24" width="550" height="420"
        name="redcoats" align="middle"
        allowScriptAccess="sameDomain"
        type="application/x-shockwave-flash"
        pluginspage="http://www.macromedia.com/go/getfl
        ashplayer" />
  </object>
</div>
```

Part V
The Part of Tens

The 5th Wave   By Rich Tennant

"...for technical support, press 7; for product information, press 8; if you're bored and just want to argue with someone, press 9..."

That's me...

In this part . . .

I have three chapters of a time-honored *For Dummies* staple: The Part of Tens. Part V is apropos for The Part of Tens because ten divided by five gives you an even number, which when I went to school was two. So why three chapters? Because I have thirty tidbits of information to share with you, which, if you do the math, is logical; three times ten equals thirty.

But seriously, in this part of the book, you'll find ten sections on how to create trouble-free Flash Web sites, ten sections on dealing with clients, and ten sections on optimizing the site.

Chapter 14

Ten Tips for Creating Flash Sites That Work

*I*f you build it — you know, a Flash Web site — they may come. And if they do come, by all means you want them to stay. In order to make them stay, you must have a Flash Web site that is a notch or two above cool. And in order for you to have a site that is a notch or two above cool, it has to be a fast-loading, bug-free site with crisp images. In this chapter, I show you ten things that are imperative for creating a Flash site that works.

Optimize Images Before Building the Flash Site

Flash is all about panache and polish. Even though the application has great drawing tools, most Web sites will need photorealistic images in addition to great vector artwork. And if you're not a da Vinci of the vector realm, photorealistic images — also known as *bitmaps* — are definitely needed. So then, your task is to have bitmaps that look great and load fast. I know what you're thinking — isn't that impossible? Well, no it isn't. By default, Flash compresses images to 80 percent quality. You can change this globally in the Publish Settings dialog box (which you access by choosing File➪Publish Settings), and you can apply different compression to individual images by changing the image's properties in the document Library and then looking at a preview in an itsy bitsy little window, which doesn't tell you much. The true results of the compression setting are not readily evident until you test or publish the movie.

A better solution for optimizing images for a Flash movie is to do the work in a stout image editing application such as Macromedia Fireworks or Adobe Photoshop:

1. **Resize the image to dimensions suitable for your Flash movie — like, you know, so it fits on Stage — and then change the resolution to 72 ppi (pixels per inch).**

2. **Compress the image when you save it by using the Export command in Fireworks or the Save for Web command in Photoshop.**

   Both applications let you preview the compressed image alongside the original. You don't need a whole lot of experience to master optimizing an image in either program.

3. **Choose the appropriate file format (JPEG or GIF), depending on your image content:**

   • If you're optimizing a photorealistic image of a person, place, or thing, choose the JPEG format.

   • If your image contains large areas of solid color, such as a logo, choose the GIF format.

4. **Apply enough compression until you start to see some pixelation and then use a higher setting.**

Do all of your work with the image magnified to 100 percent so you can see the true effects that the current compression setting has on the image. Remember, you can apply higher compression to smaller images that will be seen briefly in your Flash movie.

Don't Put All Your Eggs in One Basket

If you're designing a Flash Web site for a client with beaucoup information, you may be tempted to put it all in one Flash movie. Don't — especially if the client's information includes lots of images and the odd video or two. A photographer's Web site is a prime example. When you design the gallery section of the site, you could put each and every image in the document Library and display them as a movie clip slide show, in which each image displays for three seconds on the timeline before the next appears. The easier solution is to create thumbnail versions of each image and store these in the document Library. Create a button for each thumbnail that, when clicked, loads the full-sized JPEG image into a target movie clip, using the `loadMovie` action. (I show you how to load external content into a movie clip in Chapter 7.)

You can do the same thing with Flash video. Create a separate SWF movie for each video you want to display in the Web site and then use the `loadMovie` action to load the video into a target movie clip.

Get the Bugs Out of Your Scripts

With the advent of the Script Assist button, a degree of automation returns to ActionScript. You may think you can just create ActionScript code 'til the cows come home and then publish your movie. If you adhere to this assumption, you may be doing a lot of work for nothing. Remember that guy, Murphy? You know, the one who wrote the law that says anything that can go wrong will, and that the chance of an open-faced jelly sandwich landing face-down on the carpet is directly proportional to the cost of the carpet per square yard? Well, he's the same guy who, despite your best-laid-out plans, is going to put little gremlins in your ActionScript. If you wait until it's time to publish your Flash Web site before you test it, you may have more bugs in your movie than you care to deal with. You can go back through every bit of code you've written, add breakpoints, and use the Debugger as outlined in Chapter 13, but hey, that's a lot of work.

The easiest way to ensure you have bug-free Flash movies without investing an inordinate amount of time and a huge amount of money in hair-coloring products that promise to get the gray out is to use the Test Movie command early and often. Use the command the first time you make a major change in your movie, such as adding a new movie clip with a lot of animation or creating ActionScript for a button. If you test your movie each time you make a major change, when you do encounter a bug, it's most likely in the item you last created. If you do methodical testing at every stage in the process, you won't be faced with a logistical nightmare at the end of the project.

If you run into a problem with your ActionScript, and the ActionScript contains a variable used elsewhere in the movie, make sure the latest instance of the variable is spelled the same way as other instances of the variable in your movie.

Label Your Frames and Scenes

One of the easiest ways to troubleshoot a faulty ActionScript is with the Movie Explorer. You use the Movie Explorer's visual outline to find a keyframe, symbol, or other object you suspect may be causing the hiccup in your ActionScript. By default, a keyframe is referenced by its path and frame number. That makes it kind of difficult to figure out exactly which keyframe contains the faulty ActionScript. If, however, you give each keyframe a distinct label, it's much easier to figure out what the frame does. Then, when you're troubleshooting your document and scrolling through the Movie Explorer, your built-in sensor (or censor depending upon the type of bug you're after) says, "Aha, I'll bet this is where Murphy planted the bug." And if you've done a good job of creating meaningful labels for the keyframes, you're probably right.

When you assign actions to a movie clip object, you are working with a labeled instance of a symbol. Give it a unique name that identifies what the instance of the movie clip is used for, and it will be easy to troubleshoot the movie clip with the Movie Explorer.

Use Named Anchors

Some people prefer to do things the old-fashioned way. You spend your time creating cool buttons to go from point A to point B in your movie, yet people still want the luxury of their browsers' Back buttons to get back to previously viewed content. Well, you can cater to these Neanderthals who don't realize all the trouble you've gone through to add cool navigation to your site. In order to cater to people in love with their browsers' Back buttons, you add named anchors. A *named anchor* is like a frame label on steroids; modern Web browser Back and Next buttons link to them like white on rice. You create a *named anchor,* as follows:

1. **Select the keyframe in which you want to add the named anchor.**

2. **Choose Window⇨Properties.**

   The Properties Inspector opens.

3. **Type a name in the <instance name> field.**

   For safety's sake, type a name that does not contain spaces. Your movie will be viewed by a wide variety of browsers, as well as being viewed cross-platform, and not all browsers and operating systems recognize spaces in filenames and tags.

4. **Choose Anchor from the Type drop-down menu.**

   When the movie is published and it advances to the keyframe after the one on which you've added a named anchor, the user's browser's Back button can be used to navigate to the keyframe with the named anchor.

Create Linkage

When you have a movie clip that needs to be displayed on command, you can easily do so when you create linkage to the movie clip. When you create linkage, you give a movie clip an identifier that can be referred to with ActionScript using the attachMovie action. This is like loading an external movie on command, but you're referencing content that is within the movie. This is a great option when you have small movie clips that need to be displayed when users pass their cursors over an object. To create linkage to a Library object, follow these steps:

1. **Choose Window⇨Library.**

   The document Library opens.

2. **Right-click (Windows) or Control-click (Macintosh) the object to which you want to refer with linkage and choose Linkage from the context menu.**

   The Linkage dialog box opens.

3. **Click the Export for ActionScript check box.**

   The Export in First Frame check box is also selected by default. Do not uncheck this box because, in most instances, you want the item available in the first frame of your movie.

4. **Type a name in the Identifier field.**

   Use a descriptive name that contains no spaces.

5. **Click OK.**

   The dialog box closes and the object can now be referred to with ActionScript by its identifier.

Make Your Site Skinny with Symbols

Lots of stuff in a movie can break the user's bandwidth bank. When you're using some of the same objects again and again, you're ahead of the game when you convert them to symbols. Alternatively, when you know you're going to be using the same object over and over again, you can use the New Symbol command (Insert⇨New Symbol) when you first create the object. This opens the New Symbol dialog box, which prompts you to select a symbol behavior type (Button, Graphic, or Movie Clip) and to enter a name for the symbol. After creating a new symbol, or converting a current object to a symbol, the new symbol appears in the document Library.

Whenever you need to create a carbon copy of the symbol, simply drag it out of the document Library on Stage. This creates an instance of the symbol.

Symbol instances do not increase the file size of the published movie because the Flash Player creates the symbol instance based on the information in the original symbol in the document Library.

After you create an instance of a symbol, you can transform it with the Free Transform tool or apply a color effect to the symbol instance. You can also use the <instance name> field in the Properties Inspector to give the symbol instance a unique name, which can then be addressed with ActionScript.

Create a Separate Layer for Your ActionScript

Did you ever try to find something and couldn't? You know, like a pair of your favorite socks or stockings? Well, if you put your socks or stockings in their own separate drawer, then you'd know where they are at all times, except during the obligatory trip to the washing machine where at least one pair of your favorite socks ends up a solo act — how socks orphan themselves is still a mystery to me. The same thing is true of actions. If you put them all in the same place, then you know where to find them when debugging your Flash movies.

When you assign an action to an object, it's always right where it should be, attached to the movie clip or button to which you assigned the ActionScript. However, a frame action is attached to a keyframe, and if you have lots of keyframes interspersed with lots of frames that are allocated on lots of layers, the keyframe with the action that has your movie screwed up eight ways to Sunday is going to be hard to find. You'll make your life a lot easier if you create a separate layer for all frame actions and position this layer at the top of the hierarchy. Then when you need to debug ActionScript code you've assigned to a keyframe, you know right where to look for it.

Use Comments

Another way to make your life as a Flash Web designer less stressful is to use comments. Comments are little notes to yourself. You can add a comment in one of two places: in a keyframe or within the ActionScript itself. When you create a comment, create one that will make sense in three or four months when you have to revise the Flash movie. When you create a comment, be brief, but not so brief that you don't understand the comment. When you need to add a comment to ActionScript, you can do so by following these steps:

1. **Click the Script Assist button to exit Script Assist mode.**

   You're going to manually type your comment.

2. **Position your cursor at the start of the line of code after the spot where you want your comment to appear.**

3. **Press Enter or Return.**

   This creates a blank line where you can type your comment.

4. **On the blank line, type two forward slashes (/ /) followed by your comment.**

   If your comment is lengthy, stop typing when the text reaches the end of the Script pane — text doesn't wrap in the Actions panel. Press Enter or Return to create a new line, type two forward slashes, and then type the rest of your comment. Repeat as needed to keep your comment within the border of the Script pane. Otherwise, you'll have to scroll to read the full comment, which can be annoying.

You can also create comments on keyframes:

1. **Select the keyframe you want the comment to appear on.**

2. **Choose Window⇨Properties.**

   The Properties Inspector opens.

3. **In the <Frame Label> field, type your comment.**

4. **Choose Comment from the Type drop-down menu.**

   Flash displays the comment on the keyframe preceded by two green forward slashes. The reason for the two forward slashes is so that Flash reads this as a comment instead of as a frame label and also so you will recognize that this is a comment and not a label. If the comment is obscured by other keyframes in close proximity, position your cursor over the keyframe that contains the two green slashes, and a tool tip appears with the word *Comment* followed by your comment. Such efficiency.

Think Modular

Objects and effects that you create with ActionScript — especially the cooler and more complex things — involve lots of frames and keyframes, plus quite a few lines of ActionScript. These cool effects generally take a while to create. When you get something that's especially good, there's no sense in re-creating it in another movie; convert the effect into a movie clip and then click the icon that looks like a pushpin to pin the document Library in which the movie clip is stored. This keeps the pinned document Library visible, even when you open another document. Open the document in which you want to use the movie clip and then drag the movie clip from the pinned Library into another current document. Here's how to convert an effect into a modular movie clip:

1. **Select all the frames and layers used to create the object or effect.**

   The frames are highlighted.

2. **Choose Edit⇨Timeline⇨Copy Frames.**

   The frames are copied to the clipboard.

3. **Choose Insert⇨New Symbol.**

   The Symbol Properties dialog box appears.

4. **Choose the Movie Clip behavior type, name the symbol, and then click OK.**

   Flash enters symbol-editing mode.

5. **Select the first frame and then choose Edit⇨Timeline⇨Paste Frames.**

   Flash pastes the frames, objects, and layers into the movie clip using the same layer names.

6. **Click the Back button to exit symbol-editing mode.**

   The movie clip is stored in the document Library for future use.

If you want, you can delete the frames you just copied and put the movie clip in their place. You can now use the movie clip in other movies by opening the file, pinning the document Library, and dragging the symbol on Stage or into the current document's Library. The symbol is now ready for use in the new document.

Chapter 15

Ten Tips for Working with Clients

● ●

In This Chapter

▶ Create a survey

▶ Create a site mock-up

▶ Get client approval

▶ Be specific

▶ Include everything

▶ Create a contract

▶ Get payment up front

▶ Get feedback frequently

▶ Get written feedback

▶ Bill for everything

● ●

The title of a brilliant rock album advised, "We're Only in It for the Money." As a Flash Web designer, you work with clients. Unless you're independently wealthy, you create Web sites for friends, or you play with Flash as a hobby, you need to generate a profit from your work. When you're dealing with clients, this can be tough. The client is always the client, and each client is different. If you're going to survive working with clients and still keep your sanity, you need to do a few things. In this chapter, I show you ten things you should do with every client.

The information in this chapter should not be considered legal advice. When you create the forms and templates for your contracts, be sure to seek the advice of a competent attorney who can advise you as to whether or not the contract is binding in the area in which you do business.

Create a Client Survey

Every aspiring Web designer has a Web site. On your Web site, you likely have information about yourself, information about the services you offer, and examples of your work. If you're a beginning Web designer, the examples will be faux Web sites you've created and uploaded to your server. If you're an experienced Web designer, you'll have an actual portfolio on your site with links to the sites you've created. No matter which type of portfolio you create, the method to your madness is to get a warm or red-hot prospect to want you to create a Web site. You might think that this stage is as simple as your client picking up the phone and calling you after viewing your Web site. However, Web designers can and often do get clients from distant locales. Therefore, sometimes the only way you can establish a preliminary contact and know what the client needs is to create and post a customer survey on your Web site.

Customer surveys can be kind of lengthy, so I advise against using a form created in Flash. Instead, you'll have to rely on its butt-ugly — that's a technical term — HTML counterpart to gather information. In your questionnaire, you need to get the following information:

- ✔ **The potential client's contact information.**

- ✔ **Whether or not the client has procured a domain name.**

- ✔ **Whether or not the client will provide edited text, images, and so on for the Web site.**

- ✔ **The client's expectations and why he wants a Web site.** This should be a definite reason, such as promoting a product or expanding the customer base. If the client says he just wants a Web site, this should raise a red flag — the client has no earthly idea of what his expectations are.

The information from your client survey will help you establish a line of communication and eventually will be used to create your proposal and price quote.

Create a Static Mock-up

After your initial meeting with the client, you should have a pretty good idea of what he wants for the final Web site. But sometimes your vision and the client's vision are diametrically opposite. If this is the case, and you create an extensive Flash Web site using your vision, the client won't be very happy when he sees the end result. Therefore, you should always create some kind of mock-up for the client to look at before you launch Flash.

The mock-up doesn't need to be elaborate. You can easily create a mock-up of the banner and the navigation menu in less than an hour by using the powerful tools built into Macromedia Fireworks. After you have these areas laid out, you can create the area of the page where the initial content appears. Typically, this will be a combination of text and images. Of course, you don't know what the client wants to say because at this stage of the square dance, you may not have a contract. That's right, if you don't have an extensive portfolio or don't come highly recommended, some clients will want to see something before they sign on the dotted line.

What's that? You don't have your clients sign on the dotted line? If you fall into this category, please fast forward to the "Get It in Writing" section of this chapter.

So then, how do you flesh out the area of the page where the content will appear? I generally use clip art, type or paste in some Greeked text like *Ipsum lorem,* and then copy the text to fill in the areas. You want to hedge your bet on the design and present a variation or two.

Refer to Chapter 2 for a killer technique on creating more then one client mock-up in Fireworks without cracking a sweat.

For a plethora of cut-and-paste Greeked text, point your Web browser to `www.lipsum.com`. Or for something a bit more light-hearted, check out `www.malevole.com/mv/misc/text/`.

Get the Client to Sign Off on the Design

Now comes the fun part: presenting your design to the client. If you've done your homework and have assessed the client's needs correctly, one of your mock-ups will suit the client's fancy. After the client decides on the winning mock-up, get the client to sign the mock-up. In fact, you might consider having a stamp made that says *Approved By:* on the first line and *Date:* on the second line. Stamp each of the mock-ups, and when the client swoons, whip out your pen — or felt-tipped marker if you print your mock-ups on glossy paper — and ask the client to sign. After the client signs off on the design, file it in the client's folder in case there are any questions later.

Dot the Eyes and Cross the Tees

If you're new to the Web design game, chances are you don't have a portfolio and need to follow the scenario presented in this chapter, which is creating the mock-up and presenting it to the client. If, however, you're an experienced Web designer with a portfolio, the contractual issues will come *before* you submit the mock-up and have the client sign off on the design.

When you write a contract, make sure you list everything you're going to do for the client. You should list every phase of your work, such as optimizing photos, scanning images, publishing the Web site, optimizing the site for search engines, uploading the site to the server, submitting the site to search engines, and so on. When you list every phase of the project, your client sees the added value in the services you're providing. The added value justifies the cost of your services.

Also list contingencies, such as what happens if the client is late delivering material you need for creating the site. After all, if the client is going to hold your feet to the fire on the delivery date, you need to hold your client's feet to the fire as far as the delivery of needed material. You should also cover legal issues, such as the venue in which any disagreements that require the services of an attorney will be resolved.

You also need to cover the client who waffles — you know, changes her mind. Time is money, and if the client significantly changes the design from what she originally signed off on, you need to include a clause that covers this eventuality. Changes should be billed at your hourly rate. You do have an hourly rate, don't you?

Another factor you need to cover is additional online material you need to create, such as extra sections of the site or supplementary images the client supplies that you must optimize for the design. In my contracts, I add a clause that if the total scope of the site exceeds what is listed in the contract, the client will be notified so that an agreeable fee for the additional work can be negotiated. You may want to consider doing this on an hourly basis as well.

Cover the Bases

When you create the client's Web site, make sure you cover all the bases. Do everything you've listed in your contract. This may sound blindingly obvious, but when you're creating a complex Web site, it's easy for small details to slip through the cracks. When you're done with the Web site, the contract can serve as your checklist. Go through every paragraph and clause of the contract. For example, if you say you're going to submit the site to six search engines, make sure you have done so.

It's also important to document that you've done everything listed in the contract. One problem that arises is documenting sundry details like submitting the site to search engines. Your client won't know the results of search engine submissions for several weeks. Therefore, you should take a screenshot of the site being submitted to each search engine and keep this with the client's file. If any questions arise after you've completed the site, you have all the documentation needed to prove you've done what you said you would.

Get It in Writing

Never do business on a handshake; it will always come back to haunt you. Make sure your client signs and dates your original contract. If minor changes are to be made, cross out the original and then write in the revision. Both you and the client need to initial the revision. If the client requests significant changes in the contract, rewrite it — or tell the client to take a hike. Then make sure all additional client requests — with the exception of really small requests — are handled with a change order. Now, I know what you're thinking — that's a lot of paperwork. The change order doesn't need to be anything elaborate; a quick note to the client on your letterhead will suffice. Leave an area for the client to accept and date the change order. Include an SASE with the change order and don't do any additional work until you receive the signed change order.

Get an Initial Payment

When you submit the contract to the client, make sure you add a payment clause. Always ask for an initial payment of at least 40 percent of the total contract price. Because this is a Flash design and you won't have anything to show the client until your initial prototype is published, 40 percent of the total price is a fair initial payment. Your contract should also include an additional 40 percent payment when the site has been published and uploaded. At this stage of the process, you'll request feedback from the client on the final design. Typically, you'll have to do a few things to satisfy the client. The final 20 percent is paid when the client signs off on the site.

Get Frequent Feedback

When you achieve a milestone in your Flash design, contact the client for feedback. For example, when you've created the interface for the site and the first section of the site, publish the Flash movies and upload them to your Web server in a separate folder. Send the client a quick note telling her what you've done along with the URL where she can view the work in progress and request feedback before going any further.

Get Feedback in Writing

When you request feedback from a client, don't rely on a hasty telephone call where he tells you, "Yeah, it's great. Rock on." Unless you've recorded the conversation — which may or may not be legal in the state where you live — this won't hold up in court if the client pitches a hissy fit when you're done with the site. If it's an important part of your design, get the client's feedback in writing. If you rely on e-mail for client feedback, after you receive the client's feedback, send an additional e-mail to the client acknowledging and thanking him for the feedback.

Bill for Extras

Your contract states everything that you and the client have agreed to. Your contract should also have clauses for extra work. When you perform extra work, generate an invoice immediately and send it to the client with the invoice for the applicable incremental payment. For example, if you perform the work at the final stages of the project, send the invoices for the extra work with the request for final payment.

Chapter 16

Ten Tips for Promoting the Site

*A*fter you create the site and upload it to a Web server, your client is going to expect visitors. Well, just because you build it doesn't mean that visitors will come flocking to the site. The site has to be optimized for search engines and then submitted to the most popular search engines. In addition, you'll have to tell your client how to publicize the site. In this chapter, I show you ten things that you can do to promote a site.

Choose a Meaningful Domain Name

If your client has not already chosen a domain name, advise her to choose a domain name that describes the business but is short and easy to remember. Sharonsflowersbouquetsandgreetingcards.com is way too long for users who are manually typing the URL in the Address field of a Web browser. Plus, it's hard to remember. However, SharonsFlowers.com tells what the business does, is easy to remember, and doesn't contribute to an onslaught of carpal tunnel syndrome when Web surfers type the name in the Address fields of their favorite Web browsers. Remember, if the site name is not available as a .com, you can also choose from the following: .net, .biz, .org, .info.

Optimize the HTML Page in Which Your Flash Site Is Embedded

You can't do a whole lot within Flash to vault a site to the top of a search engine's results page for keywords pertaining to your client's business. You must do all of this work outside of Flash. You can, however, add information to the base HTML document in which your Flash Web site is embedded to make your site more recognizable to search engines.

Search engines look for tags (which I cover in upcoming sections) and text. However, all of the text in your Flash movie is embedded in the movie and cannot be read when search engines access your site after you submit it. You can, however, greatly influence the site's rank within a search engine by creating a meaningful title for the Web page. You do this in an HTML editor, such as Dreamweaver, by changing the pages' properties. Create a meaningful title that describes what the Web site is promoting. For example, if you were adding a title to a Flash Web site for a wedding photographer named Joe Smith in Tampa, Florida, a good choice would be this: Joe Smith Wedding Photography, Tampa Bay, Florida.

Add Meta Tags

The default HTML page created when you publish a Flash movie includes just enough information to play the movie in the viewer's browser and includes nothing that will make your site more visible to search engines. You can, however, add Meta tags to the HTML document in which your Flash Web site is embedded. One Meta tag that the search engines use to index a site is the `Keywords` tag. Keywords can be a single word or a phrase that search engine users are likely to use to find a site that contains certain information. You can add up to 255 keywords in the `Keywords` Meta tag. When you're working with a client, ask the client which keywords she thinks Web surfers would use to find a site like the one you're designing. Then you've got to be a bit of a magician and come up with variations of the keyword, such as common misspellings. If the client's business is regional, you should also include the city and state in which the client does business as keywords. You can add keywords in your favorite HTML editor. Each keyword or key phrase must be separated with a comma. The following is an example of keywords for a photographer's Web site:

```
<META name="keywords" content="Joe Smith, Photographer,
        models, Orlando, Florida, FL, model, glamour,
        fitness, modeling, lifestyle photography,
        product photography, fashion photography,
        television, Tampa, Tampa Bay">
```

Research High-Ranking Web Sites

When you do your initial consultation with a client, ask him who his competitors are and then get the URLs for their Web sites. Armed with this information and the keywords suggested by the client, you're ready to go to work. Follow these steps to get keywords that are relevant for your client's Flash Web site:

1. **Go to your favorite search engine.**

2. **Type one of the keywords supplied by the client.**

   The search engine returns a list of URLs along with a description of each site.

3. **Click the top-ranking sites from the search.**

   The first ten will tell you what you need to know.

4. **As you peruse each site, ask yourself whether the business is similar to your client's.**

   If so, it's a viable keyword. If not, repeat Step 2 with the next keyword on your client's list. Your goal is to find the keywords that return Web sites of businesses similar to your client's business.

5. **When a keyword returns a site of a business similar to your client's, view the source code.**

   In Internet Explorer, you can view the code by choosing View⇨Source. In Netscape Navigator, you can view the source code by choosing View⇨ Page Source. Either command opens the source code in Notepad (Windows).

6. **Analyze the source code and pay particular attention to the keywords. Copy the keywords and use the ones that you think are pertinent for your client.**

7. **Navigate to the Web sites of your client's competitors.**

8. **Analyze the source code and keywords used on your client's competitor's home page.**

   This information enables you to fine-tune your list of keywords.

Add Alt Text

When you add an image to an HTML page, you have a provision for adding ALT text. This text tells Web site visitors who are viewing only text what the image is all about. Search engines also examine ALT text when indexing your site. If you add ALT text that mirrors your keywords, your site has higher relevancy and will rank higher than sites that don't mirror keywords with ALT text. The problem, however, is that in Flash, you have no way of adding ALT text to images. You can, however, add some images that will never be seen to the HTML page in which your Flash Web site is embedded, as follows:

1. **In your favorite image editing program, create a new document that is 8 pixels by 8 pixels.**

   The background color of the document should be the same color as the background color of your Flash movie. Or, if you've changed the background color of the HTML page in which your Flash movie is embedded to a different color, use this color for the background color of the document you're creating.

2. **Save the document as a GIF file.**

   A single-color GIF file with these dimensions has a file size of about 4K.

3. **Use your HTML editor to add the image to the HTML page in which your Flash Web site interface is embedded.**

4. **Add ALT text using some of the keywords from your Keywords Meta tag.**

Add Text to the HTML Page in Which Your Flash Site Is Embedded

Search engines also search the first few paragraphs of text in a Web page. Savvy Web designers always include several of the keywords in the text on the home page. In Flash, however, all the text is embedded in the Flash movie. You can add text to the page in which your Flash movie is embedded, as follows:

1. **Open the HTML document in which your Flash movie is embedded.**

   This task is easier if you open the document in a WYSIWYG (What You See Is What You Get) HTML editor like Dreamweaver.

2. **Press Enter or Return several times.**

   This adds several lines with no text to the document. Your goal is to add enough lines so that the text you type will not be visible in the browser.

3. **Type the desired text.**

   Don't just type keywords because major search engines may reject a bunch of keywords that are not part of a paragraph. Type a meaningful paragraph that describes the client's business or what is in the Web site. Some Web visitors will actually scroll down to the text out of curiosity.

The text should be similar to the welcome message you see on any Web site home page. But the trick is to use as many keywords as possible in the text. If for example, if your client is Joe Smith, a fashion photographer from Tampa, Florida, your first line of text may read like this:

```
Joe Smith is a fashion photographer doing business in
        Tampa, Florida.
```

Tell the World

In addition to marketing your site on the Web, your client also needs to market the site in their printed media. This is easily done by adding the site URL to every piece of printed literature that gets sent to existing and potential clients. The URL for the site should also be included in all printed media, such as letterheads, business cards, brochures, catalogs, and so on. If your client advertises, advise him to add the site URL to all TV ads and printed ads. If your client purchases radio ads, the URL should be spoken at least once in the ad.

Get Web Sites to Link to You

Search engines give higher relevancy (rank sites higher) to sites that are linked to other sites. When you are designing your client's Flash Web site, ask her for the URLs of businesses that complement but do not compete with her business. Add these links to the Links section of your Flash Web site. In addition, your client should ask each of the businesses on the Links page to include links to *her* URL on *their* sites.

But once again, the nature of a Flash Web site works against you; all the links are embedded in the Flash movie. You can easily add these links below the text you've added to the HTML page in which the Flash Web site is embedded. The search engines will record this information when your site is searched for indexing.

Promote the Site in Blogs and Forums

Another way in which your client can draw attention to his Web site is by listing the URL whenever he posts information to a blog or forum. If the blog or forum is relevant to your client's business, many people who see the URL will visit the site. If your client's site features tutorials or information pertinent to a forum, tell your client to answer posts where forum users are requesting this type of information. However, instead of having your client answer the question, tell your client to direct the forum user to the section of your client's site where she can find the information. Remember to refer them to the URL where the Flash Web site loads and then tell them the section of the site where the information can be found. After doing this for a while, the forum users will perceive your client's site as a valuable resource and will visit often. If your client has items for sale, the increased traffic is bound to boost sales.

Submit Your Site

After you've done everything possible to the HTML document to increase your client's visibility to the search engines, the next step is to submit the site. There are gobs of search engines out there, and your Web hosting service may offer submission to several sites as part of its service. However, the only way to be sure something is done is to do it yourself. Therefore, you should submit your client's site to the major search engines. As of this writing, the best search engines are

- ✔ www.google.com
- ✔ www.msn.com
- ✔ www.yahoo.com
- ✔ www.lycos.com

Navigate to the site's home page and look for a link that says something like "Submit your site." Each search engine is different, but most ask you for a list of keywords and a description of the site. You won't be able to paste a gazillion keywords when submitting the site. Most search engines limit you to 25 keywords and a brief description of the site. The description appears when the site is listed in the search engine's results for a relevant keyword. If you've done your homework, you'll know exactly which keywords to enter and will be able to write a concise description that gets the job done.

Appendix

Flash Internet Resources

· ·

*F*lash is a super-popular application, but it's not the easiest application in the world to master, which is probably why you bought this book. In addition to the pearls of wisdom in this book, you can surf for other ports on the Web.

As of this writing, I waxed my board and actually surfed to each site to verify that it's still there. But you know how the Net is — here today, gone tomorrow. Therefore, by the time you read this appendix, some of these sites may have gone the way of the Dodo.

Flash Training and Tutorial Resources

Lots of sites offer Flash training. Listed in this section are some of the more popular sites, with examples of what types of training you can expect to find there.

www.computerarts.co.uk

The Computer Arts site, which is the digital counterpart of a print magazine, features news, product reviews, and extensive tutorials that cover all sorts of digital design programs, including a plethora of learning tools for Flash.

www.ultrashock.com

At this site, you'll find a ton of resources to choose from. Take your pick from tutorials, user forums, downloadable FLA files, articles, games, and cartoons, which are all wrapped up in an incredibly cool interface.

www.EchoEcho.com

If you need tutorials on almost any Web design subject, including JavaScript and Flash, this is the place to be, Lee. You'll also find an archive of FLA files that you can download and dissect to see how each effect was created.

www.ellenfinkelstein.com/flashtips.html

Ellen is a fellow *For Dummies* author. At her site, you'll find Flash tutorials on easier drawing methods, changing the pace of tweened animation, creating hyperlinked text, and sculpting shapes.

www.swift3d.com

At this site, you'll find information on Swift3D, a powerful application that enables you to create 3-D Flash animations. In addition to information about the application, you'll also find tutorials on using the application.

www.actionscripts.org

Here's a site where you'll find lots of information about ActionScript. The tutorials range from beginner to advanced, so navigate to the site and take your pick.

www.flash-creations.com

This site by Helen Triolo features up-to-date tutorials on ActionScript syntax, code snippets, sound files, and sources, as well as myriad other invaluable online resources.

www.communitymx.com

At this site, you'll find Flash information and tutorials. There is also a section devoted to Flash extensions.

www.flashstreamworks.com

At this site, you'll find lots of Flash information, including tutorials and links to cool Flash broadband sites.

www.were-here.com

This site is chock-full of tutorials for ActionScript and Swift3D, including tutorials that show you how to create mouse trails, arrays, drag-and-drop movie clips, and dynamic text, as well as how to control a movie clip with a slider. This is an excellent and well-respected source for free Flash tutorials.

www.flashkit.com

Here is another site for great Flash tutorials. You'll also find sections where you can download sounds for your Flash movies, and much more.

www.lynda.com

This site is packed with Flash tips, downloads, links, and techniques, as well as many free resources, including articles about color, inspirational Web sites, tips, and resource links.

www.flzone.net

This site features tutorials, extensions, Flash source files, and sounds, as well as demos and forums.

www.moock.org

On this site, you'll find answers to technical questions and Flash examples from the mundane to the obscure. In addition, you'll find helpful ActionScript tutorials on this site.

www.macromedia.com

Macromedia has a great site with lots of pertinent and helpful information. Be sure to look under Macromedia Flash Usability to find usability tips, downloadable source files, and guidelines with extensive hyperlinks to relevant and useful information. Also, check out the Flash gallery and Site of the Day section. There's also a Designer and Developer Resource section that provides articles on writing ActionScript code efficiently. You'll also be able to download a motherload of extensions to further your Flash arsenal.

Flash Animation

Flash is all about animation. But of course, there are different methods you can use to create it. Tons of sites out there have great Flash animation, and here are a few from other Flash designers that you can use as inspiration.

www.coolhomepages.com

As the name implies, you'll find cool home pages at this site. Navigate to the different sites for inspiration for your own designs.

www.bestflashanimationsite.com

At this site, you'll find links to cool Flash sites that feature animation, as well as tutorials and resources.

www.melondezign.com

This is a Web design company, but within this site, you'll find examples of some very cool Flash animation they've incorporated into their designs.

www.webmonkey.com

At this site, you'll find useful tutorials on Flash and other Web design topics. The site features an extensive library about every aspect of Web design, and then some.

www.djojostudios.com/flash

Check out the Flash Projects and Animations sections. Trés cool.

Sound

Flash is such a cool tool for creating Web sites, but without the ability to incorporate sound, it would be pretty boring. If you're new to Flash Web design, this section shows sites where you can download loops and sound effects. You also find sites where you can purchase software that enables you to create your own Flash music loops.

www.soundshopper.com

Here you'll find a wide array of music clips, loops, sound effects, and other audio elements for your Flash productions. You can try out and purchase any of these royalty-free sounds directly from the Web site.

www.flashkit.com

That's right Ethel, in addition to being an awesome tutorial site; you can also download background music loops and button sounds from this site.

www.sonymediasoftware.com

Here you'll find software that enables you to create very cool sound loops using royalty-free samples. The main program is Acid Music Pro, but you'll find other applications that enable you to create sound loops. You can download free demo versions of software from the site.

www.groovemaker.com

This site features Groovemaker 2.5, an application that enables you to create hypnotic, nonstop, professional dance tracks in real time. You can mix them, layer in some loops, and then create a totally new remix. It offers MP3 expert compatibility and Mac OS X capabilities. You can download a free demo version from the site.

Index

BUSINESS, CAREERS & PERSONAL FINANCE

0-7645-5307-0

0-7645-5331-3 *†

Also available:
- Accounting For Dummies †
  0-7645-5314-3
- Business Plans Kit For Dummies †
  0-7645-5365-8
- Cover Letters For Dummies
  0-7645-5224-4
- Frugal Living For Dummies
  0-7645-5403-4
- Leadership For Dummies
  0-7645-5176-0
- Managing For Dummies
  0-7645-1771-6

- Marketing For Dummies
  0-7645-5600-2
- Personal Finance For Dummies *
  0-7645-2590-5
- Project Management For Dummies
  0-7645-5283-X
- Resumes For Dummies †
  0-7645-5471-9
- Selling For Dummies
  0-7645-5363-1
- Small Business Kit For Dummies *†
  0-7645-5093-4

HOME & BUSINESS COMPUTER BASICS

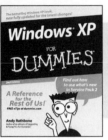

0-7645-4074-2

0-7645-3758-X

Also available:
- ACT! 6 For Dummies
  0-7645-2645-6
- iLife '04 All-in-One Desk Reference
  For Dummies
  0-7645-7347-0
- iPAQ For Dummies
  0-7645-6769-1
- Mac OS X Panther Timesaving
  Techniques For Dummies
  0-7645-5812-9
- Macs For Dummies
  0-7645-5656-8

- Microsoft Money 2004 For Dummies
  0-7645-4195-1
- Office 2003 All-in-One Desk Reference
  For Dummies
  0-7645-3883-7
- Outlook 2003 For Dummies
  0-7645-3759-8
- PCs For Dummies
  0-7645-4074-2
- TiVo For Dummies
  0-7645-6923-6
- Upgrading and Fixing PCs For Dummies
  0-7645-1665-5
- Windows XP Timesaving Techniques
  For Dummies
  0-7645-3748-2

FOOD, HOME, GARDEN, HOBBIES, MUSIC & PETS

0-7645-5295-3

0-7645-5232-5

Also available:
- Bass Guitar For Dummies
  0-7645-2487-9
- Diabetes Cookbook For Dummies
  0-7645-5230-9
- Gardening For Dummies *
  0-7645-5130-2
- Guitar For Dummies
  0-7645-5106-X
- Holiday Decorating For Dummies
  0-7645-2570-0
- Home Improvement All-in-One
  For Dummies
  0-7645-5680-0

- Knitting For Dummies
  0-7645-5395-X
- Piano For Dummies
  0-7645-5105-1
- Puppies For Dummies
  0-7645-5255-4
- Scrapbooking For Dummies
  0-7645-7208-3
- Senior Dogs For Dummies
  0-7645-5818-8
- Singing For Dummies
  0-7645-2475-5
- 30-Minute Meals For Dummies
  0-7645-2589-1

INTERNET & DIGITAL MEDIA

0-7645-1664-7

0-7645-6924-4

Also available:
- 2005 Online Shopping Directory
  For Dummies
  0-7645-7495-7
- CD & DVD Recording For Dummies
  0-7645-5956-7
- eBay For Dummies
  0-7645-5654-1
- Fighting Spam For Dummies
  0-7645-5965-6
- Genealogy Online For Dummies
  0-7645-5964-8
- Google For Dummies
  0-7645-4420-9

- Home Recording For Musicians
  For Dummies
  0-7645-1634-5
- The Internet For Dummies
  0-7645-4173-0
- iPod & iTunes For Dummies
  0-7645-7772-7
- Preventing Identity Theft For Dummies
  0-7645-7336-5
- Pro Tools All-in-One Desk Reference
  For Dummies
  0-7645-5714-9
- Roxio Easy Media Creator For Dummies
  0-7645-7131-1

* Separate Canadian edition also available
† Separate U.K. edition also available

SPORTS, FITNESS, PARENTING, RELIGION & SPIRITUALITY

0-7645-5146-9

0-7645-5418-2

Also available:

- Adoption For Dummies
  0-7645-5488-3
- Basketball For Dummies
  0-7645-5248-1
- The Bible For Dummies
  0-7645-5296-1
- Buddhism For Dummies
  0-7645-5359-3
- Catholicism For Dummies
  0-7645-5391-7
- Hockey For Dummies
  0-7645-5228-7

- Judaism For Dummies
  0-7645-5299-6
- Martial Arts For Dummies
  0-7645-5358-5
- Pilates For Dummies
  0-7645-5397-6
- Religion For Dummies
  0-7645-5264-3
- Teaching Kids to Read For Dummies
  0-7645-4043-2
- Weight Training For Dummies
  0-7645-5168-X
- Yoga For Dummies
  0-7645-5117-5

TRAVEL

0-7645-5438-7

0-7645-5453-0

Also available:

- Alaska For Dummies
  0-7645-1761-9
- Arizona For Dummies
  0-7645-6938-4
- Cancún and the Yucatán For Dummies
  0-7645-2437-2
- Cruise Vacations For Dummies
  0-7645-6941-4
- Europe For Dummies
  0-7645-5456-5
- Ireland For Dummies
  0-7645-5455-7

- Las Vegas For Dummies
  0-7645-5448-4
- London For Dummies
  0-7645-4277-X
- New York City For Dummies
  0-7645-6945-7
- Paris For Dummies
  0-7645-5494-8
- RV Vacations For Dummies
  0-7645-5443-3
- Walt Disney World & Orlando For Dummies
  0-7645-6943-0

GRAPHICS, DESIGN & WEB DEVELOPMENT

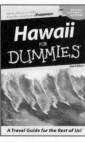

0-7645-4345-8

0-7645-5589-8

Also available:

- Adobe Acrobat 6 PDF For Dummies
  0-7645-3760-1
- Building a Web Site For Dummies
  0-7645-7144-3
- Dreamweaver MX 2004 For Dummies
  0-7645-4342-3
- FrontPage 2003 For Dummies
  0-7645-3882-9
- HTML 4 For Dummies
  0-7645-1995-6
- Illustrator cs For Dummies
  0-7645-4084-X

- Macromedia Flash MX 2004 For Dummies
  0-7645-4358-X
- Photoshop 7 All-in-One Desk Reference For Dummies
  0-7645-1667-1
- Photoshop cs Timesaving Techniques For Dummies
  0-7645-6782-9
- PHP 5 For Dummies
  0-7645-4166-8
- PowerPoint 2003 For Dummies
  0-7645-3908-6
- QuarkXPress 6 For Dummies
  0-7645-2593-X

NETWORKING, SECURITY, PROGRAMMING & DATABASES

0-7645-6852-3

0-7645-5784-X

Also available:

- A+ Certification For Dummies
  0-7645-4187-0
- Access 2003 All-in-One Desk Reference For Dummies
  0-7645-3988-4
- Beginning Programming For Dummies
  0-7645-4997-9
- C For Dummies
  0-7645-7068-4
- Firewalls For Dummies
  0-7645-4048-3
- Home Networking For Dummies
  0-7645-42796

- Network Security For Dummies
  0-7645-1679-5
- Networking For Dummies
  0-7645-1677-9
- TCP/IP For Dummies
  0-7645-1760-0
- VBA For Dummies
  0-7645-3989-2
- Wireless All In-One Desk Reference For Dummies
  0-7645-7496-5
- Wireless Home Networking For Dummies
  0-7645-3910-8